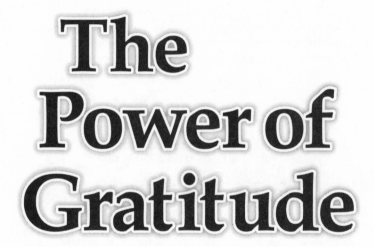

Chicken Soup for the Soul: The Power of Gratitude
101 Stories about How Being Thankful Can Change Your Life
Amy Newmark and Deborah Norville

Published by Chicken Soup for the Soul, LLC www.chickensoup.com
Copyright ©2016 by Chicken Soup for the Soul, LLC. All Rights Reserved.

The publisher gratefully acknowledges the many publishers and individuals who
granted Chicken Soup for the Soul permission to reprint the cited material.

Front cover photo courtesy of iStockphoto.com/neirfy (©neirfy)
Interior photo artwork courtesy of iStockphoto.com/pixdeluxe (©pixdeluxe)
Photo of Amy Newmark courtesy of Susan Morrow at SwickPix
Photo of Deborah Norville courtesy of Timothy White

Cover and Interior by Daniel Zaccari

Distributed to the booktrade by Simon & Schuster. SAN: 200-2442

Publisher's Cataloging-In-Publication Data
(Prepared by The Donohue Group, Inc.)

Names: Newmark, Amy, compiler. | Norville, Deborah, compiler.
Title: Chicken soup for the soul : the power of gratitude : 101 stories
    about how being thankful can change your life / [compiled by] Amy
    Newmark and Deborah Norville.
Other Titles: Power of gratitude : 101 stories about how being thankful
    can change your life
Description: [Cos Cob, Connecticut] : Chicken Soup for the Soul, LLC
    [2016]
Identifiers: LCCN 2016942612 | ISBN 978-1-61159-958-9 (print) |
    ISBN 978-1-61159-258-0 (ebook)
Subjects: LCSH: Gratitude--Literary collections. | Gratitude--Anecdotes. |
    Attitude (Psychology)--Literary collections. | Attitude (Psychology)--
    Anecdotes. | LCGFT: Anecdotes.
Classification: LCC BF575.G68 C45 2016 (print) | LCC BF575.G68 (ebook) |
    DDC 179.9--dc23

PRINTED IN THE UNITED STATES OF AMERICA
on acid∞free paper

25 24 23 22 21 20 19 18 17 16   01 02 03 04 05 06 07 08 09 10 11

The Power of Gratitude

101 Stories about How Being Thankful Can Change Your Life

Amy Newmark
Deborah Norville

Chicken Soup for the Soul, LLC
Cos Cob, CT

Chicken Soup for the Soul

Changing your life one story at a time®

www.chickensoup.com

Contents

❶

~Count Your Blessings~

❷

~Eye Openers~

❸
~Practicing Gratitude~

❹
~A Change in Perspective~

❺
~Well Chosen Words~

❻
~Grateful for Life~

❼
~Simple Pleasures~

❽

~Silver Linings~

❾

~Paying It Forward~

Introduction

"Thank you." It's one of the first things we are taught to say when we are youngsters. In a civilized society, it's part of being a polite person.

But then there's *ingratitude*, and most of us have experienced that, too — extending ourselves on someone's behalf and the gesture not being acknowledged. When you have experienced ingratitude, you never forget it.

It's been years since my son invited a friend to spend the day with him at the local amusement park. When we pulled up in front of his house after a long and fun-filled day, the boy jumped out of the car and ran inside. "He didn't say *thank you*!" my son said in amazement. I too was stunned — I sat behind the wheel of the car, speechless. Both of us still remember that boy's omission, and we wonder how that lack of thankfulness has affected that boy.

"Thank you" is the grease that keeps society functioning. But *saying* thank you and *being* thankful are two very different things. The former is part of being mannerly, the latter — well, it's the secret to a life of happiness and success.

For one thing, people will like you better. Ingratitude is one of the most disliked traits in people. It acts as a repellent. No one wants to be around ingrates. Gratitude, on the other hand, is right up there in the top ten percent of qualities people appreciate. Being likable is just the beginning. The list of consequences that come from being grateful is so long and so upbeat that it sounds more like the sales pitch of a cheesy infomercial than research-proven outcomes. Greater optimism. Higher energy. Increased creativity. Longer lifespan. Boldness in the face of challenge. Higher immune response. Greater tolerance. Increased cognitive skills.

I learned all of this as the result of being bored at work. It was during a news cycle when it seemed the stories making headlines all fell into the category of "Young Stars Having Meltdowns." Britney Spears was in her head-shaving/tattoo-getting phase and Lindsay Lohan was just beginning her string of run-ins with the law. It didn't take much time or many brain cells to write my scripts for the broadcast and, frankly, I had time on my hands.

I decided to spend some of that time looking into a hunch I had always had: that my life went better when I focused on what was going right for me, rather than lamenting the things that went wrong. This was *not* a novel idea. Charles Dickens once said, "Reflect upon your present blessings, of which every man has plenty; not on your past misfortunes of which all men have some."

What I wanted to know was: Is there anything to it? Is there actually any proof that counting your blessings, looking on the bright side, practicing gratitude — whatever you call it — actually produces quantifiable benefits? I came at it with a reporter's mindset. Do the research, examine the facts, talk to the experts. I shared what I learned in a book I wrote called *Thank You Power: Making the Science of Gratitude Work for You*. I learned that not only was there peer-reviewed scientific research into the consequences of a grateful mindset, those consequences were life altering in a variety of life affirming ways.

Being grateful puts you in a positive frame of mind. Psychologists call it the "upward spiral." Just as focusing on all the things that went wrong during the day leaves you cranky and ill-tempered, acknowledging what went right — call them blessings or "good things" — has the reverse effect. One positive thought prompts another positive thought, which is followed by a pleasant memory and so on. Each thought spirals upward into another happy moment and your mood climbs along with your thoughts.

The reason this happens is multifold. Your attention is focused on actual events that occurred — giving a concrete realness to moments most of us would likely forget or overlook if not being deliberate about recollecting them. Since the majority of most people's grateful moments involve other people — tallying those moments underscores the relationships that give life meaning, which is particularly important in today's electronically isolated existence. It also boosts one's self-esteem. "If all this good stuff is happening to me, I must deserve it."

Common sense dictates these would probably be likely outcomes of recalling positive past moments. That finding didn't surprise me. But some of the other results documented by researchers really got me excited. One professor I consulted found that when people feel appreciated, they go the extra mile on your behalf. Her experiment found that when busy physicians were given a small token of gratitude — a little bag of candy in this case — they were more elastic in their thinking and willing to consult other doctors to confirm their diagnoses. The doctors who didn't get the extra "thank you" tended to be methodical in their approach and sometimes ignored facts that didn't fit with their preliminary diagnosis.

Gratitude also helps "take care of emotional business of negative things in our lives," says psychology professor Philip Watkins, Ph.D. of Eastern Washington State University. Grateful people are able to remember past positive events, even in the aftermath of trauma. Finding things for which one can be grateful helps make the memory of a difficult experience less intrusive. Other research has found a connection between the kind of positive emotions created by gratitude and resilience. Grateful people are better able to weather life's storms.

Those positive emotions can *also* help you solve life's problems. There is a clear connection between feeling upbeat and making cognitive connections and associations. One fascinating study found that when little children were asked to recall a moment that made them so happy that they wanted to dance, they were better able to remember information they'd just been taught than children who did not get the "happy dance" prompt. That bit of research prompted me to tell my own children to think of a happy memory just before taking a challenging test at school. I figured it couldn't hurt, and the data indicated it just might help a lot!

Equally important, gratitude can help take the edge off stress.

Counting one's blessings elevates one's mood, which studies have shown can reduce the physical effects of stress. Six out of ten millennials say they are trying to reduce stress in their lives, and more than half say stress has kept them awake at night. One researcher I spoke with conducted a study in which participants were wired up so their blood pressure, heart rate and stress hormones could be measured. Then they were asked to present an impromptu speech that would count for a majority of their course grade, which put them all in a high-stress state. The participants who were given a visual cue that summoned up a positive mindset were shown to quickly de-stress in a way that those given neutral or negative visual images did not. Gratitude can have a similar impact.

Which is why this *Chicken Soup for the Soul* book may be such an important companion for you. The stories we've collected all feature moments of gratitude. Some are monumental — but most are part of everyday life. That's the magic of gratitude. It truly is the little things that matter. The sunrise and its glorious colors. The unexpected dismissal from a job and the gracious way the woman fired said goodbye. The lesson learned from taking the bus. It was raining when I first wrote this. Now as I proofread it, I am in the glow of the magnificent double rainbow that blazed across the sky. That rainbow will be on my gratitude list for today — when I look back in my journal I will be reminded of how awe-inspiring it was.

Perhaps you picked up this book because you are not naturally disposed to "look on the brighter side." The good news is you can *become* more grateful even if it doesn't come naturally for you. Hearing other people's stories of gratitude is one way to do it. In a letter he wrote in 1771, Thomas Jefferson commented, "When an… act of charity or of gratitude, for instance, is presented to our sight or imagination, we are deeply impressed with its beauty and feel a strong desire in ourselves of doing charitable and grateful acts also."

The stories in this book have been selected to act as a little pick-me-up just for YOU. There is a good chance that they will encourage you to find blessings in ways you hadn't noticed before. Researchers call it "elevation" — you and I might call the stories "heartwarming" — and studies show that people who hear stories of good deeds report literally feeling a sense of warmth in their chests and a desire to replicate in their own way the kinds of deeds they've just heard about.

There are a million different reasons you might have picked up this book. Perhaps you're a long-time fan of the *Chicken Soup for the Soul* series. Perhaps you've experienced a loss and are feeling blue. Perhaps you've heard about this "gratitude thing" and wondered if there is anything to it. The research says the answer is "yes." But you don't need to have a fancy degree and a bunch of published research to know that there IS power in gratitude. Being thankful CAN change your life — in just ONE way: It can make your life better. You're about to learn 101 different ways it already has for other people. I hope you will reach out to me and share how the Power of Gratitude has changed YOUR life!

~Deborah Norville

The Power of Gratitude

Count Your Blessings

*Count your blessings. Once you realize how valuable you are
and how much you have going for you, the smiles will return,
the sun will break out, the music will play, and you will finally
be able to move forward with the life intended for you with
grace, strength, courage, and confidence.*
~Og Mandino

Turning Up the Volume

Abundance is not something we acquire.
It is something we tune into.
~Wayne Dyer

"The movie *American Sniper* is on," I said to my husband as we settled into bed. We hadn't seen the movie, but it had gotten good reviews. Bradley Cooper plays a U.S. Navy SEAL in Iraq who later has difficulty adjusting to regular life.

We decided to watch, figuring it would take our minds off my husband's situation at work. He had been working with the same organization for close to twenty-three years, and the management, he suspected, was preparing to let him go. The signs were pretty clear and I felt his pain. He had given so much to the organization and had been such an asset to his department. But, the new management was making changes and it seemed as if those from the former "regime" were being let go.

Out with the old, in with the new. The entire ordeal was weighing heavy on his heart, as he was now being treated rather coldly and it hurt.

I wondered if *American Sniper* was the wrong movie to watch and considered changing the channel. Maybe something lighter was in order? A nice family comedy with laughter and silliness would have been more uplifting for my husband.

"It wouldn't bother me so much if I just felt appreciated," he said, while Bradley Cooper jumped out of the way of a bullet.

I nodded in agreement.

We snuggled into bed and turned the volume down as my son was in the next room studying for the PSATs. He had been taking prep tests along with his classmates for a couple of months and would soon be taking the real test.

Colleges, GPAs, and the PSAT were constantly on my mind and I wondered now, with my husband's new situation, whether my son might have to take on the burden of a student loan.

A car bomb exploded on the television and I quickly lowered the volume another couple of notches with the remote.

> *As I watched the movie, it dawned on me how trivial our problems really were.*

"You know this movie is based on a true story," I said, half thinking about my husband's situation, half watching the movie.

"Yes," he replied. "It's based on Chris Kyle's book."

I thought about all the young men who had lost their lives over in Iraq. "Incredible. Some of those boys were only a couple of years older than James is right now," I said, referring to our son.

As I watched the movie, it dawned on me how trivial our problems really were. "You know, other couples are in bed tonight wondering if their sons are safe on a battlefield; and here we are with our son perfectly safe in the next room. Our problem seems so small in comparison."

Over the next hour, the mood in our bedroom changed from depression to gratitude. How blessed we were! Our son was healthy and safe in the next room. We had a roof over our heads and could walk outside without worrying whether there would be bullets flying through the air!

As for my husband's job, he could do something else — something that he would love. And how many people can say they've been with a company for twenty-three years? That's a great run!

Looking at the big picture, counting our blessings, and moving from "dejection to reflection" has made all the difference.

It may be time for us to turn the page, but at least we have pages to turn. Our story is a good one and a happy one! We just need to remind ourselves — every so often — to highlight all those good parts.

And when it comes to gratitude, we remember to always turn up the volume.

~Mary C. M. Phillips

The Beauty of Age Spots

Years may wrinkle the skin, but to give up
enthusiasm wrinkles the soul.
~Samuel Ullman

"Don't worry, those are just age spots," the esthetician said in a reassuring tone, as she handed me a small tube of beauty cream.

"Are you absolutely certain that these are age spots?" I questioned, pointing to the dark spots on my hands.

Angie, the esthetician, smiled warmly and pronounced, "I'm 100% positive."

I let out a squeal of delight and hugged her tightly — letting the tube of beauty cream fall to the floor.

"You have no idea how long I've waited for these to appear," I confessed.

Angie looked slightly bewildered, and I realized there was no possible way I could explain my excitement. I was just a little disappointed that she hadn't mentioned the wrinkles around my eyes and the sprouting gray hairs near my temples. I was so proud of them! In fact, the whole visit was a huge letdown, but since I was using a gift certificate — given to me by a friend — I didn't want to seem ungrateful.

What Angie didn't know was that I wasn't supposed to live to see age spots, wrinkles or gray hair! At age forty, I wondered if I would live long enough to see any signs of aging. I was in the battle of my life — fighting breast cancer — and all I really wanted to see was my boys, ages nine and fourteen, through safe passage into adulthood. (And maybe a grandchild or two!)

After the five-year mark of being cancer free, I started to have hope. I saw the actual beginnings of wrinkles. I called them laugh lines because I couldn't stop giggling at the squiggles on my face; I was actually getting older! In fact, I attended my older son's high school graduation wearing no make-up, just so everyone could see my new wrinkles.

When I got my first gray hair, I quickly pointed it out to my husband. "Look, honey, a gray hair," I announced, fluffing it up so he could see it better. Mark, my husband of thirty years, always seemed a little disinterested in hair issues, but I think it had something to do with the fact that he was bald by the age of thirty.

I wasn't supposed to live to see age spots, wrinkles or gray hair.

On our thirty-fifth wedding anniversary, while I danced at our younger son's wedding, I was giddy with excitement because I had sprouted two new gray hairs and lip lines. There was no way the make-up artist was going to cover up those beauties; I simply wouldn't let her!

There was so much to look forward to because age spots hadn't made their appearance yet... (or so I thought) and I was approaching my sixtieth birthday and our fortieth wedding anniversary.

While I was taking a trip down memory lane, Angie interrupted my thoughts. "Here's another sample of fade cream that you can put on your hands twice a week before going to bed. During the day, use liberal amounts of sunscreen," she warned. And then I gasped when Angie mentioned the second option. "Of course, you can always have your age spots removed with lasers," she said matter-of-factly.

"Remove them?" I protested. "Why would anyone want to do that?"

Angie stared at me — not understanding — while I explained; "I'd very much like to keep them — all of them — if you don't mind."

She shook her head as she handed me the spot-fading cream and asked if I would like a follow-up appointment.

"No thanks!" I said with a grin. "I won't need the anti-spot cream or a follow-up appointment."

As I walked out the door of the spa, I was beaming with gratitude to have such a wonderful "diagnosis" of age spots! Absolutely nothing could have prepared me for that.

Later that year, I celebrated two milestones — my sixtieth birthday and twenty years of being cancer free. I'm absolutely thrilled to be growing older with gray hair, wrinkles, and now — age spots. I'm not sure why anyone would want to take them away or make them disappear because they are — after all — long-awaited gifts.

And I can see the beauty in all of them!

~Connie K. Pombo

The Perfect Home

Be grateful for the home you have, knowing that at this
moment, all you have is all you need.
~Sarah Ban Breathnach

For a short time I lived smack in the middle of a row of brownstones located on Chestnut Street in Springfield, Massachusetts. I wasn't crazy about being that close to my neighbors on either side, but the tree-lined street had cafés, flower shops, and a corner food market. My building had geranium planters on its stoop and pots of herbs on its broad windowsills. It even had an attic for storage and a basement for my bicycle. The front door had a good lock and my neighbors were friendly.

Nice, right? Yes, but I still found myself criticizing my living arrangement. The furniture seemed awkward, the wall color was off, and the old radiators were eyesores. I constantly pored over decorating magazines looking for the perfect accessory, thinking one more couch pillow might make me happy, or another end table in the living room would do the trick. But of course it never did. My work was going well, my social life was interesting, yet I was always looking for more. More what? I wasn't exactly sure but I couldn't settle in.

Then something strange began to happen. I started to lose track of things. I'm not talking about days or appointments. I'm not even talking about car keys or bills. I'm talking about food. I would be sure I had a can of tuna, but when I'd go to get it, no tuna. I didn't recall eating the last bit of cold cuts yet the package was gone. It was puzzling but not earth shattering. I am a busy woman, and I rationalized that I must be snacking and not paying attention. What was I supposed to do? Tell the doctor everything else in my life was on track, but it appeared I was blacking out and eating food?

One morning, I stood dumbfounded at the open refrigerator door for close to a minute. The cool air washed over my bare knees while I stared at an empty shelf. I knew I wasn't crazy, and I was certain I hadn't been sleepwalking, but today a bright blue plastic container of leftovers that I had placed there last night was gone. I sat down and made a list. From what I could remember over the last week I had lost a couple of apples, some cheese, a can of soda, and the last pieces in a loaf of bread. Only my cat and I lived in this apartment, and Smoochie was only nine pounds and couldn't have done this.

From the very day I found her pitiful home, I never again found fault with mine.

Did I have mice? A rat with superpowers that could open the refrigerator? A raccoon? Something was going on but I couldn't get a handle on it.

That afternoon, as I opened my kitchen window for a breeze, a movement caught my eye. The neighbor across the street was trying to keep his huge, playful dog from charging into the house with muddy paws. It was a funny battle, one that the man ultimately lost. I smiled at the sight of brown prints trailing up the steps and into the doorway. But it gave me an idea. That night I sprinkled flour on the kitchen floor, a messy job to be sure, but one that would let me see where this critter was coming from by its prints. Once I figured that out, I would block his access. Knowledge is power. I went to bed confident that I was going to solve this mystery.

The next morning I got out of bed excited to get downstairs, visions of a giant sandwich-eating rat swirling in my brain, but at the kitchen door I stopped short and let out a startled gasp. My plan had worked all right, but instead of being happy, I was suddenly fearful. There were human footprints everywhere. And they led over to the closed basement door. I froze in place. Why did it have to be in the cellar? Scenes from old horror movies played in my head. I shouldn't go in the basement — that's where the killer always hides.

I tiptoed across the floury floor and put my ear on the old wooden door. Nothing. I quietly cracked it open. A white outline marked the edge of each step going down. "Hello?" I could hear my voice crack with the tension. "Who's down there?" Silence. "I'm calling the police." Nothing moved. I remember vividly to this day how the hair on my arms stood straight up.

I flipped the light switch and began creeping down one step at a time, ready to bolt at the slightest sound, but the basement was small and I could clearly see there was no one hiding in the room. The ghostly looking footsteps continued across the floor and up the steps to the outside hatch door. I followed them, easing the hatch open and peering out with nervous eyes. Nothing seemed amiss except I realized my lock was so rusty it had fallen out of the wood and was hanging by one screw. At this point I could barely see the flour, but little bits of white clearly stretched across the alley toward a Dumpster that belonged to the adjoining property. I inched over to their trash area, the pounding of my heart loud in my ears. Everything was still. A few birds chirped. A dog barked from the next street over. I rallied my courage and peeked behind the huge container.

I stared down at a makeshift tent of plastic bags, pieces of cardboard, and bits of what looked like torn T-shirts. There was a pitiful bedroll of sorts, and women's clothes hung off a stick. Without getting too close I could see a few items: a cup, a tube of deodorant, some dishes. And my blue plastic container. My heart broke and I started crying.

As I placed a new lock on the hatchway door, I tried to recall how many times I had left my laptop out on the kitchen counter. Or my phone. Or my watch. I couldn't come up with a number but I knew it was a lot, and never once were any of those items touched.

That night, before sunset, and every night that spring and summer, I hung a bag containing a hearty sandwich, a piece of fruit, and a container of chocolate milk on the handle of the basement hatch. I never caught even a glimpse of the woman in all that time, but she took the bag. Then one day late that fall she was gone — her camp abandoned, my sandwich left untouched and still hanging on the latch.

From the very day I found her pitiful home, I never again found fault with mine. Humbled and grateful, I stopped looking for fulfillment in owning things, stopped fretting about my surroundings being perfect, and found an inner peace that has kept me steady through the years.

~Jody E. Lebel

Thanks for Messing Up My Life

Find the good and praise it.
~Alex Haley

In January 2005, I committed my wife Ginny to an Alzheimer's facility after caring for her at home for seven years. As is often the case with home caregivers, the experience made me an emotional wreck. I had never been a pill taker; now I was on Xanax, Ativan, Celexa, Citalopram, Motoporal, Lisinopril; I learned new groups of medications, like SSRIs, and all the "pams."

It was not only the beginning of the new year, but also — literally — of the wreckage of my life, because shortly after I put Ginny in that facility, my Odyssey minivan and I met a cement truck head-on. The truck survived.

My vehicle was squashed into a tangle of steel, the front half a gaping hole. The steering wheel and parts of the dashboard hung from the space where the driver's door once was. The vinyl seats, springs and wires dangled from the chassis, which looked like Swiss cheese.

Thanks to my seat belt, I wasn't strewn in the street like the pieces of my car. But they had to cut me out with the Jaws of Life. And that was after I was burned in the fiery wreck; I am left with patches of white where skin was taken for grafts to cover the burns.

I was broken — up, down, and around. Gratitude? Well, I was alive. And thanks to the doctors and nurses of the Trauma Team of the

Oregon Health Sciences University, my body was fixed. Most everything that could have been broken, fractured, or torn had been. Muscles lost their bindings; tendons and ligaments had been disconnected and strewn about under the skin. Wrecked as I was, I could be thankful: I was whole — although the nurses in the ICU referred to me as "Humpty Dumpty."

Fortunately, my head didn't need fixing. The only noticeable injury there is a one-inch dent in my forehead from the airbag.

That was my 2005: a broken body for me, and a broken mind for Ginny. I didn't feel much gratitude.

I hoped 2006 would be a year of renewal.

The first step was to fix my body. The doctors inserted metal plates to connect my broken bones, tied together the body parts, and repaired the fractures. I continued to improve. Ironically, "progress" for me was a move upward into the bright light of wholeness. For Ginny, "progress" meant continual degradation, movement downward into the darkness of dementia. As I saw the possibility of my wholeness and functionality returning, I witnessed her inexorable deterioration and destruction. Our nearly sixty years of marriage would end eight years later, on December 13th, 2013.

> *I could weep over what I couldn't do, or I could be grateful and seize upon what I could do.*

After living comatose and supine for several months, I learned to raise my upper body and sit in place at least fifteen seconds without falling over. Then I learned to scoot down on a board from the side of the bed and transfer from bed to wheelchair. As time went on, my body re-learned how to stand. Then the inevitable — to take a few steps holding on to the parallel bars. Although most of my travels now are in a wheelchair, I can walk short distances.

There was one more ledge to climb before I could approach independence: I needed a place to live. At seventy-three, one year following my accident, I entered an Assisted Living Facility.

But I found dependency.

I didn't know what it meant to live in an assisted living facility, a congregate, ordered, smoothly oiled, and systematically regimented life. I learned that my free spirit didn't fit in. My freedom and individuality were constricted. I was "Room 108," not "Dick," not even "Humpty Dumpty."

In the beginning of my new life, like many people in the assisted living facility, I sat in my room and stared out the window. I saw people on their bikes — I used to cycle as my means of transportation and exercise. I saw people running — I had run daily, ran 10Ks and marathons. And I had been a triathlete; I mourned the reality of never doing that again.

I also pondered my accident: I had been dead, and was brought back to life. I had been broken, and sewn back together. I was repaired — bodily. I faced my choices: I could weep over what I couldn't do, or I could be grateful and seize upon what I could do.

I had been a writer and a professor. So I began to write about my life in an assisted living facility. Perhaps my writings could teach others about this kind of life, including the professionals who worked with the elderly and the disabled. It turned out, they did. The essays were used in professional development, in teaching workshops, in college classes.

I transformed incidents that happened to me or that I witnessed into vignettes about living the dependent life; I was honest, and critical, but identifying the absurd and the humorous. As one reader said, "I would have cried if it wasn't so funny."

Eventually, my pieces became a blog, posted twice a month by AARP Oregon.

While ideas flowed from my observations and imagination, writing — or actually typing — was not easy. My hands had been only partially fixed: the left hand was useless; my right could move and grasp, but my fingers were stiff and curled like a partial fist. I couldn't straighten them; thus I couldn't type. So, I adapted my writing to my condition: one stroke at a time. I wrote key by key with a Chewy Tube — a green, rubber T-shaped tool recommended by my occupational therapist. It is normally used to assist people to chew, or as an improved baby pacifier.

I held it in my right fist, striking one character after the other. The flurry of ideas that spilled from my imagination slowly and carefully turned into words.

My blogs have become a teaching tool for the Oregon Department of Human Services, and advocacy groups seeking to improve the quality of living for elders in assisted living facilities and nursing homes. As a resident myself, I could present an insider's view; to reveal what the public, the adult children who place their parents in such facilities, didn't see.

Not only did I use the "pen" in my new career, I created a video documentary, *The Thin Edge of Dignity*, which describes my life in an assisted living facility. It has spread around the country, used by the Ombudsman of each of the fifty states. Each Ombudsman and her/his professional staff and volunteers are advocates for elder rights. The video is also used in college classes, as continuing education for long-term care professionals, and, from the responses on YouTube, a wide swath of the general public.

And, despite being in a wheelchair, I have flown around the country and spoken at regional and national conferences. I was selected to participate in the regional meeting of the White House Conference on Aging, leading up to the meeting in Washington, D.C.

The active and committed life I lead as an elder won me placement among a select group of American elders, recognized by the National Association of States United for Aging and Disabilities, and chosen, among the elders from each state, to be the one person from Oregon listed in *50 Fabulous Older People*, a publication celebrating the fifty years of the Older Americans Act.

And these achievements were all because of that accident which left me in physical disrepair.

My yearlong ordeal in hospitals, nursing facilities, rehabilitation clinics, and living in a long-term care facility, have led me to a new career: I remain a teacher, but the classroom and the students have changed.

More important than traveling a new path, I have developed a new perspective: strangers' random acts of kindness have opened my eyes to the goodness of people — even if they took only a fraction of a moment to open a door, shove a chair out of the way in a crowded coffee house, remove my coat in a hot room — old friends' committed acts of kindness have helped me live my former free-spirited life. I see the unseen undefined connective bonds between friends — between people. I am in place to make a difference, to help form a new paradigm for the way old persons live in the institutions into which society shelves us.

Of course, I wish that cement truck had not messed up my life. But I am grateful for the opportunities that have arisen for me to continue to make a difference — to teach, to write, to travel and speak, to volunteer, to influence… to matter.

~Richard Weinman

Editor's note: To see Professor Weinman's thought provoking documentary on YouTube, type *The Thin Edge of Dignity* into your Internet browser or click on https://www.youtube.com/watch?v=UciTFCPCivI

5

My Answered Prayer

*Sometimes the difficult things that happen in
our lives put us directly on the path to the best
things that will ever happen to us.*
~Author Unknown

My husband and I went to our twenty-week ultrasound expecting to get a few pictures of our first child and then head off to the airport for a weekend away. We never made it to the airport…. We spent the next eight hours being shuffled from exam room to office to exam room. By the time we left the hospital, we had undergone an amniocentesis and were told that Down syndrome was the best-case scenario for our child. According to the doctors, it was more likely that our baby had a chromosomal defect that was "incompatible with life."

We spent the next three days praying that our baby would be okay…. We prayed for Down syndrome. Our prayers were answered and we received the most incredible gift we could have ever hoped for — we were having a daughter, with Down syndrome. We immediately named her Lily. We didn't want to spend the rest of my pregnancy thinking about our "baby with special needs" or our "daughter with Down syndrome." Instead we just thought about Lily Kathleen and what we could do to make sure she'd be as healthy as possible when she arrived.

During those last months of my pregnancy we faced one challenge after another. Just two days after confirming that Lily had Down syndrome, we saw a fetal cardiologist who told us she also had a serious heart defect that would require surgery, possibly just after birth. Weeks later we heard from another doctor that there was a possible tumor on Lily's brain that hadn't been there before. I underwent an MRI and after many more sleepless nights, the test results revealed no tumor or mass.

It felt like every time we came to grips with a diagnosis or prognosis, we received another blow from the doctors. But we continued to remain positive, and we made sure that our family and friends remained positive as well. From the moment we told them about Lily, we let them know that we were okay with the fact that our daughter had Down syndrome and would need heart surgery. Our positive outlook allowed our family and friends to share in our joy and excitement. So when Lily finally arrived, she entered this world surrounded by love and enthusiasm.

> *She has led me to people I would have never met— incredible people who do incredible things.*

The day she was born was one of the happiest days of my life. There was no sad news or awkward silence in the delivery room. Instead, there was a baby girl with the biggest cheeks I'd ever seen and fingernails that looked perfectly manicured. She had bright red rosebud lips and a mess of dark brown hair. She was not premature, as the doctors had said she might be, and she was not tiny and blue. She weighed more than eight pounds, was a healthy pink, and was breathing on her own. She may have had a serious heart defect and a chromosomal disorder, but she was exactly what we had prayed for.

Four months after Lily was born, she had open-heart surgery to correct Tetralogy of Fallot and an atrial septal defect. I was terrified to hand her over to the doctors that day, but I knew in my heart that she would be okay. We had come too far in our journey to have it end so soon. Much to our delight and relief, she came through the surgery without complications and was home in only four days. She may have been tiny, gaining less than two pounds in her first four months of life, but she was a fighter and she proved to everyone how strong she could be. She continues to show us that when she barely flinches while getting her blood drawn, or asks for pretzels twelve hours after a tonsillectomy. She never ceases to amaze me.

I view Lily as my guiding light. She has led me to people I would have never met — incredible people who do incredible things. She has taught me to take life a little slower — and that by doing so you get to truly enjoy the journey and rejoice in even the smallest of accomplishments. She has shown me that every life is worth living — and that no part of her or any other individual is imperfect or flawed. She has illustrated bravery, perseverance and strength that rival most adults. And she has shown me that a bright smile can be contagious and can make even the worst day wonderful. Lily teaches me something every day about myself and about others. I have direction and purpose now that she is here, guiding me to be a better mother and a better human being.

I will be forever grateful for the circumstances surrounding my prenatal diagnosis. I was given the opportunity to see my daughter as a blessing, a child who not only survived, but also thrived in spite of her challenges. Someday Lily may ask me if I ever wished she didn't have Down syndrome, or she may even wish it herself. And I'll explain that I would never want her to be anyone other than who she is, exactly as God created her. I can tell her that I wanted her always and I consider her one of the greatest gifts I've ever received.

She is, after all, my answered prayer.

~Nancy F. Goodfellow

6

Midnight Runs

*When you're a nurse you know that every day you will
touch a life or a life will touch yours.*
~Author Unknown

I became the on-call nurse for a hospice and palliative care organization eight years ago. I visit the patient's home when his symptoms become uncontrollable, when a family member spots a new sign or unfamiliar symptom, or when the caregiver needs emotional or hands-on support. I might be called to instruct an eighty-year-old wife on how to give a bed-bath to a dying husband. Then it's back to nursing basics, second nature after thirty-eight years of nursing. I simply roll up my sleeves and do it myself while the Mrs. brews me a cup of tea and gratitude.

But I am no saint, far from it. Statistically I am older than twenty-five percent of my patients, which means, "Lord, I am tired!" No one should be roused from a peaceful slumber at 3 a.m. It's exhausting at age twenty-six, and very daunting at sixty-six. Research has shown that seven hours of snoozing is the bare, healthy minimum. Interrupted sleep—not just bumbling to the bathroom at midnight, but sustained wakefulness—has serious effects on health. Succinctly, it shortens your life. We call the middle of the night "the hours of lead." That's what it feels like when I struggle to calculate a drug-dosing regimen at 2:37 a.m.

My job is however like many others, in some respects. Ten percent of the time I work for sixteen hours without time to grab a coffee from an all-night diner. Another ten percent of the time I rest for an entire shift without a single callout. The remaining eighty percent of my shifts are checkered with calls and visit requests. Patients' families frequently claim that I am a saint; I demure, saying with a straight face that I work strictly for the money — a million dollars a year. Then we all laugh knowingly. When I'm driving to someone's home on a July night under a full moon, with the temperature a balmy seventy-two degrees, and no traffic other than bread delivery trucks and slowly cruising state troopers, it's nearly pleasant! Driving home into a sunrise, knowing all my patients are comfortable, that's the happy end to a good night's work.

But there are bad times, nights when I am exhausted from a string of shifts that were filled with non-stop visits to patients whose symptoms would not resolve, who had intractable pain and wrenching nausea. There are nights when I struggle with a head cold that drains me of stamina and good will. Worst of all are the calls that come between 2 a.m. and 4 a.m. One typical visit last winter began as many do, with a shaky voice on the other end that suggested personal insecurity rather than a clear-cut clinical problem. "I'm not sure what's wrong with him; he just doesn't seem quite right. He's got cancer. Can you come out and take a look, and tell me what I can do for him to make him comfortable?"

I have everything I could ask for.

There would be no quick return to my warm, cozy bed that night, I realized while piling on layers of winter clothes. Outside the sleet pelted the storm windows. It took ten full minutes to scrape the car windshield clear. The car's engine and I grumbled with irritation, neither ever warming completely. The road was covered with four inches of fresh, unplowed snow and ice. The trip to my patient's home was a white-knuckle, hour-long slide along country roads. With each slippery turn I became more irritated. Couldn't I have just given a double-dose of sympathy and reassurance by phone and stayed safe and comfy at home?

My destination was a two-hundred-year-old farmhouse that looked its age. The driveway hadn't been shoveled during the previous storm and the back stairs were a ramp of virgin snow. My bad humor had nearly reached a boil as I knocked on the mudroom door. I knocked a second time, then a third, pounding with my mittened hand. Was I at the wrong home?

The patient's wife released the door's two latches and then the dead bolt. She braced the door with both of her frail, blue-veined hands against a sudden blast of ice-filled wind. "Come in, come in," she exclaimed, "Don't bother with your boots, just come in out of the storm. The furnace seems to be out but I have a fire in the living room, where George is, to keep him warm. Oh my goodness, you are an angel to come out in this weather!"

My anger instantly vanished as I approached the sleeping patient slumped in his tattered easy chair by the fireplace. The meager fire showed his half-finished cup of tea and plastic cup of vanilla pudding on the chair beside him. "He can't seem to wake up anymore, not even to swallow his medicine," she informed me. His ragged breathing rattled ominously beneath a small mountain of blankets. "Would you like a cup of tea to warm you up?" she asked with hospitality that made me wince at my prior irritation.

As my octogenarian hostess shuffled to the kitchen, I removed the cup and pudding from the chair and sat down as quietly as I could. I slid my hand beneath the covers and felt the thready pulse beneath his cool, parchment-thin skin.

My professional attention drifted away. I thought of my warm, healthy wife at home who'd probably have fresh coffee waiting when I returned at dawn. I thought of the new roof on our own renovated farmhouse and the furnace that never failed. I felt my own pulse's healthy rhythm and my strong lungs that minutes before had created white puffs in the air as I shuffled through the snowdrifts toward this decrepit house. I noted my trusty car, my neighbors who probably would have shoveled my driveway for me by the time I reached home. I thought of my well-stocked pantry, the cord of firewood in the mudroom, and even my dog that would keep one ear cocked for me, eager to greet me on my return.

And I thought of my nursing job that pays our mortgage, puts our kids through college, and provides me with a million dollars worth of tea and gratitude with each visit.

"Thank you so much for coming out; you are an angel," the patient's wife said, her eyes welling with tears as she handed me my warm cup of tea. "Would you like sugar or milk?"

No, I thought. I have everything I could ask for.

~Thom Schwarz

Because of Facebook

Family is not an important thing. It's everything.
~Michael J. Fox

When Facebook appeared, I wasn't interested, as I prefer face-to-face communication or talking on the phone. But my friend Karen would call from Manhattan for our weekly Sunday evening chats and give me reports about my grandchildren and some mutual acquaintances she followed on Facebook.

"It looks like Sara had a fun time on her field trip. If you'd join Facebook, you could see for yourself," she said, trying to entice me. "And you'll never guess who I found — some old friends from Lansingburgh High School."

"That's great, but it's just not for me. Besides, why should I when I can get all the news from you?"

My ten-year-old granddaughter, Sara, showed me her Facebook page and how to download photographs. "See how easy it is?" she said, promising to help me choose a photo for my homepage.

I was tempted, but still not convinced. That is, not until my phone rang one night a few weeks later. It was my brother, shouting, "I found Teddy. That is, Teddy found me!"

"Slow down, Chuck. Are you talking about your son, Teddy?"

"Yes," he cried, "it's a miracle!"

Years ago, while in nursing school, I had introduced Chuck to one of my classmates. They fell in love, got married, and had a precious, golden-haired son named Teddy. But when the baby was two years old, Chuck and his wife divorced. It was a sad day because no one on our side of the family was allowed to ever see Teddy again — not my brother or our elderly father, whose heart was broken. Teddy was lost to us, and we mourned as if there had been a death.

Now, years later, Chuck and Teddy (now Ted — thirty-four years old, husband, and father of two) had reconnected. Ted had been trying to find his father for years. It was only when Chuck joined Facebook to stay in touch with buddies from his fortieth high school class reunion that Ted was finally able to contact his dad.

While Chuck talked, I grabbed my laptop and logged onto Southwest. com. Before we hung up, I had booked a flight. Chuck would drive north from his home in Florida and pick me up at the Norfolk airport. I would be part of the historic meeting when father and son were reunited.

> *Now that he and his son have been reunited, I know that Chuck will hold on tight.*

Two weeks later, Chuck and I were in a family room filled with toys in a two-story brick home in Virginia Beach. I gazed at the handsome young man seated on the couch next to his gorgeous wife and two smiling children: my nephew Ted, Lauren, three-year-old Sophia, and six-month-old Baby Teddy.

Chuck looked affectionately at Ted and asked me, "Don't you think he looks like Dad?" I looked appraisingly at Ted's deep set, brown-almost-black eyes, the contour of his brow, his strong chin, and saw a younger image of our father. I agreed, "Definitely!"

Baby Teddy was the spitting image of his grandfather Chuck. When the little guy crinkled up his face in a toothless grin, he looked just like my brother when he was a cheerful, chubby baby. "And this little guy looks just like you," I said.

I wanted to hear everything about Ted's life but refrained from making him recite every bit of the past thirty years.

I started with, "So, where did you go to high school? College?"

Looking at his 6' 2", well-muscled frame, I asked, "What sports did you play?"

And nearly as important, "What professional teams do you like?"

I was relieved to hear "The Yankees and the Dolphins." Yes, definitely his father's son.

The next afternoon I watched Ted with his children in their back yard. I caught a glimpse of the youth within, the playful and loving spirit, as he blew soap bubbles with Sophia. He cradled Teddy and spoke softly to the baby, who looked deeply into his father's eyes as if understanding every word.

On Saturday night, Chuck and I volunteered to babysit. We played "Pass the Baby" until Teddy started acting hungry — rooting around on his grandfather's arm, and when he didn't find what he was searching for, tried to put his entire fist into his mouth. I offered him a bottle, but he sputtered, scrunched up his face, and wailed. In between sobs, he glowered at us as though we were the enemy. Finally, he cried himself to sleep, exhaustion winning over hunger.

Around 11:00 p.m., Lauren and Ted walked through the door. Chuck and I cheered, "Hooray! Mommy and Daddy are home!" Teddy had awakened and was beyond being consoled. He nearly leaped out of my arms at the sight of his mother.

Too soon it was time for us to leave. In the driveway, I lingered as long as possible and hugged Ted, Lauren, Sophia, and Teddy one more time. From the moment I crossed their threshold, I felt welcomed and accepted, as if I had been part of their family all along.

Now that he and his son have been reunited, I know that Chuck will hold on tight and not let Ted go again. As we drove to the airport, we laughed and talked about the past few days, exclaiming how thankful we were that we'd been blessed with a second chance.

And it was all because of Facebook.

~Kathe Kokolias

Gifts from Dark Places

It's not what happens to you in life that defines you;
it's what you do with your life as a result.
~Author Unknown

The young woman sitting next to me looked around the new-mom's group nervously. Her eyes darted from person to person as we played with our babies on the floor of the church basement. Suddenly she blurted out, "My mom says I should let my daughter cry more, but that doesn't feel right to me. She's only four months old! Do you think that is okay? I don't want to upset my mom." I sat in stunned silence. Her words opened a door within me that I hadn't realized was closed.

My mother had died when I was fourteen. Her fight with cancer intersected with my adolescent delusions that I had the world all figured out. The day after her funeral, I returned to my freshman year of high school and pretended my world was fine. I cheered for the sports teams and sang in the choir, while inside I was frozen with fear and broken with grief. I had no idea how to ask for support. I hid my true feelings as much as I could, thinking that I was protecting myself.

At twenty-six, I married a man whose love for life was contagious. He taught me to play golf, waterski, and face fears. We explored far-away places and hiked, biked, kayaked or skied wherever we traveled. Together we chipped away at the "no-kids" policy I'd created, as our desire to start a family overcame my intense fear of dying young. When my first pregnancy ended in a miscarriage, the grief nearly derailed my courage. A year later, I became pregnant again. We carefully monitored every step in growth and development. When twenty weeks passed, my fear turned into hopeful excitement. At last, we would be a family.

Nothing prepared me for the joy to come. When the midwife handed me a squirming baby girl, my heart opened wider than I could have imagined. The baby re-anchored my broken mother-daughter bond. Yet life is bittersweet. My husband's mother—who'd been so thrilled to become a grandmother—was fighting her own battle against cancer. She enjoyed gazing at this perfect new baby. Despite pain and weakness, she lovingly held her as often as she could until passing away when our daughter was six weeks old.

> *I'd been so busy feeling angry over what I didn't have, I couldn't see what I'd been given.*

The emotional highs and lows untethered me. As a mother, I was deeply in love with this new baby. Yet once again I was slogging through grief. Short on sleep, and overwhelmed by parenthood, I became angry. It all felt so unfair. I missed my mom. I grieved for my mother-in-law. I felt cheated out of a mother's guidance and help.

I sought out new-mom's groups for support. So that early winter morning, as I cradled my daughter in my lap, surrounded by the circle of new mothers, I understood the intensity of the new mom sitting next to me. She didn't want to let her baby "cry it out," but the conflict between her own instincts and her mother's unsolicited advice was tearing her apart. I felt bad for her.

Then I had an epiphany. I saw something I never knew was there.

My mothering experience was completely different. I navigated without blueprints or flight plans. I had no advice-givers, yet I was finding my own way. I'd been so busy feeling angry over what I didn't have, I couldn't see what I'd been given. I was liberated. Losing my mother at a young age was traumatic, yes, but it gave me resilience, independence, and perseverance. I relied on those qualities, especially now with the fresh loss of my mother-in-law.

I felt a sense of gratitude. My losses created—oddly enough—a unique advantage. They'd taught me I could chart my own course. I would be okay.

Until that day, I'd focused on the sadness, resentment, and anger, rather than what had been left in its wake. Gifts from my darkest moments had been waiting patiently for me. Time spent wrestling with grief taught me empathy, strength, and compassion. When I've felt overwhelmed, my wise inner voice has been there to guide me. I only needed to pay attention. That moment in the church basement reorganized my beliefs. It helped me become the parent... the person... I needed to be. I am deeply grateful for that.

~Katie O'Connell

Million-Dollar Moments

Some people don't believe in heroes.
They've never met my dad.
~Author Unknown

From upstairs, I can hear the restless kids. "We're ready, Mom!"

"Just a minute!" Where is it? I rummage through my top desk drawer until I finally unearth a small white envelope. Holding my breath, I peer inside. Two crisp twenty-dollar bills lie folded together like a buried treasure.

There will be ice cream after all.

"Last one in the car is a rotten two-scoop sundae!" I shout in victory. Then, I whisper a prayer of thanks to our silent benefactor of simple moments: my dad.

For longer than I care to admit my father has been slipping me envelopes. Not often, of course; he's too thoughtful for that. His generous gesture is infrequent enough not to insult, yet regular enough to be abundantly helpful.

"There's something on my desk for you," he whispered in my ear shortly after we arrived for a recent visit.

"Dad..."

"I got a larger tax refund than expected," he said, waving off my objection.

It was transparent, but typical, of the excuses he'd conjure for just such an occasion.

Ultimately, I took the envelope, which is why we're standing in line at the ice cream parlor today, faces pressed to the freezer case glass. The thirty-something flavors spread before us are symbolic of the number of delicious moments my father's envelopes have added to our lives.

If only he knew where those twenties have taken us.

From the simple pleasure of a spontaneous summer snack to an occasional trinket from the toyshop, the trea-sured twenties have sprinkled many ordinary days with magic. Being able to say "yes" — at least some of the time — to a tempting treat or a matinee movie, is a blessing to any money-conscious mom.

> *"You can't always return a favor, so you help the ones you can."*

On many occasions, with savings stretched tight, Dad's extra cash fills the gaps at the grocery store. Other times, the secret stash steps up to the plate to purchase baseball cleats or a First Communion dress.

In truly difficult times, an envelope covers the costly antibiotic that both cures a feverish child and humbles a mother's heart.

Now, one twenty lighter, we settle onto stools with our super-scoop sundaes, feeling all is well with the world. I wish I could tell my father's grandchildren why they're indulging in ice cream today. But the painstaking secrecy with which my dad passes the bucks prompts me to maintain the mystery: our secret to the end.

Just the same, I want to shout my gratitude from the rooftops for the things my father has done. The list would be long, an extravagance of generosity I'll never be able to repay.

"You can't always return a favor, so you help the ones you can," Dad has said.

I look forward to that, my turn to treat. To prepare, I'm starting a collection of envelopes for a future time, when I hope to stuff them as skillfully as I seem to drain them today.

Until then, I'm acquiring smiles, simple abundance, and a dose of humility with the gracious gifts from my dad. And a thousand memories of the million-dollar moments tucked into his small, white envelopes of love.

~Judy O'Kelley

Standing Out

Valor is stability, not of legs and arms,
but of courage and the soul.
~Michel de Montaigne

We all have days that stand out as good days. It might be when we find the right person, or get married, or when we hold our newborn infant in our arms. One day can change everything, and for me, that day came within the walls of a small church in a small, quiet town.

On that day, in the presence of sixty or so gatherers, my son was married. What might have appeared to be a run-of-the-mill celebration was anything but. John, you see, had returned from Afghanistan the previous year, alive, but without his legs.

One of the most significant days in my own life was when I left a combat zone knowing I had survived the ugly war of my generation. The only time I had seen tears in my father's eyes was when I departed for Vietnam. He was no dove. He'd been at Pearl Harbor and lost two brothers in the "big war," and he hated watching another generation go to their own untimely deaths. Seeing me off to that "damned useless war," as he called it, couldn't have been easy. He realized, more than I, what a waste it would be if I, like so many young men, didn't come home.

I did return with my body intact, but unfortunately, my experiences in Vietnam were like so many others in wartime. The ravages of PTSD created some very dark days. Flashbacks often haunted my dreams. Drinking eased the power of lingering nightmares, but an invisible force pressed down on me like a lead weight. I became a great pretender, as my smile never reached my eyes. There were days when I was swallowed by a black hole and it took all my strength to claw my way out into a world of shadowed gray.

There were many who tried to help, but from the desperate place I occupied, they often seemed no more than circus acrobats performing an absurd ritual. Even though I was able to hold down a job, alcohol became my god, leading to ill-advised choices. There were times when the struggle did not seem worth the effort. It would have been easier to fall into a dreamless sleep with no more regrets about the past, closing the great doors of consciousness.

The past is not something you can stick into a folder marked Confidential and stash in a file cabinet, nor can it be packed in a box and thrown into the back of a closet. Yet, in the end, I reasoned that giving up was a coward's way out. Before too many unrecoverable, precious years passed, fate intervened as a new light entered my life. Her name was Mary. With her understanding and patience, she helped me toward sobriety and a renewed taste for the good things life still had to offer, even to the point of wanting a family.

***

As my offspring grew to adulthood, I prayed no more young men and women would ever again have to make the horrible sacrifices of my generation and my father's. But it happened again, and when my son was headed to the other side of the world, my sentiments were much the same as my father's had been on the day I shipped out. "Don't make him suffer as I have," I quietly breathed.

John did suffer, but at least he did return, leading to his day of triumph inside the little church. What he had endured, and the determination he'd shown to become whole again, were inspiring beyond anything I could have imagined. In my war, I had been spared the bodily pain and agony he had the misfortune of enduring, so I had felt sure most of his dreams had ended the day his limbs were blown away.

But I had sold him short. I thought back to the times I watched him at baseball practice from a distance down the left field line. I guess I believed I'd make him too nervous if I were obvious, that he'd be embarrassed if I were to see him fail.

I was as wrong then as I was more recently. He always strived to do as well as he could, both physically and mentally. And through the anguish of his convalescence and rehabilitation, he beat back the psychological demons and became spiritually stronger than ever before. My son overcame something most of us never have to physically confront, and he did so magnificently.

But there was another ingredient that made his recovery possible. As in my life, there was an understanding and devoted woman. It was the most important element of his recovery — the tenderness and loyalty that can soothe the hurt when all else fails. Encouragement always came from his mother and myself, but would his dedication to persevere and recover have been as strong without the young woman who patiently waited? I'm not sure even John knows the answer. But she stood by him, literally, every step of his long and winding path to recovery.

> *My son overcame something most of us never have to physically confront, and he did so magnificently.*

We were all so proud to see John waiting at the altar as Sherry walked down the aisle toward him. He was ready and able to take the hand of his beautiful bride and determinedly stood next to her on his new legs.

I sat in the church on that important day and watched as the woman of his dreams approached. My heart strained toward him; beating like the day I'd first seen him come home from overseas in a wheelchair. I took his mother's hand and squeezed it a little too hard. She patted my arm and I knew she was feeling the same emotions.

The bride touched her grandmother's golden locket, which was pinned to her shimmering white dress. Her beaming father delivered her to the spot next to my son. His smile told me we had done a good job at getting our children to this special moment.

The day John was born was important beyond measure, but this day, a day of triumph over tragedy, was more important still. My son took his bride's hand. All the hopes which any young couple might have as they start a life together were etched on their faces. John and Sherry's eyes shimmered as they exchanged vows and rings.

The union was blessed. They were now one as they turned and came down the aisle, their faces wreathed in smiles. John gave his mother and me that big, gleaming smile and a thumbs-up. Sherry smiled at us and said, "Thanks for raising such a wonderful man."

Everyone gathered outside to send the couple off in a hail of rice. There was never a thought about his disability during the event, and I realized that I had a son who was a stronger, better man than I.

I would sleep well that night, for I knew John's future would be filled with realized dreams. No challenges were insurmountable for him and Sherry. With that knowledge, I was content with a day that would keep giving, a day that provided food for the soul — one that still drips memories as sweet as honey from a comb. That, my friends, is as good as a day can get.

~Jay Seate

The Power of Gratitude

Eye Openers

*Gratitude always comes into play; research shows that people
are happier if they are grateful for the positive things in their
lives, rather than worrying about what might be missing.*
~Dan Buettner

11

The Right Place

*There are no extra pieces in the universe. Everyone is
here because he or she has a place to fill, and every
piece must fit itself into the big jigsaw puzzle.*
~Deepak Chopra

I shoved another can of soup onto the shelf, wondering where my life had gone. I was too old to be doing this. With each successive can I stocked, I found another reason to grumble. When you are wearing a nametag while pushing soup cans onto a shelf, and the first digit of your age is a number higher than two, certain facts become indisputable about the trajectory of your life.

I was working two jobs and still not making ends meet. My failing marriage was affecting my relationship with my daughter, too.

When a shopping cart bumped my back it seemed like a physical confirmation that I was out of sync and in the way. So I muttered "no problem" to the woman's apology and continued to push cans into their appropriate slots.

There was a little girl sitting in the shopping cart staring at me, her eyes bright with that gleam children get when they want to tell you something. She had a coat on that was perhaps a little too warm for the weather, and a funky tasseled hat with a rainbow pompom. Her eyes were huge and blue and took me back ten years to when my daughter was her age and loved hats like that. I smiled at her as she stared at my ponytail. When she saw that she had caught my eye, she spoke: "I have red hair just like you."

"Molly," her mother said. "Don't bother the man while he is working."

As I turned to say she wasn't bothering me, the child reached for her hat.

"No, Molly, leave it — "

It was too late. The hat was off and on the floor, revealing a skull without a strand of hair. The smooth alabaster skin intensified those bright eyes. Now they peered, boring into me, waiting for a reaction. In that instant, conflicting thoughts ran through me. Assuming the reason for the hair loss, I felt sympathy for the girl. Then I thought, "Why am I in this situation?" which immediately made me loathe myself because, considering the three actors in this small drama, I certainly had the easiest role.

> *"The day that photo was taken was the last time I heard her laugh... until today."*

"Redheads are the best!" I said, giving her a thumbs-up.

She giggled hysterically. "My brother has brown hair and it's nice... but... I like mine better. Mommy says it will grow back in two months." She held up three fingers then grabbed the errant one and pushed it down.

Her mom had scooped the hat up and slipped it back on Molly's head. Then she glanced at me and said, "I'm sorry."

I told her it was okay; there was nothing to apologize for. Nodding, she pushed the cart down the aisle, visibly upset. Molly waved and said, "Bye, Mister," and I waved back.

I resumed stocking the shelves, feeling a deep sadness at their situation. I also felt a little stupid that I hadn't caught on sooner, or had anything better to say.

I'd made it through two more aisles when I looked up and saw that Molly and her mom were in the section opposite me. A man was with them now, and when the mom saw me she touched his arm, whispered something to him, and then headed in my direction.

As she approached, she fumbled in her bag, not looking up until she was very near. I could see she held back tears. She touched my arm and said, "I wanted to thank you."

She was still searching through her bag and I had the bizarre thought that she meant to tip me. I couldn't imagine what she was thankful for. What she handed me instead was a photo of Molly. She was smiling and her face was framed by flaming red curls.

"That was taken two months ago, before the chemo."

"She's beautiful," I said, dumb for any other response.

"I wanted to thank you," she repeated.

"For what?"

"She loves to talk to people, and she loves to take her hat off. I think she actually likes being bald." She managed a little smile, and I chuckled.

"Good for her," I said.

"Yes, it is," she said as if trying to convince herself of it, "but, when she does take off her hat, people usually react awkwardly. I don't blame them. I mean, what can you say? And then they wind up talking to me instead of her, and she gets so sad."

Tears ran down her cheeks. "When she spoke to you, you barely even looked at me, and…" She couldn't go on for a moment. "…you made her laugh." Now the sob that she had been stifling escaped, but she caught it quickly. She nodded at the photo as I handed it back to her. "The day that photo was taken was the last time I heard her laugh… until today."

My breath caught at her words. "I'm sorry," I said, my voice choked with emotion. It sounded as empty as every other time I'd heard or said it.

She nodded. "I want you to know how much it meant to her that you treated her like a normal kid."

I looked at her. "She is," I said.

"Thank you."

"My thoughts are with you and Molly."

"My name is Maureen."

I told her my name and said, "Good luck, Maureen."

She turned and walked back to her family. They headed to the registers.

Despite my feelings of helplessness, I suddenly knew I was exactly where I was supposed to be that day.

~Thomas Behnke

12

The Couch
and the Grouch

Make your home as comfortable and attractive
as possible and then get on with living. There's
more to life than decorating.
~Albert Hadley

Every morning I sit in my comfy old recliner with a cup of coffee. Reading my Bible and praying helps me start my day. But a few months ago I found myself doing more than these rituals. I began grumbling as well.

You see, my recliner faced our living room window — and the couch beneath it. The old and worn and dirty blue couch. Its matching chair was in no better condition. My mind would then wander to the kitchen. The table and chairs in there were also shabby and outdated.

"We need new furniture," I complained to my husband Allen more than once. His reaction was always the same. We simply couldn't afford to replace anything. And then he would get a certain look in his eyes. Did I read defeat?

"It's embarrassing," I explained. It was getting to where I didn't want to invite guests over. I could only clean and rearrange so much! Would they notice the small cigarette hole in the couch, the sewed-up tear on the blue recliner's back, the worn spots on the kitchen chair cushions? Would they think I was a poor housekeeper?

I'm not a complainer most of the time, and I didn't like becoming a grouch. Allen was a hardworking man who had recently retired. My writing and speaking income didn't amount to much. What extra money we did have was often spent on traveling, something we both enjoyed immensely.

Allen took my complaints personally. "I'm doing the best I can," he said. That was true — on the outside of the house. He painted, tended the garden, mowed the lawn, pruned the trees. Why couldn't he see that the inside was important too? Was he just interested in how our neighbors perceived us? Did he care about what mattered to me?

One morning, while sitting in the old recliner — a hand-me-down from Allen's mother — I was jolted by a verse I read in the Bible. The apostle Paul told his readers that he had learned the secret of living with lots — and living with almost nothing. "I have learned to be content with whatever I have," he wrote.

> **The couch had to stay and the grouch had to go.**

It dawned on me at that moment that I had allowed my discontent to rob me of my joy. And it was beginning to affect my marriage. I hated to admit it, but the couch had to stay and the grouch had to go!

"I'm sorry I've become such a complainer," I apologized to God. "Thank you for all the good things you have provided for me. If it weren't for Allen, I could be living in a box. Please forgive me for not being content with what you have provided for me through this wonderful man."

I vowed that day to be content. What a relief to give God my desires and leave it at that! Whenever I was tempted to become a grouch again, I thanked him instead for all his provisions — and there were lots! I also found it helpful to think about those who would give anything to have my old furniture!

It's interesting how things have a way of working out when we truly trust God. A few months after I stopped complaining, my father passed away. And what did I inherit? His almost-new couch which was perfect for our living room — and his oak table and chairs that fit into our country kitchen beautifully!

We then bought a recliner and drapes at a Black Friday sale. And we had the joy of giving our old furniture to two needy families!

I am no longer a grouch — and I have my couch! And I will continue to be grateful for all that God has given me — and not given me. There is something to be said about contentment!

~Cathy Mogus

13

Note to Self

*The only real mistake is the one from
which we learn nothing.*
~John Powell

There was a noticeable shift in our routine the evening my mom sketched stationery. My mother, a lover of schedules, sent me to bed at the usual time of 9:30 but instead of turning in as she normally did, she remained in the living room.

When I didn't hear the tinny voice of a news anchor through the TV or the familiar swoosh of water streaming from the kitchen faucet, I wondered what kept my mother up past her bedtime. I found her hunched beneath our sole lamp, sketching. When I asked what she was drawing, my mother covered the page with her arms and ordered me back to bed.

A wave of resentment rose in my belly. Hadn't I begged my mother for pastels? And what about the construction paper she had denied me only a week ago? "Unless you intend to eat it for lunch, put it back," she'd said. Yet, here she was drawing in a pad that had to cost at least as much as the construction paper.

"It's not fair," I said before stomping my feet all the way to my bedroom.

That night, as I lay in bed gazing out the window, past the rooftops where chimneys puffed white smoke that swirled against the sapphire sky, I cursed my life. Why couldn't I be like the other kids at school who owned scratch-and-sniff stickers, and who ate Twinkies and Moon Pies at lunch? I fell asleep that evening believing I was the unluckiest girl in the world.

The next morning, the bags under my mother's eyes were darker and puffier than usual, and she yawned twice while stirring the pot of oatmeal. "Drink your juice," she said, pointing at the kitchen table.

"I don't want any," I said, still sullen from the night before.

"There are plenty of kids who don't have juice. You do, so drink up."

My mother often reminded me that there were many people less fortunate than us, people who didn't have beds to sleep in, or food in their fridge. But that morning, I didn't want to

> *I realized she had stayed up much of the night to spare me the ordinary.*

hear it. I covered my ears with my hands and thought, "So give those people my juice. I don't want it."

She sprinkled a spoonful of brown sugar on top of each bowl of oatmeal and carried them to the table. "I suppose you don't want any of this either," she said. That's when I noticed that a stack of paper sat next to my juice glass. I stepped closer and saw a perfect reproduction of Minnie Mouse on the top sheet. I glanced quickly at Mother, who stared at the oatmeal in her bowl, but the slight pink of her cheeks told me that she had made the drawing. When I fanned the sheets, Tinkerbelle, Papa Smurf, Winnie the Pooh and Charlie Brown leaped to life.

A month earlier, when my teacher Mrs. Hunter announced our class would complete a pen-pal project, I'd asked my mother to buy me stationery. At the drugstore, we learned that a pack of ten cost close to seven dollars. "You'll have to use regular paper," my mother said. But now I realized she had stayed up much of the night to spare me the ordinary.

Later that morning my classmates displayed their sheets of stationery while I blanketed my desk in my mother's drawings. "That's awesome," Sandi, the girl who sat next to me, said, pointing at my mother's sketch of Smurfette. "Wanna trade?"

For a second, I thought about swapping the drawing for one of Sandi's pink sheets of paper embossed with Strawberry Shortcake, but then I thought of my mother hunched beneath our lamp. I shook my head. "My mom made these for me," I said proudly.

"Cool," said Sandi. "My mom can't even draw a stick figure."

As I wrote letters to children in Ghana, Vietnam, Nicaragua, and Korea, I imagined their smiles as they opened the envelopes containing my mother's stationery, and for the first time, I realized that I was the luckiest girl in the world.

~Alicia Rosen

14

Two Seconds on the Microwave

*He who loves with purity considers not the gift of the
lover, but the love of the giver.*
~Thomas à Kempis

I have a touch of obsessive-compulsive disorder. Okay, perhaps it's more than a touch. I can be plain old neurotic. When I use the microwave at work and the person before me has not cleared it, leaving forty-five, ten or even just three seconds on the timer, it annoys me. It's a silly thing really, but it's inconvenient that I have to push "Reset" prior to entering my desired amount of time. Besides, it's the principle of the thing: it should be cleared.

When the same thing started happening at home, I was annoyed. My boyfriend John stops by to use my kitchen during his lunch break since he works right by my apartment building. A few weeks ago I was about to put a bowl of soup in the microwave when I noticed there was a "2" on the screen indicating it had not been cleared after John used it at lunch.

Didn't he know these little things bothered me? I let it go and forgot about it until a day or two later when I noticed a "1" left on the screen. Day after day there would be time left on my microwave. It wasn't a big enough deal to focus on it more than a couple of seconds, and I honestly forgot about it quite quickly, but I still experienced a moment of "Ugh! Men!" each time I discovered the microwave timer had not been cleared. Why was John doing this to me? Was he trying to push my buttons? Then the other day, I received my answer.

John came over in the evening to have dinner with me. I was about to place a bowl of vegetables in the microwave, when once again I noticed the "2" and finally had my opportunity to give him grief about his new bad habit. With what I hoped was a lighthearted smile, I said, "Hey! What's with you leaving time on the microwave all of a sudden and not clearing it when you're done? Are you trying to drive me crazy?" I wanted to use a playful, fun tone while also letting him know I found his new routine irritating.

> I gave him a kiss and said, "You're a wonderful man."

John's brow furrowed and he looked confused. And then he explained: "If I press stop before the time is up, the microwave only beeps once instead of three times. I don't want to wake you." I had recently begun working the night shift and sleeping during the day. While John was making his lunch in the kitchen, I was asleep in my bedroom at the other end of the apartment.

I felt my face redden with embarrassment and for a moment, I was speechless. Humbled, I walked over to where he was standing and wrapped my arms around him. I gave him a kiss and said, "You're a wonderful man."

Now, when I see two seconds left on the microwave, it's a reminder to appreciate the thoughtful, caring man I am blessed to have in my life.

~Savannah Dee

Something about Mary

At times our own light goes out and is rekindled by a
spark from another person. Each of us has cause to
think with deep gratitude of those who have
lighted the flame within us.
~Albert Schweitzer

Every time I sat down with my family and scanned through photos — holidays, trips, vacations — there was always something missing. Me. It was not simply because I was the one behind the camera, but because I avoided being photographed. I felt I always looked awful in photos. There were a few photos of me on my birthdays that always made me wince. I didn't hate the way I looked generally, I just wasn't very photogenic. So, when it came to family photos, I was MIA.

Then I met Mary. I was attending a writers' conference in North Carolina and she was a photographer who specialized in headshots for writers. As a budding writer, I needed a decent headshot for business cards and social media. I decided to give Mary a try.

The day of my appointment arrived. I wore a simple solid-colored top and understated jewelry. I checked the mirror and felt I looked okay, but I was sure the photos would not reflect that. By the time I had my photo session, it had begun to drizzle. My hair had started out nicely, but I knew the rain would flatten it down and frizz it up.

I reluctantly walked into the room. Mary greeted me with a sunny smile. She was casually dressed, with her dark hair pulled back from her pleasant face. I felt myself relax in her presence. I was sure she could sense the negative attitude I had about my appearance because she immediately began to reassure me. She promised my photos would be wonderful.

Mary led me outside onto the lush grounds of Ridgecrest Conference Center. With the bright new green of spring and flowers blooming everywhere, it was the perfect backdrop for photos, even on a cloudy day. She posed me by a small water feature and then on a bench nestled under some trees. The whole time she snapped pictures, she talked about how sad it made her that so many woman thought so little of their appearance and how much this hurt their self-esteem. Looking through the eye of her camera, she told me something amazing. She told me that I was beautiful. I was both surprised and skeptical.

A subtle bond began to form between us. As we strolled over to a rock column, Mary began to share some things about herself, personal problems that she had. We seemed to naturally fall into that type of friendship. Standing me in front of the column, she told me how to pose my body, how to angle my head. She was cheerful and encouraging and I began to feel a tiny seed growing inside me.

The session ended. We made arrangements for me to come back the next afternoon to pick out the photos I wanted to buy. She told me that she had difficulty remembering names and tried to make an association with my name. I volunteered "Debbie Does Dallas," sure she would get the reference. She didn't. Did I mention that I was at a Christian writer's conference? I found myself in the awkward position of explaining to Mary that this was the title of a well-known porno movie from the 1970's. I quickly assured her I had never seen it. She was laughing.

The next day, I sat down by Mary's laptop, apprehensive about reviewing the photos. The first one was already on the screen. I was stunned. Was that me? I looked great. As she scrolled through photo after photo, I realized it would be hard for me to choose. I loved them all. Even the rain looked more like sparkles in my hair than drizzle.

The more excited I got, the bigger Mary's smile grew. She was pleased with herself, not just because I liked the pictures, but because

I liked myself in the pictures. Mission accomplished. I wrote my check, filled out an address form, and gave her a big hug and an even bigger thank you before I left.

Back home, I posted one of my pictures on my Facebook and Twitter pages. I put another one on my business cards. I got so many compliments that I was over the moon.

Just a couple of months later, I was excited to hear that I was going to be interviewed for the local newspaper. After the interview, I was told that a photographer would be out to my home later that week. Oh no! I knew that wonderful Mary could take pictures that I loved, but what would this photographer do? I went to the Internet to research tips for being photographed. Then I picked an outfit and practiced

"You look like a different person. You are radiant."

the way I should sit or stand. I also practiced smiling into the mirror. I had learned a great tip for that. Clench your teeth. Smile with your eyes. It feels very fake, but it works well.

The day of the photo shoot came. Like Mary, this photographer directed me in my pose, how to tilt my head. He adjusted the lighting in the room. I clenched my teeth and smiled with my eyes. That picture made the front page. Wow! It looked great. I would probably have chosen a different outfit, but I was feeling good about myself in photos. I had Mary to thank for lighting that spark.

The next year, I attended the same conference. Waiting in line to sign up for my photo shoot, I noticed that I caught Mary's eye, but I wasn't sure she recognized me. On the day of the shoot, another woman was just finishing her forms and payment when I walked in. Mary's face lit up. "Debbie Does Dallas" she said. She remembered. The other woman looked a little shocked until Mary explained the reason for the reference.

After exchanging bear hugs, Mary and I walked out into the sunshine. She stopped on the steps.

"I am astounded at how much your countenance has changed," she said. "You look like a different person. You are radiant." Once again surprised by her words, I felt the tears in my eyes as I told her that she was largely responsible for that change. Then I saw the tears in hers. We walked the rest of the way with arms around one another's waists. The affection between us was strong and sweet.

Chatting like the old friends we felt we had become, she once again directed me through my photo shoot. I shared with her my secret on how to get a great smile every time, delighted that this was new to her.

She showed me the pictures. "Look at you. You have just bloomed." That was because she had a green thumb with people. Once again, the pictures were wonderful. But what was even more wonderful was seeing my new friend Mary again. I have a whole new outlook on myself, my relationships, and my future.

~Debbie Acklin

16

The Grateful Chauffeur

Appreciation is a wonderful thing. It makes what is
excellent in others belong to us as well.
~Voltaire

My daughter and I had just returned home after a concert at the middle school. Still in her long choir dress, Emily handed me a sealed envelope. "Chloe asked me to give this to you," she said.

Curious, I opened the envelope and unfolded a plain white sheet of paper. Emily's friend had written me a letter in cursive handwriting:

Dear Mrs. Laufer,
Thank you for driving me everywhere this year. I really appreciate it.
Sincerely,
Chloe Hoffman

Along the borders of the paper, she'd drawn daisies and rainbows and colored them with markers.

My eyes teared up. Chloe was thanking me, when I really should have been thanking her. Somehow this girl had made me appreciate all the things I took for granted in my life.

The day I met Chloe, I was already a chauffeur, but not a grateful one. It seemed all I did was drive my daughter places. On that particular day, I'd agreed to shuttle Emily to a JV football game.

"Can we pick up Chloe on the way?" she asked.

"Where does she live?"

"The trailer park."

"That's hardly on the way," I said. "Am I a taxi service?"

"Please?" Emily begged. "Chloe needs a ride."

"Oh, all right," I said with a sigh.

That afternoon, we parked outside the trailer where Chloe lived. Emily climbed up the steps and knocked on the door while I waited in the car. The trailer sat on a tiny plot. The siding and awnings could have used a fresh coat of paint. Long grass grew around the wooden steps, and a rusty vehicle sat in the carport. I'd forgotten that people lived this way.

After a little while, the girls came out from the rundown mobile home and got into the car. Emily introduced her friend, a thirteen-year-old with crystal blue eyes and a bright smile. The difference in the girls' physical features was striking. Chloe was short and small-framed, her blond hair cut in a pixie style, while Emily was tall and big-boned, with long dark hair and cow-brown eyes. The girls started talking about how they were wearing their school's colors. I dropped them off at the game and went home.

Compared to Chloe's trailer, my two-story house looked like a castle. In fact, all the houses in my subdivision did, with their big garages, large yards, and careful landscaping. I'd become accustomed to this neighborhood, but I hadn't always lived like this. I remembered the apartments my husband and I had rented early in our marriage, and later, the military quarters. After seeing where Chloe lived, I felt thankful that we now had a nice house.

The next time I picked up Chloe, it was to take the girls to a matinee. Emily disappeared inside the trailer and didn't come out. Waiting in the car, I kept looking at my watch. The girls would be late if we didn't leave soon. I got out, walked up the front steps, and peered through the screen door. When I knocked, a boy with features similar to Chloe's appeared.

"I'll get them," the boy said.

It was very quiet inside. Were the kids home alone?

When the boy didn't return, I called through the screen. "Emily!"

"Shhh!" Emily said, as she walked toward me. "Chloe's mother is sleeping."

Oh, so they weren't alone, after all. The mother was sleeping. That must be why Chloe's mother never drove her anywhere. She worked nights and slept during the day. I knew another mom whose work schedule was like that. She was there if her children needed her, but sound asleep most of the time. What a life that must be! I'd worked in the past, but always during the day. I was fortunate my husband's income allowed me to stay home now.

> *I'd been so quick to judge Chloe's parents without knowing the whole story.*

Driving Emily and Chloe became a habit. I took the girls to the library, school dances, and the ice skating rink. The two grew to be best friends, full of smiles whenever they were together. Since Emily's brother had gone to college, Emily didn't have a sibling at home, and I felt grateful that she had a friend who was as close as a sister.

A few months passed. When I picked up Chloe and dropped her off, Mr. Hoffman was often home. He'd wave to me from his yard, and I'd wave back.

"Was Mr. Hoffman laid off from his job?" I asked Emily.

"I'm not sure," she said. "I just know he's not working much any more."

That would explain why Chloe never seemed to have spending money when she went shopping with us. I felt thankful my husband's job was secure.

One Saturday afternoon, Emily wanted me to drive Chloe and her to the bowling alley, and it wasn't convenient for me. I'd already made plans to have my neighbor come over to help plan a block party.

"Can't Chloe's mother drive?" I asked.

"She's sick," Emily said.

Sure, I thought. I figured the woman was dodging responsibility, as some parents do, letting someone else pick up the slack. As a stay-at-home mom, I was used to having working mothers take advantage of my time and gas while they were busy with their own lives. It was a reflection of the sad state of parenthood these days. But it wouldn't be fair to blame Chloe, so I took the girls.

Eventually, my patience wore thin. When Emily came to me asking for another ride for her and Chloe, I'd had enough. "I don't see why Chloe's parents can't drive you two once in a while," I said. "Her father seems to be home a lot, and her mother can't possibly work seven days a week."

"Her mother's sick," Emily said.

"Again?" I said. "She always uses that excuse."

"It's not an excuse. She has cancer."

Oh. Chloe's mother wasn't dodging responsibility. She had cancer. "What kind of cancer?" I asked, my voice softer.

"Ovarian, I think."

"Why didn't you tell me?"

"They didn't know what it was at first."

"That must be terrible." All traces of resentment slipped away. I felt ashamed that I'd been so quick to judge Chloe's parents without knowing the whole story. Now I saw the last six months in a new light. Mr. Hoffman had been home taking care of his wife. No wonder Chloe always appeared happy to be getting away from the trailer park. What a dismal situation!

In the days that followed, I found myself being thankful for my family's good health. We were so fortunate to have never been touched by a serious illness.

"What's wrong, Mom?" Emily asked as I stared at Chloe's letter through my tears.

"This is beautiful," I said. Chloe's words warmed my heart. They made up for all my time and gas. She didn't take me for granted, as most teens would have. On the contrary, I'd been the one taking everything for granted, and I had so much to be thankful for! I kept Chloe's letter, with its colorful daisies and rainbows, and now, whenever I reread it, I remember to count my blessings.

~Mary E. Laufer

17

My Wiser Self

Envy is a waste of time.
~Author Unknown

It was 3:00 a.m. and I was sitting on the couch watching television. An infomercial for some wondrous product blared through the quiet night, promising it would change my life. "If only it were that easy," I thought. Sleep had eluded me once more. I stared blankly at the TV as my mind wandered, making a mental list of how I wished things would change.

I got up and shuffled my way to the kitchen for another cookie. My worries seemed to subside as the sweetness of the chocolate chips filled my senses. "Chocolate really does make everything better, even if only for a few minutes," I thought. My late night dates with the TV and cookies had become a habit, my way of comforting myself.

I admitted to myself I had fallen victim to the Green-Eyed Monster. Having a pity party in the wee hours of the night had become a regular routine. With my husband and children asleep, the house was quiet. It was just me and the television and the chocolate chip cookies to help ease my envy.

Lately it seemed everyone I knew was moving on and I was just an observer. My friends had new cars, vacations, designer clothes and new homes. Yet my world was standing still. We continued to live a simple lifestyle. I was convinced my life was boring and I needed a change.

The next day was Sunday and we decided as a family to stay home and de-clutter some of our closets. I tried hard not to think of my friend who was on a weekend ski trip.

The kids were to put their outgrown toys and clothes in large plastic bins. My husband would clean out the hallway closet that had become a catchall for everything. I would work on our bedroom closet. Once our bins were full, we would go through them and decide what to donate, keep, or throw out.

I was in the midst of full-force cleaning when a fleck of blue caught my eyes. There on a shelf, squeezed between old purses and shoes, was my teenage diary. I had written it in a spiral notebook over a three-year period. Looking at the worn cover decorated with my hand-drawn doodles I couldn't help but smile. Inside, I saw my teenage handwriting. All of the letter "i's" were dotted with cute hearts and my exclamation marks were tripled to show my super excitement. It was obvious I was a happy teenager. I decided to take a small break from de-cluttering to read some of my diary entries.

> *Now, as an adult, how could I have been so blinded by material possessions?*

Sitting in my kitchen with a steaming cup of tea, I grabbed a chocolate chip cookie and started to read. After reading several pages I began to realize that, although I had many obstacles as a teen, I had a positive attitude and I expressed my gratitude often about my family, friends and the teachers who helped guide me. I had a zest for life even when it was difficult.

I was ready to get back to cleaning when I flipped the pages of the diary one more time. Call it fate, but one sentence jumped right out at me: "I promise myself to not be jealous of my friends anymore and not care if they have better things than I do. I want to be happy!" My younger self had just opened my eyes.

Growing up I lived in a housing project in Brooklyn, New York. We managed with bare necessities, and yet, as young as I was, I had come to terms with it and learned to accept and be grateful for what I had. Now, as an adult, how could I have been so blinded by material possessions? I had more than enough. After all, here we were cleaning out our overstuffed closets to donate to others.

That night at 3:00 a.m., when I normally would have had my pity party, I took out a notebook. With a pen in one hand and a chocolate chip cookie in the other, I started to write: "Dear diary, it's been a while since I wrote my thoughts. I am grateful for…" And so it began. As my gratitude list got longer, my spirits lifted. I dotted my "i's" with hearts and my explanation marks were tripled!

I've been keeping my diary for seven years now. My late night pity parties are now replaced with a good night's sleep. The Green-Eyed Monster took a little time to leave. If she does return every now and then, I remind myself of all the things for which I am grateful. I focus on what I have, and not on what I don't. I am grateful for my family, friends, health, pets and my home. I am also grateful to my teenage self, that girl who taught her older, but not wiser, self to count her blessings.

~Dorann Weber

18

My Renewed Joy

Kindness is a language which the deaf
can hear and the blind can read.
~Mark Twain

There was a knock at the door on that cold St. Louis winter day. My three-year-old hugged my leg as I turned the knob to open it. It was my neighbor from across the street. "I'm heading to the mall, want to come?"

I smiled hesitantly. I was still getting used to accepting help — people reading for me, or taking me places and guiding me as I walked. It was a constant reminder that I was now dependent on the kindness of others.

I was in the happiest period of my life, caring for my three-, five-, and seven-year-old sons. And without warning, my vision closed in, leaving me in total darkness. The retinal deterioration robbed me of my sight in only eighteen months. No cure. No surgery. No hope.

I spent nights awake, wondering what my life would be like. How would I care for my sons? How deprived would they feel by having a blind mom?

I tossed and turned, but no answers came — only a wave of anxiety as I faced a monster I could not defeat.

"You have to wait, sweet thing," I said to my three-year-old when he wanted cereal. I first had to find the correct box and make sure I poured the milk carefully and slowly to avoid overflowing the bowl, to avoid making yet another mess.

"Where is Daddy?" he asked.

Their father worked long hours to keep the family fed. And help from family was scarce as my mom was busy with her own trauma, because my dad, coincidentally, was also losing his sight. I inherited the gene from him, but his took much longer to manifest. He was fifty-five and I was only thirty.

"Can I come over and help?" my mom would often ask.

I did need her, but I couldn't put more burdens on her. "I'm okay. Don't worry. The boys and I are fine," I said.

I wasn't fine. Yet while I fought fear and worry, I managed to cook and clean. My memory sharpened and I memorized phone numbers to call for rides to my boys' soccer practices and Cub Scout meetings.

But in that cold December season, when Christmas carols echoed everywhere and most families around the neighborhood prepared to celebrate, I sunk deeper into my sorrow. Decorating the house, shopping for gifts, and baking cookies were tasks that seemed to mock my inability to get them done.

Christmas morning came, my first as a blind person. Three pairs of little feet bounced around our bed. "I want to open presents!" one of the boys shouted. "Me too!" his brothers echoed.

I felt around at the foot of the bed to find my robe, slipped it on, and followed their cheerful voices into the family room, where a pine scent filled the air. For a brief moment, the joy of my little boys made me forget I couldn't see.

Then my new reality set in. "Okay, we have to do this in order," I instructed. "Daddy will give one present to each of you and you will open it when we tell you to do so."

"Me first!" our youngest shouted as he ripped the wrapping off. "Wow! This is cool!" he screamed. Everything in me longed to see the expression on his little face. What had he opened? What made him so excited? I blinked back tears and chided myself—why couldn't I just enjoy what I was hearing? But the more they oohed and aahed, the more I was overwhelmed by my desire to see.

I rose from the couch. "I'll be right back." I felt my way along the wall back to our bedroom. My eyes burned as I fought back tears. I sat on our bed and said to myself, "Lord, why is this affecting me so? Please help me to understand. Show me how to cope... I don't know how."

As I silently cried, my husband came in. He put his arms around me. "What can I do for you, honey?"

"I'm okay." I brushed the tears off my face with the back of my hand.

"Mommy, Daddy, can we open some more?" the boys called out.

"I'll be there in a minute," I whispered to my husband. I yanked a tissue from the box on our dresser, and tried to swallow my pain with a deep sigh.

"This is the best present of all!" my oldest shouted! "How did you know, Mom?"

> **I didn't need eyesight to relish the moment with them.**

His words struck me. I froze. How did I know? Of course I knew. I knew what each of them wanted, what they wished, what they loved and exactly what made them excited.

I didn't need eyesight to know all about my sons. Without being able to see, I could still love them, care for them, please them and even discipline them.

A dark veil lifted from my heart. I didn't need eyesight to relish the moment with them, to delight in their shouts of surprise when they opened another present. I savored their silly comments. And I found a fresh new joy in their "I love you, Mom."

"Thank you," I whispered. But I was thanking God for opening the eyes of my heart. That day I learned to appreciate the richness I had in my three happy little boys.

And because of them, eventually I became a happy mom, a secure wife, and a fun friend again!

The day after Christmas I called my neighbor. "Want to head to the mall? Lots of bargains out there."

She helped me to the passenger seat and we took off.

Sometime prior, she had asked me if, after losing my sight, another sense had developed.

"Yes," I said, "my sense of humor did."

We joked and laughed while we rode to the mall. Holding on to her arm, we visited stores. With minute detail, she described items on the rack and we came home with bargains. Those shopping trips became our yearly routine.

I quickly learned to dare to expect great things, because each day without eyesight gave me the insight to see what makes life worth living, what brings significance to my days, and how I see each season shine with renewed joy.

~Janet Perez Eckles

19

Body Beautiful

Love yourself first and everything else falls into line.
You really have to love yourself to get anything
done in this world.
~Lucille Ball

The sunlight peeking through the cracks in the Las Vegas-style "blackout" curtains that adorn my bedroom signals the beginning of another day. I reluctantly throw off the covers and drag myself toward the bathroom.

Am I a positive person? Yes. Am I a positive person immediately upon awakening? No.

I step on the scale and inwardly groan at the number that greets me. It doesn't even matter what the number is that day. I am never pleased with it. After facing the scale, it is time for the daily "inventory" that takes place in front of the unforgiving mirror in my dressing area.

Furtively glancing about to make sure that no one is around to make fun of me, I gently tug back at the "parentheses" that appear around my mouth. I ponder the possibility of one day resembling one of our country's founding fathers. I wonder how to make the mouth-parentheses disappear without engaging in medical procedures that may result in my looking like I was caught in a windstorm.

Years ago, the late Nora Ephron wrote a wonderful book entitled *I Feel Bad About My Neck*. I now get that. I have lost weight, which is good… except now it looks like someone let all the air out of my neck, which is not so good.

I turn to analyze my profile. Have you ever met a woman who doesn't complain about her abs? I am no exception. Thanks to thirteen major abdominal surgeries starting at the age of fifteen, I had a "mom apron" long before I became a mother — and that area definitely did not improve with age or childbirth.

My back hurts. What else is new?

Every woman has a "go-to" feature that she loves to showcase and for me, it has always been my legs. But you know what no one warns you about? Saggy knees. Knees! Knees are not supposed to sag. Faces? Perhaps. Breasts? Don't get me started. But apparently, gravity also hits you in the knees... literally. A few years ago, my brilliant friend who is also a bestselling author wrote about the "smiley faces" that she claimed were threatening to appear around her knees. At the time, I thought it was funny, especially because she is annoyingly gorgeous and smiley-face-free. Now I want to yell at her for not including a disclaimer that her knee story was actually a cautionary tale.

Turning away from the mirror, I put on my glasses (because my eyes are also not what they used to be) and slog downstairs for a cup of whatever beverage is within reach. It could be coffee. It could be the cats' hairball medicine. I am not awake enough to notice.

Except that today is different.

Today — I have had an epiphany.

The number on the brutally honest scale that makes me groan also reflects the fact that I am healthy when too many cannot say the same — and that I have more than enough to eat whenever I wish.

The "parentheses" around my mouth reflect many years of laughter. The faint lines on my cheeks are marks left by dimples inherited from my father. How lucky I am to have had a number of reasons to laugh when so many have experienced much more difficulty and challenge in their lives. And when I see those dimple lines, I also see glimmers of my late father, which makes them even better.

A bust line that I could tuck into my waistband also nursed a healthy infant. More importantly, it is a healthy bust line. When so many women of all ages are fighting for their lives because their breasts have been invaded by disease, I realized how fortunate I am. My own personal health "scare" turned out to be nothing more than a "scare."

The "mom apron" borne of so many surgeries? Those surgeries were performed by wonderful specialists who eventually enabled me to bear a child that I was never supposed to be able to have. An abdominal flaw seems a small price to pay in comparison to the experience of motherhood and the beautiful young woman who lights up my life every day.

Back pain? While admittedly uncomfortable on occasion, that back pain is also a badge of honor. It is a back that has twisted, arched, flexed and withstood years of athletic demand and punishment. It is a back that supported a healthy pregnancy and allowed me to carry a child in my arms for years thereafter. It is a back that allowed me to lift, physically support, and care for a dying husband. Whatever pain I experience as a result of all of these experiences is treatable. Even the most excruciating moments are only temporary for me.

> The "parentheses" around my mouth reflect many years of laughter.

The legs with the hint of smiley-faced knees are legs that still work — and they work well. Those legs kicked off the covers this morning. Those legs worked when I put feet to floor to get out of bed. They are strong and muscular. I can dance, hike and lift weights. How many would give anything to have healthy legs and are instead challenged by illness or infirmity that has robbed them of the ability to even stand?

Finally, the eyes that are not working as efficiently as they once did still do their job nonetheless. My eyes permit me to work. They take in the beauty of the outdoors. They read incessantly. They have seen my child grow up. They have cried tears of deepest sorrow; they have cried tears of joy, happiness and celebration. It saddens me to think about the many who can no longer see or perhaps worse, have never seen the sights with which I have been blessed throughout my life.

So in consideration of all of these realizations, I decided to endeavor toward changing my attitude. I now focus on what I have, rather than what I may have "lost" through years of living what has been and continues to be a beautiful life.

And to my mind, I have a "beautiful body" to go with that beautiful life — faults, flaws, wrinkles, "aprons," smiley-faces and all.

Did these realizations change me forever? Not entirely. I still periodically tug at the mouth-parentheses and scowl at the scale. I squint when trying to read street signs and curse because I can't wear an amazing backless dress. But while I am yelling at the scale and pulling at my face and laughing at all of the rest of it, I remember to be grateful and rejoice with an attitude of gratitude. Despite societal expectations and all the attendant body image issues that we women have, I am filled with gratitude for a body that has lived well, worked well, and continues to carry me quite well through all of life's adventures.

~Carole Brody Fleet

The Power of Gratitude

Practicing Gratitude

*Life is not about receiving at all times; it is a combination of
being thankful for what you have as blessings and sharing
those blessings with others who need a little fraction of
what you have.*
~Catherine Pulsifer

20

The Blessed List

The best time to love with your whole heart
is always now, in this moment, because no
breath beyond the current is promised.
~Fawn Weaver

arlene was poised and elegant as she made her way to the sofa in my counseling office. In her late sixties, she spoke with confidence but also with a twinge of anger in her voice. Her husband had recently retired and she was feeling the pressure of being with him 24/7.

"He's driving me crazy!" she lamented. "I give him instructions on the simplest things, like making coffee or operating a blender, and then I end up repeating myself ten times before the task is completed. For goodness' sake, the man was an engineer for forty years! Have I spoiled him so badly that I've made him helpless? The truth is, no matter how much you love a guy it's not easy to be around him all the time. I used to miss him while he was at work. Now I miss missing him!"

We both laughed, but I got her meaning. So I suggested she do two things. The first was to write a blessed list. That's a list of everything she loved and valued about her husband, everything he was or did that blessed her. The second was to persuade her husband to see a doctor, just to make sure there was nothing wrong with him.

Two weeks later, she returned with a lengthy list of her husband's wonderful attributes. He was a good father and grandfather; he was an excellent provider; he was funny, faithful, and protective. The list went on and on. As she finished reading her copious list to me, she laid it on her lap and said, "I really have to thank you. Your gratitude exercise has changed the way I look at things. It made me realize what a great man I'm married to — even if he does drive me crazy at times."

"Keep reading your list," I offered. "Read it at least three times a day for the rest of the month, then once a day after that. Add to it when you think of new things or when he does something that is especially endearing. The list can never get too long."

Earlene came to see me a couple more times for some encouragement and accountability. She was a quick study, and she practiced what she was learning. I encouraged her to keep reading and focusing on her husband's favorable qualities.

> *"I was reacting so negatively until I realized all the good my husband brought into my life."*

Three years passed and I received a letter with Earlene's name and a Montana return address. She was living with her daughter, and she came across my card when she was going through some old papers. "I wanted to give you an update on my life. Four months after I came for counseling, I finally convinced my husband to see a doctor. The doctor discovered he had a brain tumor. He died five months later!"

"I am so grateful I had made a blessed list," she wrote. "It changed my heart. I was reacting so negatively until I realized all the good my husband brought into my life. My paradigm shifted and I was able to love him as he ought to be loved before he died. I shudder to think of what would have happened had I not come to see you. I would have grumbled and groused until it was too late to show him how thankful I was to be his wife. Embracing appreciation in place of my frustration was a gift to him, but it was a gift to me as well, one I will never forget."

While I have always believed in the benefit of gratitude to improve mood, Earlene's letter helped to strengthen my conviction. Now I recommend writing a blessed list not just for folks in relationship challenges, but also for those feeling the pain of grief and loss, as well as people who struggle with self-esteem issues. As Earlene's list confirmed, an attitude of gratitude can make all the difference.

~Linda Newton

21

Gratitude Is an Action

We cannot live only for ourselves. A thousand fibers
connect us with our fellow men.
~Herman Melville

I felt as though I'd been punched in the stomach. The call came on a chilly fall evening. My son Matt was on the line, confessing the sins of his compulsive gambling, completely blindsiding me.

"Mom, my life is crashing. I'm in a lot of trouble and I need help," he said, his voice quivering. "I don't know what to do."

I listened patiently as he spelled out the consequences of his ugly addiction — abandonment, anxiety, embezzlement, and unemployment. My heart ached as Matt's pain became my own. I tried to process it all, but found it impossible to believe that I had been completely clueless to the charade I had believed was his life. Had there been signs? Could I have done something differently?

The next morning, I flew 2,000 miles to be with Matt and help him pick up the pieces of his shattered existence. He had barely slept and was much thinner than when I last saw him. The devastation was evident on his face and he looked well beyond his twenty-six years, his face pale and drawn. Newly married, his wife left immediately and his friends disassociated themselves from him as quickly as possible.

After an initial appointment with a psychologist specializing in addiction treatment, we headed to a Gamblers Anonymous (GA) meeting. Modeled on the same twelve-step principles as Alcoholics

Anonymous, GA would be a big part of Matt's path to recovery. We were greeted by an older man in torn jeans and a black T-shirt. Sporting a long, scraggly gray beard and wearing a knit hat, he could have easily blended in with the city's homeless. "Welcome. I'm Jim. Is this your first time?" he said.

Matt muttered, "Yeah. I'm a gambler. I need help."

"Well, you've come to the right place," Jim confirmed. "Have a seat."

Nearly thirty men and women of various ages and ethnicities were gathered in the room. One by one, they shared their heartbreaking stories of loss and devastation, broken relationships and economic ruin. Some, like Matt, were new to the program. Others had not gambled for over twenty years. All shared their hope for better days and gratitude for the program, the fellowship and the opportunity to turn their lives around.

I found it hard to imagine that there was a way back from the utter destruction of addiction. For Matt, the idea that he would ever be whole again was unfathomable. Yet, in this room, with this community, we would eventually learn that gratitude is more than a feeling, but rather an action. I would also learn that gratitude was something that was not exclusive to addiction recovery, but rather something to be incorporated into my life each and every day.

The months that followed were difficult. Matt needed ongoing treatment and was unable to work; thus, I had to provide substantial financial support. His former employer, out to seek both justice and vengeance, insisted the prosecution press for the harshest possible punishment. Matt was out on bond and confined to the state in which he lived. We hired an attorney and checked Matt into an in-patient treatment program. His days were filled with therapy, GA meetings, community service and court dates.

I flew back and forth a dozen times that year. I was deluding myself, thinking that things couldn't get worse and that there was no way a judge would send my son to prison. This was, after all, his first offense. He was remorseful and making progress in treatment. I was wrong.

I will never forget the day that Matt was sentenced to eight months in a state penitentiary. We arrived at the courthouse with his attorney and treatment center personnel. As we waited outside the courtroom, we noticed that a circle of thirty of Matt's friends from the recovery community had formed on the courthouse steps. With arms linked, they chanted the Serenity Prayer, in unison, asking for acceptance, courage and wisdom.

The group made their way upstairs and met us in the hall. By now, twenty more friends had arrived, demonstrating their support for Matt and our family. They gathered once again, taking Matt and me into the fold. One participant led the group in expressing gratitude for the ability to be present and supportive, and expressing the hope that Matt would remain safe and strong no matter what the sentence. They affirmed that, no matter how difficult the coming months might be, they would not abandon us.

> *We need to be active participants in our lives and those of others, expressing our gratitude by doing.*

That day, I experienced true gratitude for the first time and understood that it was not simply an obscure concept reserved for recovering addicts. Each individual in that circle was grateful for the opportunity to be supportive, no matter how his or her own life was going. Gratitude was demonstrated by action, not simply by words or thoughts.

My life has been forever changed since that experience. I take the time each morning and each night to acknowledge the blessings in my life. Our family's health, safety, livelihood, friendships — these are just a few reasons to be grateful. But showing gratitude simply by saying "thank you" is not enough. We need to be active participants in our lives and those of others, expressing our gratitude by doing.

There are unlimited ways to demonstrate gratitude and I have chosen to incorporate as many into my life as possible. When someone I know is ailing or grieving, I make an effort to check in and see what I can do to help. Sometimes, just sitting silently with someone who is in pain can make a tremendous difference. I volunteer my time as a crisis counselor on a weekly basis. I smile at strangers in the elevator, or help my neighbor carry in her groceries. I am far from perfect, but I try to contribute positive energy to the world.

Matt has turned his life around, and while we will never forget those horrific days, we can now look at them with greater perspective. I tell my story of finding gratitude to inspire others and as a testament to the strength and spirit of community.

~Cara Rifkin

22

Finding Five

*A personal journal is an ideal environment in which
to "become." It is a perfect place for you to think, feel,
discover, expand, remember, and dream.*
~Brad Wilcox

During my years of teaching kindergarten, my favorite lesson was about the Thanksgiving holiday. I loved introducing the students to history by sharing the story of the first Thanksgiving and allowing them to dress like a Pilgrim or Native American for a special Thanksgiving celebration.

Each child brought a snack to share with the class, and we practiced counting skills, sorting skills, and even patterning with the goodies before they were eaten. Our school cafeteria prepared a traditional Thanksgiving dinner, and the holiday felt more meaningful to me than the other holidays. I loved hearing what each child talked about when we took turns sharing our thanks.

One day, when I was online researching different ways to celebrate Thanksgiving with children, I read "The Legend of the Five Kernels." There are many versions of this story, but suffice it to say that there is a tradition that involves placing five kernels of corn at the seat of each guest. Whether this is to commemorate the fact that the Pilgrims subsisted on five kernels of corn per day during tough times, or whether the five kernels represented five things the Pilgrims were giving their thanks for, is unclear.

I became excited about using the five kernels approach with my students as a way of starting a conversation about giving thanks. Instead of using five kernels of corn, I placed five candy corns on each child's desk and asked them to share five things for which they were thankful.

That custom in my classroom led to my decision to include gratitude in my daily journal. I decided to list five blessings about each day. A sample list for one day might have included that I was blessed with all green lights when I was running late for school; the principal complimented me on my new bulletin board display; my students behaved well; my coworker surprised me with a helping of her homemade cheese bread; and the headache I had before lunch went away after I ate.

After several days of writing down my blessings, I read the lists and realized everything was all about me. Shouldn't I be blessing others?

After that revelation, my journaling changed.

Not only did I list five blessings that happened for me, but also five ways in which I had reached out to bless others. A sample list of the blessings I tried to give to others might have included that I blessed my friend by watching her class during my planning time so she could go next door to the hospital to check on her sick husband; I duplicated copies of a special worksheet for all the kindergarten teachers, not just for myself; I shared my Play-Doh rolling pins with the new teacher across the hall; I volunteered to take ticket money at the ballgame for a sick worker; and I found extra supplies for someone whose supplies had run out.

> *By hunting for the blessings in my day, my mind was focused on the good, not on the disappointments.*

As I journaled this new way, I found myself becoming a more positive, caring person. By hunting for the blessings in my day, my mind was focused on the good, not on the disappointments. By thinking of ways to reach out and help someone, my mind was focused on others, not on my own little problems.

In the past, I often had magnified the negative and minimized the positive, but now I was magnifying the positive and minimizing the negative. There wasn't anything magical about the number five; I just chose to list five because it was the number in the "Legend of the Five Kernels." I realized quite quickly that I had way more than five blessings occur to me each day, and I even managed to perform more than five good deeds for others each day as well.

I take the time now to review my journal and reread all the blessings I've received and the blessings I've made happen for other people. It helps put things in perspective. I am much more thankful nowadays, and giving thanks is not just something I do in November. It has become a year-round lifestyle.

~Helen F. Wilder

23

A Gift Returned

*When you give and carry out acts of kindness, it's as
though something inside your body responds and says,
"Yes, this is how I ought to feel."*
~Rabbi Harold Kushner

It was two weeks before Christmas and my heart was full of joy and gratitude. I had been employed at my new job for two months and I loved it. This job, as an advisor to the students of an online college, made it possible for my husband Tom and me to move to Colorado to be closer to our new grandchildren. We were even going to be able to buy a house.

I stomped the crystalline snowflakes from my new boots (I hadn't needed any in Arizona) and proudly walked through the doors of the tall golden building in the Denver Tech Center. "Good morning," I chirped as I strode to my office cubicle, but no one replied. I looked around and no one was smiling back at me. My friend Luanne motioned me to a deserted corner of the office.

"People are being laid off! Lots of people," she whispered. Seeing my face turn a bit ashen she countered, "Oh, I'm sure you'll be fine. They just hired you."

As I walked to my desk all I could think was, "Last in, first out. I'm gone." I felt a little faint and shaky. I started my computer and pulled up the list of students I needed to call. My job was to encourage and inspire our at-risk students, the ones who were missing assignments or earning a failing grade.

It was hard to focus on my work as I watched my manager step over to various desks and ask employees to follow him to his office one at a time. Occasionally I heard angry words or a door shut just a little too forcefully. My coworkers' eyes darted about the room from face to face. We all felt disaster was imminent, but we had no power to stop it. One woman walked past my desk as she was escorted out of the building, clutching her box of personal items. Tears were streaming down her face. "You don't do this to people before Christmas!" she shouted as she left the office.

At 10:28 a.m. I felt a tap on my shoulder. It was Chris, my manager, leaning in and whispering in a low voice, "Please stop what you are doing and come to my office immediately." I could feel everyone watching me as I took the long walk past their cubicles. This manager, the one who had been so eager to hire me two months before, was about to fire me.

> *"The one thing I did not expect to hear today was 'thank you.'"*

What would I tell my husband? My dream of buying a house in Colorado was his dream too, but we needed both our incomes to qualify for a mortgage. What if it took a long time to find a new job? How would I find one I liked as much as this one? Who would hire me, a sixty-year-old woman? Worries and fears swirled around in my head as I walked into Chris's office.

"Please sit down," he said. He shut the door behind me and handed me a packet of information. The director of our department was in the office, too, and both men looked beaten and weary. My thoughts turned to the pain they must be feeling as they were forced to do this right before the holidays. The director explained that the orders came from the corporate office out east. There were papers I would need to sign and procedures I would need to follow that were outlined in the packet.

I nodded as they droned through the reasons for the massive layoff, but I hardly heard a word. They had spoken these words many times that morning and would have to repeat them many more times before the day came to an end. I felt sorry for them.

When I didn't say anything, Chris asked me, "Do you have any questions? Are you going to be okay?" I took a deep breath and assured them with more confidence than I felt that I would land on my feet.

Then I asked, "How are you doing? This must be brutal for you." The two men admitted to the pain and exhaustion they were feeling and I was compelled to encourage them. I smiled and shook Chris's hand. "I am so appreciative that you hired me two months ago. I have loved this job and my husband and I could not have moved here without it. Thank you so much."

I turned and shook the director's hand and told him how grateful I was to have met and worked with him too. The two men looked at each other and shook their heads.

Chris rubbed his weary face and said, "The one thing I did not expect to hear today was 'thank you.'" He chuckled quietly.

At the conclusion of our meeting, I took my "walking papers" and boxed my personal belongings. I hugged a few coworkers and told security I was ready to be escorted down to the lobby.

When I told my husband that my job was gone, he replied, "Then we have to make some plans."

"Oh," I moaned, "I am not ready to start the job hunt just yet. I have to process this first."

"No," he smiled, "I meant we need to plan where we will eat lunch. I am taking the afternoon off so we can walk and talk." Tom's calm demeanor assured me that we would be okay.

That night, as I pulled my cell phone out of my purse to plug it in, I noticed I had a voicemail from a number I did not recognize. I had kept the ringer off all day. I listened to the message and could not believe what I was hearing. It was from the recruiter for a different online university. The woman said that I was highly recommended by my former manager. The director at the new university wanted to meet me Monday morning! They had a position open that was perfect for me. "Anyone who can be so grateful as they are leaving a job would be amazing coming in to one!" she said.

I had always thought of thank yous as little gifts that you give to others to brighten their day, gifts that are never returned. However, the day that I was hired to a new job just hours after being laid off I knew that my gift of gratitude had been returned to me in abundance.

~Lindy Schneider

24

Out of Darkness

The struggle ends when the gratitude begins.
~Neale Donald Walsch

I always say that there are two kinds of people in the world: People with issues, and dead people. Regardless of what external circumstances life has given us, we all face issues steeped in the darkness of internal, mental chaos. As a professional counselor, I have spent more than 18,000 hours working with people who are lost in the lightless realm of shame, sadness, fear, and anger. I have stood outside the cell doors of people locked away in solitary confinement, and I have sat in luxurious rooms while working with celebrities on television. I've worked with people who are so destitute that they do not have a place to live and billionaires who can buy everything but peace; and through it all, I have seen that absolutely everyone faces internal darkness at some point.

It would be difficult to convince me that there is not a lot of suffering in the world, because I have chosen a career path that puts me face to face with it every day. When we lose our way, there is one universal countermeasure to the suffering we experience, and this antidote works for everyone, across all cultures and circumstances: Gratitude.

At the lowest point in my life, when I was struggling in the deepest depths of my own darkness, I had difficulty seeing even an ounce of light. I had heard that expressing gratitude in times of pain was helpful, but I felt like I was experiencing too much real hurt to actually trust what sounded to me like some mysterious, "out-there," transformative power. Also, at the time, I was so overwhelmed by the emotional pain I felt that I could not think of anything for which I could be thankful. But as anyone who has ever been to their lowest depths knows, desperate times call for desperate measures, and if there really was anything to this idea of gratitude, I figured it couldn't hurt to give it a shot.

I remember the night it happened. I sat down on the ground and took a couple of breaths as if I was going to meditate. I couldn't meditate at that point, however, because I couldn't concentrate. I tried to think of things for which I was grateful, but all that kept coming up for me was what I "didn't have," and the emotional agony I felt. I found myself crying, thinking about what was hurting so badly, and then something strange happened. As I was sobbing, I took in a deep breath to get myself under control, and in an instant it hit me in the most genuine way: *At least I have my breath.* And so I said "thank you" for my breath. The moment I said that, I said it again. I really thought about my breath and how I could breathe (which, when you're hyperventilating from crying so hard and then stop, becomes very present); and in the few seconds I was thinking about it, I realized that I had a few seconds of reprieve from the emotional pain. In the following moments, I found myself thinking of the reprieve, and then I noticed that I was no longer crying.

> *I was fascinated that expressing gratitude got me out of such an utterly helpless dark spot.*

Just as an addict might be desperate for a drug that brings any sense of relief, I found myself equally desperate to hold onto that moment of reprieve, so I started to say "thank you" for the most basic things that came to mind. I was sitting on the ground at the time, and, never having been a very flexible person, I noticed that my leg was really uncomfortable, and then it hit me: *At least I have legs.* That temporary discomfort in my legs got me to stop thinking about my emotional pain for another instant, so I thought, "I'm really thankful for my legs."

Then I said "thank you" for my arms and hands and fingers. I started expressing gratitude for my entire body and then for my basic senses, and after I said "thank you" for my hearing, I started to recognize some other things in my life for which I was genuinely grateful.

Gratitude got me through that moment. As a highly introspective person, I was fascinated that expressing gratitude got me out of such an utterly helpless dark spot. I thought about it a lot through that evening, although I have to be honest that a lot of the painful thoughts returned that night.

The instant my eyes opened that next morning, the first thought that came to me was, "Thank you for letting me be alive." I started my day off thinking of all the things for which I was grateful. The pain still ebbed and flowed throughout my day, but it was less than the day before. And so I made saying "thank you" a priority for myself as frequently as possible. Waking up expressing gratitude in the way I did affected me so powerfully, however, that I can tell you this: Not a single instant of waking up from that moment forward in my life has ever occurred without me saying, "Thank you for letting me be alive."

From gratitude for my life to gratitude for even having that difficult experience, I have witnessed the profound effect that gratitude can have. I am so genuinely appreciative that I had that low point, because it taught me a pathway to peace. More than that, however, what I carry with me to this day is that I don't have to wait until I am through darkness to express gratitude for it. Recognizing that I will learn from any tough time allows me to say "thank you" even in the midst of the most intense shame, sadness, fear, or anger, because what I am grateful for is the lesson I know will result from that pain.

I am who I am today because I made it through my darkest experience, just as you are who you are because of the obstacles you've faced and overcome. We all have issues, and as long as we are alive, we always will. Suffering is a part of life, but so too, is gratitude. And whether you are incarcerated or free, a billionaire or homeless, a celebrity or relatively unknown to the general public, you will inevitably encounter some kind of internal darkness at different points. When you do, I hope you find gratitude, because I have no doubt that gratitude is the fastest possible path to the light.

~Christian Conte

Editor's note: To listen to Publisher Amy Newmark's Chicken Soup for the Soul Podcast interview with Dr. Christian Conte please go to chickensoup.podbean.com/e/friend-friday-dr-christian-conte-of-vh1s-familyl-therapy-talks-to-amy-about-anger-management-and-gratitude/

25

The Summer
that Almost Wasn't

Look for the blessing in all situations.
~Wayne Dyer

W hen new families sign up to join our small pediatric practice, I tell them there are advantages and disadvantages to our size. On the plus side, because we are just two doctors, we get to know our patients very well. (I recognize most parents' voices on my voicemail even when they don't leave their names.) We take turns being on call every night and we don't employ nurses, so my partner Terence and I are the only ones giving advice and we're on the same page about things like the judicious use of antibiotics and the importance of vaccines.

On the downside, we are just two people and we, too, need to have some quality of life. Because we are on call every other night, every other weekend, and for one or two weeks straight when the other is on vacation, we may not always come into the office on weekends and we close early on Fridays. Folks are mostly okay with that.

And while I have recognized the downside for our patients since we opened our practice seven years ago, until recently, I hadn't thought much about a downside for us, the doctors.

Then something unexpected happened.

Right after the Fourth of July, my partner had an accident on his bicycle, breaking six ribs, a clavicle and his scapula in ten places.

He had surgery and would be out of the office for an indeterminate amount of time.

We had covered for each other in crises before, when Terence's nephew died suddenly and tragically, and when my brother was diagnosed with cancer. We have a 100% "family first" policy at work. Whenever one of us has to cover the other due to family emergencies, our attitude is, "Do what you need to do. Take as long as it takes." And that's exactly what I said this time. And I meant it. Mostly. Because in my gut I knew this time was different. This was six weeks. In summer. In New England, where those few warm months are precious to us.

> *I decided to savor every small moment of summer pleasure I could.*

I tried to maintain a positive attitude. I reminded myself that our practice is small. On-call nights aren't usually very busy. Some nights I don't get called at all. I told myself that solo practitioners live like this every day. And for the first two weeks, I didn't even think about the other weeks that would follow. I just pretended my partner was on vacation. No problem. Piece of cake.

But the rest of the summer loomed, with no sign of relief. My partner optimistically predicted he'd be out for six weeks, but admitted that his doctor had said it would take nine months of physical therapy before they would know how much shoulder function he'd get back. Could I conceivably be on call for nine months straight? I was beginning to get grumpy. Clearly I needed a strategy.

And my strategy was to change my mindset. Instead of complaining about missing my summer by non-stop working, I decided to savor every small moment of summer pleasure I could. Instead of just taking a quick dip in the pool after work, I floated serenely, gazed up at the swaying oak trees and soaring swallows and declared myself the luckiest person alive. I didn't just re-plant the window boxes on my deck. I sat on my lounge chair afterward, imagining that I was seeing each portulaca, each Swedish ivy, each geranium grow and bloom before my eyes. An hour's walk on the beach became a meditation. Even though my cell phone had to tag along, I'd turn my face to the sun and thank my lucky stars I lived so close to the ocean.

During the summer that almost wasn't, I packed as much summer living as I could into each outdoor experience I had. A simple backyard barbecue? I literally ate it up. An invitation to sail on a friend's boat? What could be more sublime? Another friend's beachside clambake? It didn't get any better than that.

So even though I was constantly on call, even though I dealt over the phone with allergic reactions, tick bites, earaches and colic, I still relished every drop of summer happiness each day.

Terence ended up coming back in six weeks as predicted. I had my first day off all summer. No remoting into our electronic health records from home. No fielding frantic calls from worried parents. No checking my cell phone obsessively for service. And though I was glad he was back, happy to share office hours and trade on-call days, I'm still glad for the experience of gratitude. Still grateful for the summer that almost wasn't.

~Carolyn Roy-Bornstein

26

The Blessings Box

Life's challenges are not supposed to paralyze you,
they're supposed to help you discover who you are.
~Bernice Johnson Reagon

The house seemed huge and empty. There was no talking, laughing, crying, stomping, thumping, music playing, television blaring. It was all gone.

My children, who were now nineteen and twenty years old, had both left for college at the same time. They moved too far away for quick visits and I found myself alone, struggling with this depressing change in my life. I had devoted my life to raising my children and although I worked, it was either at their school or from home where I would see them every day.

As the days turned to weeks and weeks to months I found that my loneliness and anxiety was only getting worse. I found a part-time job that got me out of the house. My husband tried to be around more and we worked on our marriage, but still, I felt like I was in mourning, dealing with the loss of my children, the family we once had. I suddenly had no purpose, no reason to get out of bed in the morning, no motivation to do anything.

My son Eric lived hours away in Virginia now and was active in ROTC and school. My daughter Emma lived even farther away from our Maryland home, in Vermont, and kept busy with school, her church and a job. She also fell in love with a young man she met at church. My kids were doing what I always prayed they would do — grow up and become respectful, serving adults — but I missed them terribly.

Of course, Emma's time was preoccupied with school and her new love. We adored him as well and when he asked if he could surprise Emma at Christmas by driving down from Vermont we were all thrilled. Suddenly the entire family was going to be together to celebrate Christmas. As excited as I was, I could not help but dwell on the fact that this time would go by quickly and in a matter of a few weeks, I would be back again in my empty, cold house. As hard as I tried to enjoy life with all the holiday festivities and kids home, I dared not let myself get too happy because I knew that once they left and the holidays were over I would be more depressed than ever.

After Kyle surprised Emma we all gathered in the living room to exchange some gifts. I smiled at all the happy faces and the love that filled the room. The house echoed with Christmas music, laughter and talk; a fire crackled and popped and sent a warm glow throughout the room. Having my kids at home was the best Christmas present ever. And then Emma handed me a wrapped gift. I slowly unwrapped it and held it in my hands. It was a wooden box.

"I made the box from old barn wood," Kyle said, smiling. And I knew immediately how special that was because Kyle was a carpenter and tore down old barns for the beams and timber.

"And I did the wood burning," Emma followed up.

I ran my fingers over the intricate scrolls and curves of the word "Blessings" and the flowers and vines Emma had burned into the wood. On the underside she had burned: "Merry Christmas, Love Emma and Kyle."

"It's a blessings box," Emma said. "You write down things you are thankful for and put them in the box. Then you can read them later when you're feeling down or sad and remind yourself of all the good things in your life."

That night, while the family was all there and the house seemed full of love and joy, I cleared a spot on my nightstand for the box. I wrote down the first thing I was thankful for and dated the paper: "Blessed to remember that no matter how far away my kids are they will always be my kids." I folded it up and tucked it into the box.

The next night I did the same thing. "Thankful for my husband and all he does for me."

And the next night, before bed, I wrote: "Thankful for the big house that can accommodate the family when they come to visit."

And the nights after that: "Blessed that I have a job to go to each day." "Thankful that I'm in good health." "Thankful for my parents."

I wrote down my blessings and prayers and things I was thankful for, no matter how big or small, for each night until the kids left.

> *With each note I tucked in that box, I was reminded of all the good things in my life.*

The holiday decorations came down and the house was once again empty, cold and lonely. My husband worked each day and I did too, but when I came home I felt like I was being swallowed up in the cold and loneliness of the house. As I changed into my pajamas one day after work, I spied the blessing box sitting under a pile of books and I quickly pulled it out. I ran my fingers over the box and the dovetail woodworking that was so carefully and thoughtfully done. I ran my fingers over the words and flowers and smiled, remembering the two special people who had made this gift for me.

One by one I pulled out each piece of paper, unfolded it, and read. I read them out loud so I could hear clearly what I had written.

"Thankful for the big house that can accommodate the family when they come to visit!"

I breathed in deeply as if trying to suck in the chill in the air, and the silence. I remembered the holiday season when the kids were home and thought about future visits. I thought about how not even distance can take my kids away — they will always be my children, and our home will always be their home. With each note I tucked in that box, I was reminded of all the good things in my life, all that I had to be thankful for.

As each week passed, and I wrote a note for the box nearly every night, it helped me to stay focused on the positive. And when I needed a lift or a reminder, there was always a word of encouragement in the Blessings Box.

Now I write notes weekly and re-read my notes of thankfulness often. It has helped me cope with depression and anxiety and has given me a new outlook on life. I'm learning to embrace the quiet times and even the big, old, empty house that has blessed us with so many memories and promises of more to come.

I am blessed and forever thankful for a daughter who recognized a need in her mother and helped her to cope and adjust with a simple idea, a precious gift that has changed everything — a blessings box.

~Jennifer Reed

27

In Thanks for What We Have

Gratitude turns what we have into enough, and more.
~Melody Beattie

I sat pensively and waited for Kathleen to speak. Being called to the human resources department is a little like being called to the principal's office. She was smiling, so I took that as a good sign.

"Annmarie," she said. "A food bank in Philly that serves the elderly is asking for help. Since it's almost Thanksgiving I thought this would be a good company project to pursue. What do you think?"

"Sounds like a great idea," I said. "What would you like me to bring?"

"Well," she said. "I'm sure whatever you donate will be appreciated but that's not exactly what I had in mind as your mission. I'd like you to organize the event and see it through."

"Well, um, errr… sure. I guess so." As I stuttered through my response, all I could think was, "What? Why me?"

"Great! I knew we could count on you, Annmarie. Good luck, I know you'll do a great job."

I walked back to my office without a clue as to where to begin. This was in 2009 when the U.S. economy was on life support and fading fast. Overtime at our company had been completely canceled. The rise in unemployment forced the families of many of our employees to live on one paycheck when they had been accustomed to two. How could I ask my coworkers for more?

That evening I drove home filled with negativity. Then I remembered a time long ago when the pickings were pretty slim at our house, too. My mother often joked that it was never a secret to the neighbors when Dad was out of work as it always coincided with the milkman skipping our house on his route. The Pennsylvania steelworkers went on strike regularly in the sixties and milk delivery was always the first luxury to go.

Then a new strike came along, and Mom wrote her customary note to Jim the milkman asking him not to deliver any more milk until further notice. In the morning Jim picked up the empty bottles, including the one with Mom's note, and left the usual gallon of milk.

Two days later Jim picked up the empties and left four quarts of milk. Then he got back in his truck. This time he wrote his own message on the flip side of Mom's. It read, "Kids need

> *It's a comfort to know that when times are tough, good folks chip in.*

milk." Jim ran back to the porch and shoved the note down between the milk bottles.

The strike went on for three months and Jim left four quarts of milk every other day as usual, never collecting a dime from us.

Once the strike was over the milk delivery continued as usual and every week he collected, but only for the milk he had delivered the previous week. He never referred to the three months when he delivered a gallon every other day without charge.

The memory of Jim's kindness went a long way to spark my enthusiasm. Maybe this wasn't a lost cause. These were hard times but I invested all of my hope in the kindness of the human heart. Perhaps I'd be in for a pleasant surprise.

The next morning I posted signs about our food drive all over the cafeteria and on every bulletin board I could find. Each sign read: "Thanksgiving food drive to support the elderly poor of West Philadelphia! Donations of non-perishable food items are greatly needed."

After I finished tacking up the signs I gathered a few empty cartons from the mailroom and hoped for the best. I'd planned to send out a few reminder e-mails as we got closer to Thanksgiving but it was never necessary. Instead, within a few days I had to locate empty office space to store the massive number of contributions we had accumulated. By the end of the week I was recruiting volunteers to help me pack the mountains of bottles, cans and boxes. I couldn't keep up with it by myself.

One of my coworkers, Maggie, made the rounds with me every day from one department to another to pick up the canned goods and other items. Maggie was a bit past sixty years old but pushed our food cart around with the energy of a woman half her age. She smiled her way through every pickup area, making a fuss over each item she placed in our cart. Everyone knew when Maggie was passing through. Her gratitude was so genuine she inspired everyone to dig deep and help.

As we were making our rounds one day I asked her where she got all the energy and enthusiasm.

"Annie," she said, "everyone in this building has a J-O-B. With the unemployment rate hovering at ten percent, what's not to be enthusiastic about if we can help someone less fortunate? It's Thanksgiving and I can't think of a better way to be grateful for keeping our jobs when so many have lost theirs, no matter how much overtime gets cut. Sure money is tight. When isn't it? But people need food."

As I listened to Maggie I could hear our milkman's words echoing in the background. "Kids need milk."

I witnessed a great return on my investment in the kindness of the human heart. It's a comfort to know that when times are tough, good folks chip in, if for no other reason than out of gratitude for the misery they have been spared.

Though our company is located in the suburbs, many of the six hundred rank and file employees reside in Philadelphia. Through this annual event I've witnessed Philadelphia's long-standing motto, "The City of Brotherly Love," come to life every year. Our contribution grows annually in direct proportion to my gratitude for such boundless generosity.

~Annmarie B. Tait

28

The Third Sentence

Each time you say hello to a stranger,
your heart acknowledges over and
over again that we are all family.
~Suzy Kassem

The sun's not quite up, but I am. I'm sitting at my desk with a stack of postcards, pen in hand, thinking and writing. It's not quite as idyllic as it sounds. My hand's starting to cramp up from clutching the pen too tightly. My knee bangs against the desk as I shift in my wooden chair. I knock over my coffee mug.

This is all my customers' fault. They're the type of people who scour the Internet for hours looking for the absolutely perfect gift for their roommates, girlfriends, babysitters, or uncles. They love that my one-person online shop can personalize a gift with a name, date, or favorite quote. They send me e-mails about the sweet old woman who'd owned an apple orchard, inspiring apple-shaped ornaments stamped with "Gram" for every grandchild. They share the importance of a "breathe" ring for a niece with cystic fibrosis or a girl's need for a handmade keychain that must arrive before her boyfriend ships out to Afghanistan.

During my first three years in business, I simply jotted a chirpy "Thanks!" on my receipts and stuffed them into packages for mailing. After all, a generic "thank you" worked for the big-box stores — why shouldn't it work for me? I never heard a peep of complaint from customers, but I felt increasingly dissatisfied. It might be proper business to be bland and formal, but it didn't feel like me.

My mom trained me to write thank-you notes at an early age.

> *My mom trained me to write thank-you notes at an early age.*

When I was lucky, I got to write them on little folded cards with pretty pictures on the front and a tiny square of white inside for the message. When I was unlucky, I was forced to use notebook paper with empty lines that seemed to stretch on forever. With that in mind, this fall I printed colorful postcards and began to handwrite notes on the back. At first, my notes were only two sentences:

> *Heather,*
> *Thank you for your order! I hope you enjoy your handmade keychain.*
> *Michelle*

By November, holiday orders began to pile up and I started writing a dozen or more postcards a day. Logically, I should have stopped. Successful businesses are all about streamlining and efficiency. Instead, I started to challenge myself to add a third sentence, one that made a special connection with each individual.

> *Melissa,*
> *Thank you for your order! I hope your actress friend enjoys the typewriter ornament. Congratulations on your play, too!*

> *Sean,*
> *Thank you for your order! I hope your class enjoys the handmade bookmarks. They are lucky to have such a caring teacher!*

If we hadn't shared any e-mail contact, this extra sentence proved challenging. Sometimes I'd add something about the item ("This airplane ornament is extra special. It's the only one I made this year!") or the customer's name ("Winter is such a pretty and unusual name. You're the first one I've ever met!"). I might try to make a connection based on their location. "I've never been to Kentucky," I wrote to a woman who bought a cowgirl-themed bracelet, "but I imagine it's filled with beautiful horses."

Months later, the third sentence still sometimes proves elusive, but I continue to try. Why do I spend time on something destined for the recycle bin? Like all small business owners, I know only too well the worries about late supplies, unpaid invoices, and technology snafus. It's easy to become discouraged. Writing notes to my customers reminds me why I chose this unconventional path and why this occupation makes me happy. I do it for myself as much as I do it for them.

~Michelle Mach

29

The Grateful List

*When you are sorrowful look again in your heart, and
you shall see that in truth you are weeping for that
which has been your delight.*
~Kahlil Gibran

"A thankful heart is a happy heart," I'd cheerfully chant as I rushed around my home, picking up after five little ones under the age of five. With a total of seven kids, I had my hands full. My hair was always in a semi-neat ponytail—most days. I took my shower, taught the kids, and got dinner on the table just as my husband walked in the door—most days.

From time to time, I would sit them all down and ask them to share one thing they were thankful for—especially if there was excessive arguing and complaining. I would write our responses on the white board and call it The Grateful List.

My football enthusiast might say, "I'm thankful that one day I will be in the NFL."

My daughter the "Daddy's girl" might say, "I'm thankful for Daddy."

My three-year old reader would gleefully declare, "I'm tankful that I can read."

Allysa, our oldest, and already a preteen, would say, "I'm thankful that one day I am going away to college and I can't wait."

Of course I would tell them that I was appreciative to be the mother of such grateful children. This always seemed to change the atmosphere and make everyone smile, if only temporarily.

Then they all grew up, so fast. Had I known time would fly by at warp speed, maybe I would have held them more, or let my home get a little messier, or skipped a shower or two. I homeschooled for fourteen years, so you would think I got plenty of time with them. On most days, however, I was being their teacher, not their mom. I remember visiting a museum in Indiana, and my son Eric said to me, "Mom, do we have to read every one of the outlines on every animal and every person here?" I guess he was asking me to be a mom that day, not a teacher.

When Allysa was ready for college, she chose a small private school in New Jersey. So far away, and yet we knew it was the perfect choice. It was set on the side of a hill with beautiful surroundings and the people were wonderful. Allysa wanted to be an elementary education teacher. She always worked well with kids, so I knew she'd make an amazing educator.

The first Thanksgiving she came home we all noticed a change in her. She had grown emotionally and spiritually. Where was the knucklehead teen who had left our home? That know-it-all had been kidnapped, but we all liked this new young lady. We enjoyed a wonderful Thanksgiving together. As a matter of fact, I had the flu, and Allysa stepped up and prepared the entire meal with the help of her little sisters and her dad.

The table was set, and as was our custom, everyone shared what they were thankful for. Allysa told us she was thankful for our family. As if choreographed, we all gasped and then laughed uncontrollably. She had been short on compliments since around the age of fourteen.

Allysa's freshman year was a time of growth; she took a mission trip to Mexico, she volunteered with a future teacher's outreach in the inner city of New York, and she participated in a weekly worship event called, "Jacob's Ladder." By her sophomore year she was not the same person.

During spring break of her sophomore year Allysa came home via Ohio in order to visit her cousin and best friend, Faith. Faith had recently given birth to Amari, Allysa's goddaughter. She spent a blissful week holding the baby and hanging out with family. Grandma Gloria made her favorite meal: pork chops, mashed potatoes, and green beans. She topped it off with Allysa's favorite dessert, Gee Gee's delight: a decadent treat with pound cake, strawberries, chocolate pudding, and a heaping scoop of whipped cream. My mom told me she just sat there and watched Allysa eat. They laughed and enjoyed one another all day long.

Finally after a week in Ohio they headed to our home in Michigan. Allysa, her cousins, and the baby had what seemed to be a great day for travel. My sister insisted that Faith drive the SUV, as we all agreed it was a safer vehicle. A couple of hours into their drive, I spoke with Allysa on the cell phone and excitedly told her that based on where they were we would see her in about an hour. Fifteen minutes later our lives would change forever. There was a freak accident when something in the road caused Faith to swerve. The SUV toppled and within seconds Allysa was gone. She was the only one who did not survive.

> *My grateful list helped me to focus, to move forward, and to heal.*

One day, I lay listlessly on the sofa in agony, longing to hear Allysa's voice or to see her face. I kept asking that disempowering question: "Why?"

Then something came over me and I slowly rose and got some paper. I began to make my list:

1. *She lived twenty-one years*
2. *She knew she was loved*
3. *I was honored to be her mom*
4. *She had a great life*
5. *We had a great life with her*
6. *She had so many friends*
7. *She had a deep spiritual life*
8. *I know I will see her again*

The list went on and on. Before I knew it, I was smiling and felt so incredibly grateful. Would I continue to long for her smile and her presence? Yes, but I was so thankful for what I had been given.

I hung the list on the refrigerator and made copies so that I could see them in various places throughout my home and in my car. My grateful list helped me to focus, to move forward, and to heal.

Recently, I met a young mom who had lost her eighteen-month-old baby to a rare disease, and I could sense her pain. I asked her a simple question: "What is one thing you can tell me about your baby?" She perked up and with great pride told me about his dimples and how his smile lit up a room. She told me what his favorite toy was: a Superman figurine. She talked about how he walked so early and could talk clearly at such a young age. Before she knew it, she was so thankful for her little one's life. She began her grateful list.

Zig Ziglar, the renowned motivational speaker, said, "Gratitude is the healthiest of all human emotions." When I'm stuck, I start again with my grateful list. It always helps to get me going.

~Lynn Johnson

The Power of Gratitude

CHAPTER 4

A Change in Perspective

In a rapidly ascending balloon were two men. One watched the earth getting farther and farther away. One watched the stars getting nearer and nearer.
~George Jean Nathan, A Book Without a Title

The Rumbling

The past cannot be changed, forgotten, or erased.
However, the lessons learned can prepare you
for a brighter future.
~Author Unknown

Most mornings, at approximately 5:15, I was startled awake as the walls of my house began to tremble. The deep, rumbling vibrations were so strong that the windows rattled. Sharp bursts that sounded like firecrackers were followed by a deep bass throbbing sound again.

It was my neighbor's Harley-Davidson.

Those bikes are often referred to as "rolling thunder" and in the early hours of the morning that was putting it mildly. My neighbor's bike typically idled, rumbling for about five minutes.

In those five minutes, I lay awake in bed imagining what this neighbor was doing that required him to make my house shake for so long. I pictured him walking back into his house, pushing the start button on the coffeemaker, and slowly stirring sugar and cream into his travel mug.

Or perhaps he went back in to feed the dogs their morning meal, followed by a quick ear scratch for the pups and a goodbye kiss for his wife. Whatever the case, my daydreaming was usually followed by intense praying that the rumbling would not wake my baby.

I have a confession: I had never actually met my neighbor or his wife. Our paths had not crossed in the busyness of life. I had seen them from a distance out the back windows in our comings and goings, but neither of us had ever taken the time to have a conversation. Instead, for several years, I endured listening to the Harley, silently fuming in my bed.

One morning, the rumbling magically disappeared. To my elation, I slept in. The baby slept in. For the entire week my eyes opened to the peaceful sound of silence each morning.

A few days later, a friend e-mailed me that my neighbor had died. I felt shock, confusion and more than a bit of guilt. Through my back window, he had seemed so healthy. He did not look that old, and he was able to ride a motorcycle every day. Apparently he had been sick for several years. My friend said he was the kindest man she knew, who kept living life to the fullest despite his illness. She added, "I know you might have been wondering why you have not heard his beloved Harley in a few days."

> *I could have been there for his wife now instead of being a nameless face.*

Oh, the irony of those words.

You see, I heard the irritating sounds of a motorcycle waking me up every morning, but to this man it was pure joy. Perhaps it was this joy that helped him survive as long as he did, because he was fighting a battle I knew nothing about. Now I'm thankful that I never sent the letter that I composed in my head each morning after I researched noise ordinances. In fact, I am actually grateful that he had his "beloved Harley" and that he enjoyed it as much as he did. Now I grieve for a man I did not know.

Had I at some point taken the time to walk across the alley and say hello, perhaps I would have learned of his struggle. I can picture a conversation as he describes his love of motorcycles and racecars. Later, there would have been friendly waves and chats as we went about our lives. I could have been there for his wife now instead of being a nameless face.

My neighbor has no idea of the legacy he left behind. From him I learned something that has changed my life. He taught me to see others in a different light.

We all have our own struggles, frustrations and issues. I know my own, but it is likely I will never know the battles of people I see every day. I can choose to be provoked by circumstance or look deeper and change my perspective. What appears on the surface as simply an annoying situation — an angry person in line or someone who cuts me off in traffic — could very well be a person fighting for his life. Every day there is an opportunity for me to smile and extend the hand of kindness.

I live with plastic toys scattered on the floor and piles of dishes in the sink, and I'm always running five minutes behind, but I used to be a person who had time to notice others. I realized that I had been so consumed with my own frenzied life that I forgot to look beyond my troubles and be a light to others.

Somehow in opening the door for a stranger or bringing a meal to a friend in need, my own burdens are lighter. I find my children are watching, and they, too, are learning how to go about their days actively finding a way to help others. As my outlook has changed, I am able to see the blessings I have all around me that had been there waiting to be discovered all along.

Driving in my car, occasionally a Harley will rumble past. My kids in the back seat will cover their ears at the deafening noise, but I simply smile. I have developed a great fondness for those bikes. They have become a reminder that things aren't always as they seem.

~Katie Bangert

Fly Me to the Moon

*The only person you are destined to become is
the person you decide to be.*
~Ralph Waldo Emerson

rowing up I was often described as quiet, docile, reserved, and naïve. It was not long until I began to see myself the same way. I trapped myself in this tiny box, buying into everyone else's perception of who I was. Intimidation and fear suppressed my hopes and dreams. I was limiting myself in so many ways.

One autumn afternoon, during my freshman year in college, I saw a play on campus. It was put on by a group of talented amateur actors and I found myself in tears at the end of the show. I realized this was not due to the moving performance, or because it was such a tragic story. It was simply because I was not on stage with them. My passion for performing could not be ignored any longer, though I knew I had very few people in my life who truly believed in my ability to pursue something so "uncharacteristic" of me. The best I could think to do was not tell anyone until I could prove them wrong.

The next week I found an opportunity to audition for a local play in North Carolina. I was terrified, but I went prepared. I had a headshot — actually my high school senior portrait — and I had memorized a monologue. I got on stage in front of the casting director with my heart beating a mile a minute and delivered my sixty-second monologue to the best of my ability. At the end of my performance, the director shook my hand and gave me a script. "Five shows, $150, that's all we can give," he said. I was elated. Not only had I gotten the part, I was getting paid for it. I was a professional actress. I knew I didn't want to pursue this as a career, but I was not going to let my talent go to waste.

I began to wonder what else I was holding myself back from. I gave it a lot of thought and realized that I could go anywhere in the world. I asked myself where that would be, without letting the words "impractical" or "impossible" jump into my head. It turned out my dream destination was New York City.

Born and raised in a small military town, I was surrounded by people who had never lived anywhere else. This was their world. So naturally when I expressed interest in leaving it, they were discouraging. There were some who blatantly laughed in my face, attempting to remind me who I was: the quiet, docile, reserved, naïve girl who would not survive one day in fast-paced, aggressive New York.

Their doubts only furthered my resolve. After graduating, I filled out hundreds of applications for jobs in New York City until I finally received a call for an interview. I was interviewed by three stern women wearing business suits. As I sat through the ninety-minute meeting, my palms sweating and my heart pounding, I tried to overcome my fear as I had when I performed on stage. But I found myself taking five steps backwards. Looking at their unimpressed faces, I stumbled over my words, had mental blanks, and completely failed the interview. I was mortified. I went back home and wept for days. I had never been so humiliated and disappointed in myself.

I started to second-guess everything. Was New York the right place for someone like me? Should I just accept what everyone said about me and find a way to be content? Or should I keep trying, and possibly face failure again?

I made my decision and distributed my résumé to hundreds of New York City employers. To maintain my optimism, I also began hunting for apartments. It took two months before I received another phone call for an interview. I prepared myself for the most formidable interviewers that I could imagine. But this time, the office environment was completely different. It was casual and laidback, and people smiled and invited me to sit down. Was I still in New York? I had developed this idea that New Yorkers were aggressive, inhospitable and greedy. Yet there I was, shaking hands with the CFO of the company and having the most pleasant conversation.

I was offered the job the next day, and I gladly accepted. When I left my hometown, everyone was genuinely shocked that I was actually making it happen. It was thrilling, but I knew the mature thing to do was not to concern myself with what they thought. Instead I thanked them, for I had used their doubt as fuel. I found an apartment within two weeks, and soon after I was living in Manhattan.

> *I gave it a lot of thought and realized that I could go anywhere in the world.*

One winter evening, I went to a local coffee shop after work. I brought my laptop with the intent of hunting for part-time acting jobs. As I sipped my coffee and searched the Internet, a young girl walked in who reminded me of my fifteen-year-old self. I wondered what I would say to the teenage me if she were to come and sit at my table. It would be quite an intervention, I thought. I imagined the younger version of me staring back in awe, surprised at who I had become. I looked at this plump, wide-eyed adolescent and began to preach: "First off, you cannot control other people's thoughts or actions and you cannot allow them to dictate yours. Focus on you. Secondly, do not wait until you are brought to tears by a college play to realize what you are passionate about. Thirdly, you will experience failure, bad days, rejection… but that does not mean that you are a failure, a bad person, or a reject. Those moments only exist to make your victories sweeter."

As my epiphany came to an end, Frank Sinatra's "Fly Me to the Moon" came on the coffee shop radio. I was overwhelmed with gratitude, as the universe had given me everything I had always wanted. Nothing ever felt so surreal and natural at the same time. I was where I was meant to be, and all I had to do was allow it to happen.

~Anita Daswani

32

Every Day Is a Good Day

If you don't think every day is a good day,
just try missing one.
~Cavett Robert

"That's it. This is my last Christmas season working a retail job!" Those were the words I had uttered almost a year ago.

But here I was again, looking at aisles stocked with Christmas merchandise that we'd been receiving for the last four months. Our extended holiday hours would start the next week. I was still working retail, despite the pronouncement I'd made at the end of the last Christmas season.

I couldn't quit. I was in the midst of extensive dental work that would take another three months to complete. I needed the dental insurance and I needed the paychecks.

So here I was, locked into another holiday sales cycle, with the long hours, the demanding work, a new manager who pushed-pushed-pushed, and a store filled with stressed and irritable shoppers.

Our co-manager — the nice one, so I'll call him Angel — had a pet phrase he often used. It was his attempt to inspire us and remind us that we were in charge of our attitudes. "Every day's a good day!" he'd bellow as he unlocked the doors to let us in. "Welcome to where happy people come to work. Where every day's a good day."

Most of us, in our pre-caffeinated, still bleary-eyed state, mumbled a greeting in return. It was usually along the lines of "yeah, yeah" or "right," said as sarcastically as possible. We didn't appreciate Angel's "every day's a good day" line one bit.

And then one day I left work even more frustrated, aggravated, and angry than usual. It was one of those days when I would have given my notice in an instant. Except I couldn't. Not yet. I felt trapped.

> Whether I agreed with the statement or not, I starting replying with positive words.

For the first few minutes in the car I screamed at the top of my lungs. I shrieked. I yelled words that I typically don't use. I would be hoarse for the next two days.

That's when I knew that something had to change. I started listening to the words I told myself: "I'm too old for this. I'm too tired for this. I'll never make it through Christmas. I can't keep going like this. I don't have the energy to deal with this." I realized how negative the words I spoke to myself were.

The first change I made was in response to Angel's morning greeting. He'd say, "Every day's a good day!" Instead of scoffing, laughing or coming back with a smart aleck response, I'd answer, "Yes! Yes it is." Whether I agreed with the statement or not, I starting replying with positive words.

Next, I made a list of affirmations — positive statements to read aloud before I went to work each day:

- *I am flying through this Christmas season with ease.*
- *My energy levels are higher than ever.*
- *I enjoy my job and am thankful for the benefits I receive from it.*
- *I complete my tasks easily and quickly.*
- *I am drawn to foods that keep me healthy and give me energy.*
- *This is the easiest holiday season I've ever worked through.*

I started looking for other positive methods. I didn't want to merely survive these frantic months. I wanted to maintain a peaceful demeanor and have the energy to enjoy a happy home life after the work hours ended.

A CD with peaceful, meditative music caught my eye in the store. It turned out to be one of the best purchases I ever made. I listened to it on the way to work, to gear up for a good day. I listened to it on the way home, to calm down after a long, busy day.

One change that made the largest impact in my life was consciously developing an "Attitude of Gratitude." When I found myself reverting back to my negative, grumbling ways, I would deliberately shift my mind to an attitude of gratitude state. I would remind myself of all the good things:

- *I'm thankful that I have a car to get me here.*
- *I'm thankful that all my limbs are working.*
- *I'm thankful I can walk into work without assistance.*
- *I'm thankful to have a job and an income.*
- *I'm thankful I have eyes to see.*
- *I'm thankful I have the intelligence to do the math I need to properly do my job.*
- *I'm thankful I have a warm, dry house to go home to.*
- *I'm thankful for my children and grandchildren's health.*
- *I'm thankful the car is paid off.*
- *I'm thankful there's gas in the car.*
- *I'm thankful there are groceries in the house.*

As I started listing the multitude of reasons I had to be thankful, the list kept expanding. And as the list grew, the minor aggravations of my job seemed to shrink in comparison.

Another lesson I learned was to go easy on myself. If I had a bad day, one when I slipped back into negativity, instead of berating myself, I needed to accept my own imperfection. We all have bad days, and we move on from them.

Before I knew it, with consistent conscious thought, every day *was* a good day. One by one, they passed, and soon the Christmas season was behind us.

I not only survived, I thrived. And now I can join Angel and proudly proclaim: "Every day's a good day!"

~Trisha Faye

33

A Big Heart

Do not judge your neighbor until you
walk two moons in his moccasins.
~Cheyenne Proverb

I managed a restaurant in Shreveport, Louisiana. One of the employees was a girl named Jeanette Harmon. Jeanette was a great worker and became a good friend. She had a great sense of humor. It still makes me smile to recall her impersonation of George Jefferson dancing.

We didn't start out that well, though. When I started managing the restaurant, Jeanette had recently given birth to her third child and had also developed cardiomegaly, more commonly known as an enlarged heart. She had missed a lot of work. She was a long-time employee though, and we had a great staff that picked up the slack.

I could see that Jeanette was a real asset when she returned to work. But Jeanette had one glaring problem. She was habitually late.

Although she had a great attitude, I didn't feel like she was performing up to her potential. Jeanette was scheduled to be at work every morning at 9:00 a.m. We were always busy and everyone would work together to prepare for the day. Everyone, that is, except Jeanette. More often than not, she would come in at 9:30 or 9:45.

Firing Jeanette was out of the question, but I wanted her to understand how important it was to be on time. I gave her multiple verbal and written warnings. She would be on time for a while, but before long, she would be back to her old habits.

After a stretch of unexcused late arrivals, one particular day I caught Jeanette at the time clock and called her into the office. I asked her if she was having health problems. She assured me that she was taking care of herself, so I knew that wasn't the problem.

At the time, I had the "my way or the highway" management style and so I told her that she had been warned for the last time. If she was late again, I was going to let her go. She told me she would do her best to be on time and when she got up to go check in, I told her to take the rest of the day off. I was proud of myself for showing her who was the boss.

Three weeks went by and then I noticed that Jeanette was more than thirty minutes late a couple of days in a row. In fact, after reviewing her time card, I noticed she hadn't been on time once that week.

> *Jeanette realized money and jobs are important, but not more important than family.*

If Jeanette was going to push back, I was going to push back harder. I thought about it all day. I was going to hit her where it hurt. I demoted her to minimum wage. If that was the way she was going to act, that was how she should be compensated. Not only was her pay being cut in half, I changed her schedule to start an hour later each day, further hurting her... or so I thought.

I called her into the office at the end of the day. I was prepared for whatever excuse she had, except for the one she gave. She started crying and I nearly lost it when she told me why she was regularly late. Jeanette's three young children each had to be taken to a different place in the morning. One went to elementary school, one went to preschool, and one went to her mother's. Jeanette didn't have a car, so she was at the mercy of the public transportation system.

Nevertheless, I thought it would show weakness if I gave in, so I stuck to my disciplined plan. Today, I would call my management style stupid and arrogant.

I wasn't sure Jeanette would come back, but I hoped she would. She was there the next day at 10 a.m. sharp. But, she was uncharacteristically quiet and didn't speak to me for a few days. Then she returned to her jovial self. And it wasn't long before she was performing at her best. I tried to act like I didn't notice, but I did.

After three weeks, I asked her what she thought of the new arrangement. She said coming in an hour later gave her time to get her kids ready for school without rushing. She thanked me! She said that she probably deserved to be demoted and she might have done the same thing if she were in charge.

Jeanette surprised me. She knew stuff I should have known long before, but somehow the lessons passed me by. Jeanette realized money and jobs are important, but not more important than family. The reason she had a job was to take care of her family. I know it well now and still think about how foolish I was for not realizing it before.

That day, I paid Jeanette all of the money that she would have made had she not been demoted. It wasn't long before I gave her a raise and a promotion.

Jeanette never harbored any hard feelings. She maintained that it was I who taught her something, but I can tell you now, it was she who taught me.

The next year, when Lent came around, I gave up driving for six weeks. I did it without fanfare and have never bragged about it. I didn't do it to show others that if I could do it, they could too. I did it to awaken my empathy. It was a hard but rewarding lesson, but I can only imagine how hard it would be with three small children.

After a few years, I moved on to another job and heard that Jeanette had been promoted to manager. I was so proud of her.

I was sad to learn that Jeanette died a few years ago from complications of her cardiomegaly. I'll never forget her. She showed me how important it is to have a big heart.

~Johnny Wessler

34

Sometimes It Takes a Child

*If we experienced life through the eyes of a child
everything would be magical and extraordinary.*
~Akiane Kramarik

O ur savings were wiped out and there was nothing we could do. We were going to lose our house. Joe wouldn't even look at me. "I guess we'll have to move into Grandpa's old house."

Grandpa Mac's little house had been old and in disrepair when he was living. Now that the place had been empty for more than five years I shuddered to think how much worse it would be. But the construction firm Joe had worked at as a foreman had gone bankrupt a year ago and he had not found a new job.

We had managed to scrape by for a while with Joe's unemployment benefits and our savings. But those days were over. I had given up the privilege of being a stay-at-home mom and found a job in retail that barely paid for groceries and daycare for our daughter, Kelly.

I couldn't bear the pain in Joe's eyes now. He has always taken pride in being able to take care of Kelly and me. He loved coming home from work to Kelly flinging herself into his arms and me in the kitchen making dinner. Now Kelly was running to me when I came home from work while Joe watched with his head hanging low. He thought it was his fault that my feet hurt and my back ached from standing for hours at the cash register. He served us simple suppers while Kelly whined, "When is Mama going to make lasagna again?"

We both tried to be cheerful around Kelly as we packed to move. She was only three. As long as we didn't send her the wrong cues she wouldn't notice the poor condition of her new home.

We splurged with the last of our savings and bought paint for Grandpa Mac's house. He had been a widower for many years before he died and he had done nothing to keep the house up. I suppose without Grandma he just didn't have the will or the energy. It might have been foolish to use the last of our money in this way, but after inspecting the old house we just couldn't bear to move in to it without at least trying to make it look a bit more cheerful.

We let Kelly choose the color for her new room, knowing that it would be some shade of pink. When we showed her the color chart I held my breath, hoping she would pick one of the lighter shades. Of course she wanted the gaudiest shade of pink available. "She likes the Pepto-Bismol pink." Joe said, grinning as he shook his head.

"What's Pepto-Bismol?" Kelly asked, not knowing what to make of our rueful smiles.

"Oh, it's pretty girl pink," the salesman said, giving Kelly a warm smile. "That's what I'd call it." So Kelly got her "pretty girl pink" room and she thought it was absolutely lovely. At least one person was happy in Grandpa Mac's house.

The shingles on the roof were dry and curled at the edges and threatened to leak at any moment. Hundreds of thousands of footsteps had worn the finish off the hardwood floors and they squeaked as if in protest that they were being trod on again after all these years. The countertops were scarred and stained and one of the doors on the kitchen cabinets was warped and would not close so it stood perpetually ajar. Worst of all, the white paint on the house's exterior was brittle and cracked but there was nothing we could do about that.

One evening, as I stood at the kitchen window looking out at the back yard, Joe came up behind me and put his arms around me. "It isn't that bad, is it?"

I frowned at the unkempt flowerbeds that had gone to seed years ago, at the bare spots in the lawn that became mud puddles when it rained, and at the sagging corner of the back porch. "It is, actually," I said as I slipped out of his embrace.

One evening, I walked out into the back yard to escape the heavy heat in the house. Naturally there wasn't any air conditioning — not even a window unit. The one redeeming feature of the house was the leaning wooden fence that allowed Kelly to play outside safely.

Kelly was busy picking the dandelions that grew profusely in the yard. She grinned when she saw me and ran over to give me a bright yellow bouquet. She plopped down beside me on the bottom step and said, "I like our new house, Mommy. We have pretty yellow flowers in the yard. Most people just have grass."

She looked around the yard, beaming. "We have an apple tree and I can get one whenever I want. There are baby birds in one of the trees. And I hear the birds singing every morning when I wake up." Her eyes shifted to the lantana bush in the corner that was filled with butterflies of different colors. "We have a lot of pretty butterflies."

"I think this must be the best place in the whole world to live."

Just then we heard a loud rapping sound and Kelly squealed with delight. "And we have a woodpecker in that tall tree over there. I'll bet nobody else has a woodpecker living in their yard." She hugged her knees. "We even have a fence so I can play outside whenever I want." She wound her little arms around my waist. "I think this must be the best place in the whole world to live."

Later, when Joe came in from job hunting, he looked more relaxed than I had seen him in a long time. "I don't want to get your hopes up only to disappoint you," he said. "But I think I will be hearing back from Jones Construction. My interview went well and I have a good feeling about this one. Maybe we won't be stuck in Grandpa's old house much longer."

"It's not that bad." I said. "There's no rush. We should probably stay here at least until we have replaced our savings."

Joe looked incredulous. "Did you say it's not that bad?"

"It isn't," I said, laughing. Relief swept over his face when he saw that I meant it. It took a three-year-old to teach me how to see the blessings in our new home. There's always something to be grateful for no matter what situation you are in. You just have to look.

~Elizabeth Atwater

35

The Really Bad, Sad, Rotten Year

Human beings, by changing the inner attitudes of their minds, can change the outer aspects of their lives.
~William James

I scanned the journal entries I had written during the past year. Each one sounded pretty much the same: unhappy, disgusted, angry, bitter. Really bitter. Well, I thought smugly, I was entitled. I had every right to those feelings thanks to the miserable circumstances life had dealt me.

Between January and June of that year, my father had been hospitalized and almost died twice. Five days after he was released home, he fell and broke his hip, requiring me to move from the home I shared with my husband into Dad's home to care for him. In the midst of this, my brother became gravely ill and died within six weeks — two days shy of the fiftieth birthday party I had planned for him. Shortly after that, I lost a close friend I'd known since childhood as well as a close business associate. While that would have been enough to knock anyone off her feet, it didn't stop there. In November, my husband's best friend of thirty-five years was found dead on a hiking trail under mysterious circumstances. Then I broke my wrist. My husband had surgery. Did I also mention that two of our beloved cats succumbed to illness? And those were just the highlights.

If that year of my life had been made into a movie, no one would dare watch it. It was too tragic. Yes, I did have every right to wallow in my misery. My life was rotten. Only, there was one problem. My anger and bitterness were ruling me. I had become weepy and short-tempered. I felt exhausted and depressed. It was a grand effort to drag myself out of bed each morning to care for Dad and an even grander effort to trek back home each afternoon to attend to my own household and cook dinner for my husband.

I knew my attitude was a problem. People were avoiding me and my friends had stopped calling. Yet, I clung to my negativity. Each night I sat with my journal and wrote down my litany of woes. I re-read previous entries. I cherished my misery. It had become my new best friend.

Now I happen to have a wonderfully intuitive husband. He knew that I started a new journal each year on my birthday. And that's when I always look back on the previous year and decide what changes and improvements I'd like to implement in my life. So that particular birthday my husband gave me an extravagant leather-bound journal. Without words, he conveyed a powerful message: It was time for something new.

Yet, I still wasn't quite ready. I was still enjoying my misery. Half-heartedly, I took pen to paper and wrote a snarky preface in my beautiful journal: "Happy Birthday to me! I've decided this year is going to be different. Things are going to change for the better. Improvements are on the horizon!"

That morning, on my birthday, my father complained about the breakfast I'd served him! I burst into tears. I pulled myself together, though, because my husband and I were going to have a special dinner that evening. Those plans, however, were put on hold when I got home to find our main sewer line clogged and backing up into our bathtub. I spent a good block of time plunging and praying until I finally surrendered and left a message for our plumber. I didn't have much hope for a reply. It was already 8 p.m. on a Saturday night. Yet, as my husband and I contemplated our next move, the plumber phoned. He could come by at ten the following morning if that was all right with us. At no extra charge. On a Sunday morning. A tiny ray of gratitude pierced my gloom. "Oh yes," I told him, "That would be all right."

The next afternoon, reveling in the relief of our once again free-flowing drain, my husband suggested we take a little road trip and then have my postponed birthday dinner. We did and we had a lovely time. That night my journal entry read as follows: "I'm so grateful that we have a plumber who is a decent person and who came to the rescue right away. I'm grateful for my birthday dinner and for my husband who made it happen. I'm even grateful for my new journal."

My anger and bitterness were ruling me.

In that moment, I hadn't specifically contemplated being grateful — I just was. And it felt really good. I thought about the events of the past year. Yes, there had been much adversity, yet somehow, I had gotten through. That in itself, I realized, was something to be grateful for.

The irony of making this discovery thanks to a clogged drain was wholly apparent to me. In an odd parallel, it seemed that my heart and mind were clogged as well — with all the muck of the past year's events. I had allowed unproductive thoughts and emotions to accumulate in me until they became overwhelming. What if I kept the momentum of this one good day going by focusing on the good every night as I wrote in my journal instead of focusing on the bad?

So I tried. But old habits die hard, and on the first go-round, all I could think to write was, "I'm grateful for the good weather today." I continued to flounder for a while afterward and some nights the best I could muster were two simple words: "Thank you." Still, I kept my promise to practice gratitude daily.

Then, after a while, I noticed something. I wasn't dragging myself out of bed anymore. My husband and I often joked over dinner. Friends started to call again. I was even invited to a few parties and actually had a good time at them. By deliberately shifting my focus, it seemed, I had allowed a certain healing to take place. Little by little, the person

I used to be returned until finally I was myself again. And for that, I couldn't be more grateful.

~Monica A. Andermann

36

Why Didn't I Think of That?

If we all do one random act of kindness daily, we just
might set the world in the right direction.
~Martin Kornfeld

I started running thirty-five years ago when my daughter was three years old and I had yet to lose those last five pounds of pregnancy fat. I love running. More specifically I love to be finished running. It makes me feel virtuous and thin, it keeps my muscles and bones strong, and I get to spend time outdoors.

My running was put on hold when I got injured four years ago. The doctor didn't have to tell me not to run. I couldn't. It hurt too much. But that time has passed and I am back on the roads.

I ran my first return race yesterday. It felt great. I didn't care how fast I ran; I was just grateful to be out among my old running buddies, enjoying the beautiful weather. At the end of the race I was exhilarated. I was happy that my time was pretty good and nothing hurt.

I went over to the refreshment table and got in line for a bottle of water and a banana. An older, obviously homeless woman was there, loading up on water and bananas and ignoring the volunteer who told her the food was for the runners. She just kept grabbing as much as she could carry.

Another volunteer said to me, "There won't be anything left for the slower runners and that's not fair." I kind of mumbled in agreement.

He took the food away from the old lady and she turned to walk away empty-handed.

A young woman who was a bit ahead of me in line took her own water and banana and handed it to the homeless woman, who looked up at her with sad eyes and nodded a thank you. The young woman didn't come back to take more. She gave away her share to someone who needed it. It was a selfless gesture.

Now why didn't I think of that? I know why. Because I was thinking of myself. I was basking in the glory of my triumphant return. I was thinking of my own thirst. I barely saw that poor woman.

I ran into the supermarket a few weeks ago, rushing to buy some refreshments for a meeting that was about to start. I was grateful to see that the line wasn't too long, but then the cashier told the man ahead of me that he owed four dollars and seventy-two cents. He slowly took out a wallet that looked so old I expected moths to fly out when he opened it. He removed four singles and began counting out the change. Very slowly. The dimes, nickels, and pennies — apparently all he had — added up to thirty-two cents. He searched his pockets fruitlessly. I was sighing and looking at the clock, impatient. But the woman behind me handed the cashier the missing forty cents. The man looked embarrassed and thanked her quietly. She smiled at him and said, "Don't worry about it. Have a nice day."

Now why didn't I think of that? I know why. I was so concerned about getting to my meeting on time that I ignored a problem that was happening right in front of my eyes, one that I easily could have solved.

I had business in Orlando, Florida, so of course the plane was full of kids. It was very noisy, but one baby, in particular, wouldn't stop crying: high pitched, loud, non-stop, and sitting in my row. The young mother was trying unsuccessfully to soothe the baby and handle her three-year-old at the same time. Passengers could be heard grumbling every time the baby let out another wail.

Then a grandmotherly type approached the woman and said, "You've got your hands full! Why don't you play with your daughter for a bit and I'll walk the baby up and down the aisle? Maybe the movement will calm him enough to fall asleep. And don't worry; I'll be within

A Change in Perspective | 4

sight the whole time." The mother looked unsure, but where would the woman go? They were in an airplane together. So she passed the baby to the woman, who walked him and rocked him for only a few minutes until he fell asleep.

Now why didn't I think of that? I know why. I was thinking about two things: how annoying the baby was and how grateful I was that he wasn't mine.

These three mini-dramas happened within a few weeks of each other. I began to see a pattern. I thought about how easy it could be to solve people's problems or make their days a little better. It takes little effort to smile at strangers passing by, or to hold the elevator for the next person, or to make a phone call or a visit, to give a compliment or say thank you. To donate something: clothing, food, money, time. To say something nice. To listen.

> *I thought about how easy it could be to solve people's problems or make their days a little better.*

I remember years ago I attended a Christmas Eve mass in a very crowded church. A woman walked up the aisle with her octogenarian mother looking for a seat. There was an empty one right in front of me but as the older woman entered the row a young man said, "Sorry. This seat is reserved." I remember thinking how ironic that this took place on Christmas Eve, the night when there was "no room at the inn." As I was musing about this clever comparison a teenage girl got up and offered her seat to the woman. Now why didn't I think of that?

Going forward that's what I'm going to do.

~Eileen Melia Hession

37

Thank You Is Enough

Saying "thank you" creates love.
~Daphne Rose Kingma

As a child I was made to feel unloved, unworthy, unwanted and undeserving of anything good that came my way. The feeling stayed with me when I became an adult. I didn't like getting gifts from anyone; in fact, it was almost painful if someone gave me a gift for my birthday or Christmas. I would thank them to the point of gushing, I would send them an elaborate Thank You card and I would immediately start thinking of a way to "pay them back" for the gift. I would try to give them something of equal or greater value than whatever they had given me.

I would practically start a gift giving frenzy with gifts going back and forth between myself and friends until nobody could remember why or when it started.

I preferred to be ignored on holidays, so there would be no feeling of indebtedness or obligation. I enjoyed getting cards from people, but if anyone gave me a gift, regardless of whether it was something I really liked or not, my first thought was "What can I give them back?"

I've had people ask me to stop giving them gifts because they couldn't keep up. I think I always felt I had to buy friendship, that no one could possibly like me for being me. If I needed to get my car repaired, I'd take a box of donuts to the garage so the mechanics could have something for their coffee break. When I went to the dentist

I'd take copies of magazines I'd read and leave them in the office for other patients.

Many people do thoughtful things every day for the people around them. The things I did could be considered generous, except the reason I did them wasn't about being generous. Even if I paid for a service, like getting my car repaired or a tooth filled, I felt paying for it wasn't enough, I needed to do a little more.

I did favors for people I didn't want to do, donated money I couldn't afford to give to charities, took care of people's pets when they went on vacations. It was as if I did enough "good" things, I would deserve someone's time or friendship. I was depositing "favors" into a friendship bank so I'd be "ahead."

> *"When you let someone help you, you have given them a gift."*

I was proud of the fact I never asked for favors, never asked for help no matter how badly I might need it. If I was flat on my back from surgery, I told no one. I had taken care of myself since I was a child and I would take care of myself until I died. I didn't want to owe anyone anything.

One time, I had promised my friend Harriet that I'd help her paint her kitchen but I had the worst flu I'd ever had. I called her and told her I couldn't help her that day but if she could put it off for a week I could help later. I didn't tell her I was violently ill but my voice gave me away.

An hour later Harriet came to my home carrying a picnic basket and a sack. I told her not to come in because I had the flu and I didn't want her to catch it. She ignored me and came in anyway.

She brought a kettle of the best soup I've ever eaten; she had prepared some sort of orange drink she guaranteed would cure me. She brought a sack of various medications, tissues and a copy of the children's book, *My Secret Garden*. She said I'd mentioned it was my favorite book when I was a kid.

She changed my sheets, carried out the trash, and did a load of laundry. For the first time in days I felt like I might live.

I was lying in bed, propped up on the freshly fluffed pillows and trying to think of ways I could thank her when she said something that changed my life.

"Sometimes, the nicest thing you can do for someone, is let them help you. When you let someone help you, you have given them a gift," Harriet said, "And a simple thank you is enough."

She knew me. She knew as soon as I was back on my feet I'd be shopping for a gift for her to pay her back, because that's what I'd always done in the past.

She was right. I wasn't "thanking" people for what they did for me; I was using gifts and favors to pay them for what they did. I didn't mean to, but I was stealing their joy, taking away any blessing they'd have received for helping me. People offered their help, their friendship, their comfort because they were goodhearted and because they felt I deserved it. I finally felt "good enough."

It wasn't easy to change the habits of a lifetime and I had to make a conscious effort every time someone did something nice for me to just say, "Thank you." I didn't have to repay them or give them a gift; just saying "Thank you," was enough.

It has been a tremendous relief. I don't have to out-do anyone. When I get my car worked on, just saying "Thanks" and paying my bill is enough. When I go to the dentist, again, saying "Thanks" and paying my bill is enough.

I've learned to really appreciate and enjoy getting gifts from people; they give me gifts because they want to, not to put me in a position of giving them something bigger and better in return.

I still give gifts, but I give them for birthdays and Christmas, I give them for the right reason, not to pay someone back for something they did for me.

I carried a huge burden for years, trying to be good enough to deserve friendship. I deprived myself of joy, and I kept other people from being blessed. Sometimes the nicest thing you can do is let someone help you and saying "Thank you" is enough.

~April Knight

38

A Wedding and a Funeral

*Living in the moment means letting go of the past and
not waiting for the future. It means living your
life consciously, aware that each moment
you breathe is a gift.*
~Oprah Winfrey

A recent Saturday found me at two churches for two contrasting events — a wedding and a funeral. By the end of the day I felt like I'd spent too much time in the wave pool at the local water park. I'd been suffocated in the undercurrent of grief one moment and buoyed up by tides of joy the next.

The funeral was for a twenty-seven-year-old man. Brian was a talented athlete and an avid reader. He was a loving son, a loyal friend, a cherished brother and an adored uncle. But he was also deeply troubled. He'd been plagued by depression for years. And early one morning his mother found him dead in his room, in the home he shared with his parents.

His loss rocked our community and devastated his family. His mother and grandmother had never stopped believing that Brian could be restored to the exuberant, charming boy they'd watched grow up. And suddenly, without warning, he was gone.

The church was filled with somber, dark-clad guests. Tears fell freely. Brian's family has the comfort of their faith to help them through their loss, and the hope of a heavenly reunion, but their pain is still a raw ache. No one and nothing will be able to fill the gap that Brian left behind.

After the service my husband and I headed home. We exchanged our funeral black for wedding finery. Emotionally, I couldn't quite make the leap.

We drove in subdued silence through the tree-lined campus to the chapel at Mukogawa Fort Wright Institute. We'd eagerly anticipated this wedding of a friend in his forties who'd long shied away from marriage, but the sadness of the afternoon lingered.

Happy guests sloshed through the damp parking lot and entered the elegantly decorated sanctuary. A cellist played softly as the crowd assembled. Glowing white votive candles shimmered, and the guests chatted and laughed quietly while listening for the first strains of the wedding march.

It takes a hard knock on the head to wake us up—to force us to appreciate what we have.

And when at last I caught a glimpse of the white-gowned bride, with her radiant smile, a spark of joy flickered and then ignited in me. The ceremony was perfect. There was lots of laughter and a few poignant moments. The pastor told the assembled guests how it took a car accident to bring a confirmed bachelor to his senses. How after he'd rolled his truck on an icy patch of road, the groom had hung upside down, suspended by his seatbelt. And the only name on his lips was that of his true love, Vicky.

Sometime life's like that. It takes a hard knock on the head to wake us up—to force us to appreciate what we have.

Late that night, after the reception, the toasts and the dancing, I wandered through our home unable to rest. I watched my husband sleep for a while. Our newlywed days are long behind us and sometimes it's easy to take for granted simple joys like falling asleep and waking up together.

And then I slipped into my sons' rooms. I listened to one son mumble and another snore. I shushed my light sleeper, whose head popped up the minute I opened his door—just like it did when he was an infant and I tried to peek at him while he slept.

I crouched at the foot of my seven-year-old's bunk bed and tucked his blankie around him.

And tears caught up with me again. Mothers should never have to bury sons. The shining promise of every wedding should gleam even brighter twenty years down the road.

But life doesn't always work out that way. And sometimes it takes a wedding and a funeral to make us realize how fleeting our blessings can be, and how much we need to cherish what we have while we can.

~Cindy Hval

39

Road to Forgiveness

Forgiving is rediscovering the shining path
of peace that at first you thought others
took away when they betrayed you.
~Dodinsky

As an only child of separating and then divorcing parents, I didn't understand where I fit. I lived in an adult world where dreams were abandoned and futures were uncertain. My parents were suffering, moving, changing jobs, struggling, and healing.

And there I was from age six on, holding their outstretched hands, but only one at a time. For many years I was confused about almost everything: who, what, where, when, why and how. No one offered me any explanation that made sense.

But there was one thing I wasn't confused about: nasty people. And the nastiest of them all was my grandfather. He was cruel to everybody, not just me, and he exploded with rage if I was too loud one day or if I didn't speak up another day. I couldn't win. He told me to sit, stay, and be still, or he ordered me to leave when I wasn't welcome anymore.

One summer evening when I was thirteen we were having a formal "adult" dinner at my grandfather's house. Since I was the only grandchild I was included with my seven aunts and uncles and my grandfather. What this meant was that we all sat at a large round dining room table and listened to my grandfather talk. He wasn't interested in what anyone else had to say, and if anyone else was talking he would interrupt when he had had enough. Even at thirteen I knew that these dinners were dreaded events for everyone.

I was a pudgy young teenager. Food gave me solace when I was feeling sad, and I felt sad a lot. What I didn't realize then was that my grandfather had no respect for overweight women, and I seemed to be heading in that direction. All of the other women around that table were very skinny, so I was the outlier, and thus in danger.

At the end of the meal my aunt brought in a plate of chocolate chip cookies for dessert and put them down in front of me. My grandfather immediately changed the focus of what he was saying: "For God's sake don't put those down in front of her! She'll eat the whole damned plate!"

> *"Do you realize how much energy you are spending feeling angry?"*

Everyone turned and looked at me. I was on the verge of crying and quickly asked to be excused — no one could leave the dinner table without permission from my grandfather.

As I scurried away I heard my father try to defend me. "Dad," he said. "She's still growing. It's just baby fat."

For years I held onto the anger I felt toward my grandfather, never missing a chance to say a spiteful word about him when his name came up. Then he died when I was in college, and not long after I was recounting one of the many stories I had heard of his ruthlessness to my father over the phone. After listening to me complain about my grandfather yet again my father said, "Gwen, try to forgive him. Do you realize how much energy you are spending feeling angry? It's just not worth it."

These were shocking words to hear — especially since my dad had suffered far, far worse physical and mental abuse than I had from his father.

It took me five years to put my dad's words into action. To take them in and let them transform me, to really apply them to my emotions. Forgiving my grandfather took practice, took reminding, and took going over my feelings and adjusting them.

Finally, one day it happened. When I thought of my grandfather I felt not even a sliver of anger. For the first time ever, when I thought of him, I felt free... and thankful.

My grandfather was the first person I ever forgave, and like so many things, the first time you do it is the hardest. Since then I have had to forgive many more people, and I am so thankful that I know how to do it.

Today, I like to think that part of my father's family legacy is not the cruelty I remember, but the lesson in how to forgive and feel gratitude.

~Gwen Daye

40

A Brighter Future

*When you have a disability, knowing that you are not
defined by it is the sweetest feeling.*
~Anne Wafula Strike, In My Dreams I Dance

I felt like I had been punched in the stomach. As the air escaped from my lungs, my mind was reeling from what I had just heard.

It was 1990, and I was sitting in the office of the Director of Disabled Student Services at my college. I had been considering a particular program for graduate school, but I was still a little unsure of myself — trying to navigate my way into a career that reflected my passions. I knew I wanted to work with people with disabilities, and this seemed like a great way to get some answers. After asking what I considered to be some pretty intelligent questions, I was interrupted.

"I don't think you will ever get a job, Lorraine. But you are disabled and a female. I'm sure somebody will feel sorry for you."

What? I had spent the majority of my life doing things to feel just like everyone else, to try and get people to see me as a person before they saw my wheelchair. I worked hard at everything I did, both academically and socially, and someone was telling me I wouldn't get a job because of my abilities, but maybe could get one because of pity. It was an insult that undermined all of my effort to fit in.

One of the reasons I had chosen to attend this university was its national reputation of accessibility for people with all kinds of disabling conditions. The compact campus made getting to classes in my wheelchair manageable, and the extra time that I needed to finish my essay tests due to my limited finger dexterity was always graciously accommodated. For decades, this university had prided itself on meeting the needs of students who had serious challenges. It was hard to wrap my mind around the fact that the Director of Disabled Student Services didn't think I was employable. I left the office feeling like Charlie Brown after Lucy took away the football, and I struggled to get out the door before the tears started to flow.

It didn't feel fair. I could live with the fact that I would never drive and would always need caregivers, but a job? I always anticipated that having a job would make me feel just a little more like everyone else.

When I got back to my dorm room that day, I did a lot of soul searching. Looking back, I realized it was not entirely hopeless. I had already held a few temporary jobs. In order to gain some work experience when I was in high school, I answered phones and did some office work for the church my family attended. I had also been a reporter for the student newspaper on campus for a couple of semesters. At each position I had to be creative in figuring out ways to complete some of the duties that were assigned to me. Some things I needed were stored out of reach and some places I needed to be didn't have ramps at the entrance. That was the way the world had always been. I'd never had a problem before, so why would anyone think I would be denied the opportunity to get a job at this point? Why was somebody I had gone to for help telling me I wasn't capable?

One night, a few months later, on July 26, 1990, I was at my parents' house watching the news. The big story of the day was that George H.W. Bush had signed into law the Americans with Disabilities Act, which meant that government agencies, public transportation, and places of public accommodation like businesses, restaurants and schools had to be accessible to those of us with disabilities. I was particularly excited that the ADA included a section on employment, which said that if candidates for a job are qualified for that job, employers can't refuse to hire them because of their disability.

After President Bush signed the law, he said, "Let the shameful wall of exclusion finally come tumbling down." I felt more hope than

I had in a very long time.

In the years since the passage of the ADA, I have had some significant health issues that prevent me from working full-time. However, I regularly post to a blog that I love, which is about my experience living with a disability. It has been an honor to have been published numerous times and to write for online magazines and United Cerebral Palsy's national website on occasion.

I got an e-mail recently from the editor of a magazine in my hometown. He asked if I would be interested in taking over a column called "Hometown Heroes." The column profiles people who are doing good things in our community. It sounded right up my alley. In my response I expressed my only concern.

> *"Let the shameful wall of exclusion finally come tumbling down."*

"Nathan, I know that interviewing people goes a million times better when a reporter does so in person, and I know that private homes aren't always accessible. Would it be okay with you and do you think it would be okay with whoever I would be interviewing to ask them to meet me in a public place for the interview? I would probably always have a caregiver with me."

His simple, direct reply came early the next morning. "Lorraine, if anybody you interview is not willing to meet in a place that is the most accessible and comfortable for you, I would have trouble profiling them as a hometown hero."

Well, all right then.

The polar opposite attitude of this editor compared to the Director of Disabled Student Services on my college campus was like the difference between an iceberg and ice cream. The Americans with Disabilities Act has been on the books for the last twenty-five years. That means that for the first time in history, there is a generation of people who grew up in a country where they don't know anything different than inclusion. This editor understood that I was entirely capable of doing what he was asking of me. Whatever adjustments were necessary for me to accomplish the task were okay with him, and he expected them to be okay with members of the community as well. When I had an appointment with him in his office to discuss details, he met me outside so he could show me where the accessible entrance to the building was.

When the Americans with Disabilities Act was passed in 1990, it ensured that when I go out in public there are accessible parking places that make my life easier, as well as larger restrooms and doorways on businesses. However, I will always consider the change in perception toward people with disabilities to be the greatest achievement of the ADA.

~Lorraine Cannistra

The Power of Gratitude

Well Chosen Words

Well chosen words mixed with measured emotions is the basis of affecting people.
~Jim Rohn

41

Have a Day!

If you can't see the gift in having a child with autism,
you're focusing too much on the autism and
not enough on the child.
~Stuart Duncan

I kiss my fourteen-year-old autistic son Jacob on the head as he leaves for the bus stop and then I tell him to have a great day, a comment that comes out of my mouth without any particular thought. To me it is small talk — simply what you say when you want to be nice. But to my boy it is anything but. Jacob carefully chooses his words, for he knows how much words really matter.

"Mom, please don't say that! Too much pressure!" he replies as if he is the parent and I am the child.

I try backtracking, searching desperately for the right words. "How about, have the day you want?"

He shakes his head no.

"Make the day count?" I say, hoping that this conversation is not causing him too much stress.

"That is even more pressure," he says and begins pacing back and forth trying to find his own words to express how he feels.

I stop for a moment. If there is one thing I have learned being the mom to this incredible boy it is that sometimes we both need to stop and process the situation. After a moment or two I speak again, this time less rushed and more sure of myself.

"I think I've got it. Have a *day*, Jacob! Simply, have a day. How is that?"

Jacob smiles and says, "Perfect!" He throws his messenger bag around his neck and starts to walk out the door. Suddenly he stops. So does my heart. Seeing the panic in my eyes my boy smiles again, kisses me on my forehead and says, "Thanks, Mom, for understanding," and walks happily out the door. And as I watch him walk away, I cry! I cry because I am suddenly overcome with a huge feeling of gratitude!

I am grateful because I get to be this incredible person's mother.

I am grateful that my son has words!

I am grateful that my boy will now allow me to kiss him on his head and even more grateful that now he will reach out and kiss me!

I am grateful because he is able to advocate for himself. He is able to express how he feels, something he has not always been able to do.

> *"Have a day" means endless possibilities and hope. There is no pressure to be a certain way.*

I am grateful because for the first time ever, this year he is able to take the bus to school. Before it was just too loud, too unpre-dictable — too much!

I am grateful because while he has chal-lenges, he doesn't let them stop him from dreaming, from doing, from living and being!

I am grateful because with the right support he will go to college, find meaningful employment and get married and have his own family some day if he wants.

I am grateful because he makes me stop, live in the moment, and reconsider what I think and know. He has taught me that there are so many ways to get from Point A to Point B and most of them are a lot more fun than drawing a straight line.

And I am grateful because I finally understand what saying "have a day" really means. It is so much more than a nicety, small talk, a casual conversation. "Have a day" means endless possibilities and hope. There is no pressure to be a certain way, act in a manner that others expect, to change. "Have a day" means acceptance. It conveys tolerance and respect for difference all wrapped up in three little words. I am grateful that my boy has shown me all this… and even more grateful that he believes it!

I hide behind the big oak tree in my front yard and watch as the bus comes to a stop and Jacob gets on. He is a teenager now and teens don't want their moms watching them. But as the bus doors close and it begins to pull away I see my boy looking for me. He seems frantic, lost and alone. I want nothing more than to run to him, but instead I step out from my hiding place so he sees me, my way of offering him comfort even if it is from afar. It works! Jacob puts his palm against the glass, smiles calmly, and mouths three simple words...

"Have a day!"

~Sharon Fuentes

42

The Antidote for First-World Problems

Cultivate the habit of being grateful for
every good thing that comes to you,
and to give thanks continuously.
~Ralph Waldo Emerson

I looked in the fridge and scowled. We'd run out of my favorite coffee creamer. "This stinks," I muttered.

"What stinks?" my teenage son, Jordan, asked.

"We're out of creamer."

"So put milk and sugar in your coffee," he said with a shrug.

I shrugged back. "It's not the same. I've got a big writing deadline today and I always work better when I have coffee."

"You do have coffee, Mom. You just don't have creamer. And this sounds like a first-world problem to me."

I sighed. This first-world problem thing was his new favorite expression and frankly, I was ready for the phase to pass. "You know I don't like it when you say that. It feels like you're making fun of me for complaining about small things, but we all do it."

"You're right," he said. "We all do it, and that's why I'm not making fun of you. I'm just reminding you that if running out of coffee creamer is the worst thing that happens to you today, it was still a really good day."

I smiled. "You're a pretty smart kid."

He grinned back. "All teenagers are."

I rolled my eyes and hugged him.

That Sunday, at church, my pastor was talking about a program that provides shoes to children in Africa. "There are these fleas called jiggers that burrow so deep into kids' feet that they have to cut them out," he explained. "They get so bad that the kids can hardly walk, but their parents don't have money to buy them shoes to protect their feet."

I glanced down at my well-worn Nikes, suddenly grateful for them.

But my pastor wasn't finished. "What percentage of your household income do you think you spend on food?"

My husband and I looked at one another and shrugged. I really had no idea.

"The average family in America spends eight percent of their income on food. In Haiti, it's over ninety percent." He waited a moment to let the statistics sink in. "Can you even imagine that? Spending almost everything you have just to keep from starving to death?"

I nodded. I remembered a few years ago when my children and I had packed food to send to Haiti. We filled bags with rice, dried vegetables, and a protein powder. When I'd asked how many people that small bag served, I was shocked when the volunteer said, "It serves a family of six, and when you give it to them, those mothers act like they've won the lottery."

I looked at the bag again, knowing I'd prepare three times as much food for my own family's dinner. And that meal wouldn't be our only one for the day.

When we left church that day, I vowed to return the following Sunday, my arms full of shoes to donate.

But as the week went on, I couldn't stop thinking about those statistics. I spent some time on Google and discovered a wonderful tool called the World Wealth Calculator.

I typed in my family's middle-class income and discovered that we are among the richest people in the entire world. We're talking top one percent.

I'd been a single mom before I'd met and married my husband. My annual income was $18,500 for a family of three. We'd barely made ends meet, but we'd never gone hungry. I plugged that income into the calculator and even that meager amount placed me in the top twelve percent of world incomes.

I remembered my constant fear over having enough food for my children, and tears filled my eyes as I realized how many mothers in the world experience those fears every day of their lives.

Studies show that having more money makes us happier, but only to a certain point. People who earn less than $50,000 a year usually become happier as their income increases. But for people with annual incomes over $50,000, their level of happiness does not increase if their income goes up.

> *"This sounds like a first-world problem to me."*

The bottom line? Stuff doesn't make us happy.

I thought about all my little gripes. My first-world problems, as Jordan would say. Running out of coffee creamer. Disliking the color of my super-reliable used car. The ten extra pounds I carry because we have more food than we need.

I realized that nearly all of the aggravations in my life could be classified as first-world problems. I remembered all the times I'd found myself in a bad mood because of something insignificant. Countless times, I'd allowed small inconveniences to steal my joy.

Luckily, there is an antidote to this type of dissatisfaction. It's gratitude.

Simply being thankful for what we have.

Being happy is nearly impossible without gratitude. Without gratitude, we can't see the blessings we already have. Our glass is always half empty.

I don't want to live that way.

Now, when I look in the mirror and see a few wrinkles, I call them "laugh lines" and thank God for the friends and family who helped put them there. When I have too many errands on my To Do List, I am grateful that I have a reliable, if not beautiful, car to drive that day. And when I run out of coffee creamer, I remember that I have a son who loves me enough to remind me that if drinking a less-than-perfect cup of coffee is the worst thing that happens to me today, it will still be a really good day.

~Diane Stark

43

Being Happy Is Enough

*The happiest people don't necessarily have the best of
everything. They just make the best of everything.*
~Author Unknown

Someone on Facebook had shared pictures of her vacation in Europe. The delivery truck had dropped off a gargantuan entertainment system at my neighbor's house. And the kids came home from school raving about the new video game their friends had just gotten.

Meanwhile, we were living in a house furnished mostly with freebies and dressing our kids in secondhand clothes. And even when we and the kids had to go in three different directions at night, we didn't eat out. Ever.

I like to cook, and I'm good at it. But sometimes, you just want to be spared the hassle and the cleanup!

My poor mother-in-law, in town for a visit, got to hear the whole tirade that night. "I feel so resentful sometimes," I told her, as we cleared the table after dinner. "I know we're doing the right thing, living frugally, saving money, but it feels so hard. There are so many things I'd like to have, so many things I'd like to do, and we just can't."

She hummed once or twice, nodding as she folded a cloth napkin in silence. Then she turned to me. "You know," she said, "when you compare yourself to others, it's easy to focus on what you don't have. But there's one thing you two do that we don't see too much of in other married couples. You two make a priority of going out together and taking time to focus on your marriage. And that's a very important thing. You two have such a great marriage."

I stopped wiping the table and pondered that for a minute. I thought of the movie my husband and I had seen a week earlier, and the English country-dance we'd attended a few weeks before that. I remembered the bike rides and the concerts, the hikes and the picnics. Most of all, I thought of how happy we were together, even after twenty years. How many people can say that?

> *"You two make a priority of going out together and taking time to focus on your marriage."*

I looked around my home with new eyes. Our refrigerator is almost too small for a family of six, but it's always filled with food that is both nourishing and delicious. Our kitchen décor is cobbled together, but it comes to us from our grandmothers' homes after they passed away. And our deck overlooks a sycamore grove where our family cooks s'mores in the fire pit every few weeks.

Even without the big TV and the European vacations and the new wardrobe every season, we are... well... happy.

And you know what? That's enough.

~Kathleen M. Basi

44

A Stroke of Blessings

Reflect upon your present blessings, of which every
man has plenty; not on your past misfortunes
of which all men have some.
~Charles Dickens

Eighteen years ago, my mother had a stroke. My parents had gone out to dinner with two other couples, all close friends. As they pulled up to our house, she suffered the stroke. In a flash, her left side was paralyzed from head to toe. But she could still talk.

The image of my father dashing into our house through the side door to call an ambulance is one I'll never forget. I was sitting in the kitchen, watching *Saturday Night Live* while I waited up for them. I'd come down from Boston with my newborn daughter, Bridget, to visit my family in New York one last time before returning to work from maternity leave. I'd planned to drive home that Saturday, but my mother begged me to "stay, just one more day." Bridget and I ended up not leaving for another two weeks.

What happened next was controlled chaos: the red lights of the ambulance, my mother in ICU, the doctors and us waiting for another big stroke to come. My two brothers, two sisters, and I were frantic. My father tried to appear calm.

After four days in the ICU and no second stroke, Mom was moved into a regular hospital room. Friends and family visited her. The home phone rang nonstop. I called Julia, one of my long-time friends, a former coworker of mine in New York. Strong, but comforting, Julia always seemed to know what to say.

I sobbed as I told her the story. Mom had just celebrated turning sixty-two. How could this have happened? When I finished, Julia said, "I'm going to tell you something and I want you to take it the right way." I waited for the words that would bring me comfort. "Count your blessings."

What! Count my blessings? Hadn't she listened to anything I said? My blood boiled. I felt like I was going to have a stroke next. For fifteen years, we'd been friends. Julia knew me so well, and yet all she could say during this terrible time was "count my blessings?" I had expected better from her.

Right then, I wanted to end our friendship, but she interrupted me before I could. "I know you must be wondering how I can say that," Julia said, her voice gentle. "But when I lost my brother, people told me the same thing."

We had just become office mates when Julia's only brother died from testicular cancer, six months after it was discovered, and a few months before his wedding day. Julia said she knew it was hard advice for me to hear. She had felt the same way when someone said the same words to her when her brother got sick. But, she said, even after he died, it really helped her see the situation in a different light. Despite the negative appearance of my mother's situation, she told me to look for, then count, actually count, the blessings that appeared.

"They are there," Julia said.

I couldn't listen to this nonsense. I wanted comfort, not some wishy-washy sentiment! I hung up.

The next day, I awoke hoping it was all a bad dream. It wasn't. My mother still lay in her hospital bed, her left side paralyzed. I couldn't see past it. What was next? Julia's words came back to me. "Count your blessings." I pushed them away.

Yet, as the day went on, I began to notice, not big miracles, but small things that could be counted as "blessings." There was the kindness of neighbors, church members, and friends. I had no idea that so many people loved my parents. Day after day, they brought us food.

Well Chosen Words | 169

The mailman delivered an endless stream of cards with handwritten, comforting messages that my mother would be okay, telling us how much she meant to them.

Then there were even bigger blessings, like her doctors telling us that, since she hadn't suffered another stroke, my mother could go for physical therapy to help regain her ability to walk. Most amazing was the display of my father's love for my mother, not in words, but in his actions.

Over the next year, my mother was discharged from the hospital and moved to a wonderful rehabilitation center filled with great staff. My father visited her every day, while still working, often spending the entire day with her, while she went through various exercises to regain her strength and use of her left-side limbs. At least my mother hadn't lost her ability to talk, we joked. Not being able to talk would have killed her. Hearing her voice, normal as ever, was a great comfort. She could also still use her right hand and write short thank-you notes to people.

> *I began to notice, not big miracles, but small things that could be counted as "blessings."*

While the experience was terrifying, it made my close family even closer. While Mom was at the rehab facility, we helped my father make their home handicap-accessible. Grab bars helped my mother support herself in the bathroom and shower. A stair-climbing mechanical chair made getting upstairs easier and let her be more independent. A La-Z-Boy recliner chair for the living room allowed Mom to nap downstairs.

My father once protested my mother's shopping habit, but now he used it to motivate her to walk. His "shopping therapy" took place at a nearby Lord & Taylor. The floors there were flat, so she couldn't trip. The clothing racks provided soft bumpers for her as she walked, ever so slowly, with a cane for support. For a few moments, Mom felt normal again, like her old self. Dad would treat Mom to lunch after shopping, something she always liked to do with us girls.

My mother never fully recovered from her stroke. Eventually, though, Mom returned to doing many of the things she used to do, like meeting friends for dinner. My parents even traveled, taking a cruise, something they had done before. One benefit of the stroke? Getting upgraded to a bigger, handicap-accessible room.

Eighteen years later, we've just celebrated my mother's eightieth birthday. Today, she lives alone in an over-fifty-five community with aides to help her. Unfortunately, my father has passed.

Recently, I told Mom what one of the doctors told us almost twenty years ago in that ICU: that she might only live a few more years — ten years tops. "We should go back, wheel you in, and show those doctors they were wrong," I told her.

Over the years, there have been plenty more heartbreaking situations. Each time, I lean on Julia's advice. I share it with friends when they tell me their troubles. If they don't seem open to hearing it, I keep the advice to myself. And count the blessings for them.

~Kathy Shiels Tully

45

Broken Gifts

The soul would have no rainbow had the eyes no tears.
~John Vance Cheney

e was kneeling on the kitchen floor as I walked in from outside, my arms laden with the baby, groceries, shopping bags, lunch boxes, the mail, and other things that had been rolling around on the floor of the van.

I was filled with my normal early evening thoughts: What to make for dinner? How fast could I feed the baby? And how did my daughter put holes in the knees of her pants again? But that stopped when I saw my son on the floor, silently sobbing, his little shoulders shaking.

"Brother sad," my toddler observed, mildly dismayed. "Broken." She pointed to the pieces of pottery on the kitchen floor. There were several pieces, gorgeously fired in teal green — my favorite color.

"What happened, Bud?" I set down my load, including the baby, and bent over my brokenhearted second grader.

"It's ruined!" He looked up at me, tears streaming. "RUINED! It was for you and now it's just a piece of junk!" His face had gone red and his fists were balled up. I reached for him, but he evaded me and headed for the stairs and his room. I sighed. I'd give him a few minutes to calm down, and in the meantime sweep up the kitchen floor so no one would get hurt.

I began gathering the broken pottery. It had been a dish of some sort, crafted by my son's careful hands. It was made with so much love.

Tears collected in my own eyes and I set the pieces on the counter. I wanted this gift. And so I got out the Super Glue. Porous pottery generally glued pretty well. I could reassemble this. And I even had some nail polish in the same color. I could fix the spots where the glaze had chipped. It would be almost as good as new.

I could hear him banging around in his room. Things were getting thrown.

I went up the stairs slowly, trying to decide my strategy. He was old enough to no longer be pacified. "It's okay" wasn't going to work.

I knocked on the door and opened it in time to watch a book fly across the room. He leapt into bed and under the covers. Carefully closing the door behind me, I looked around. The room was trashed. Nothing broken though. So there was that.

"Hey," I said, sitting next to the lump under the covers. "Can I talk to you for a sec?" Silence. "I need to see your face."

> *"I wouldn't have known how much that gift meant to you if it hadn't broken into pieces."*

He pulled back the covers. Disheveled, red hair standing on end, face streaked with tears.

"I know you're mad and disappointed." His lip started to quiver. "I get it, believe me. Broken things are the worst. Especially broken gifts. You worked really hard on that, didn't you?"

He nodded. "And it's ruined! It was supposed to be a surprise and now it's not. It's nothing! It's worse than nothing!"

"Not true." I shook my head. "I'm fixing it. I can glue it. It won't be perfect, but it will be pretty close and I'm going to keep it forever."

"No, you're not! Why would you keep a stupid broken dish?" The anger was creeping back in. Disappointment does that sometimes. It pulls away all of your pretending and reveals the brokenness underneath.

"Because you made it," I said. "And that makes it worth keeping. I'm going to fix it, and wrap it back up, and stick it under the tree. And then I'm going to open it on Christmas morning with you. And I'm going to put it on my dresser and keep my jewelry in it." He studied my face, trying to tell if I was serious.

"Even though it's broken?"

"Especially because it's broken," I said. "I wouldn't have known how much that gift meant to you if it hadn't broken into pieces on the kitchen floor. But now I know. And that makes it special. Really special. In fact, I think it's pretty much my favorite Christmas gift ever."

"No it's not." But he wasn't angry. The darkness had lifted from his eyes.

"It is," I was firm. "You made it. And broken gifts are sometimes the most beautiful gifts."

"Okay," he said.

"You done up here?" He looked around sheepishly.

"I guess I'll pick up a little."

I nodded. And this time he didn't evade my hug.

~Alice Luther

46

The Family Meeting

*Documenting little details of your everyday life
becomes a celebration of who you are.*
~Carolyn V. Hamilton

"Why won't you play with me?" my older son, Seth, demanded of his little brother.

"Because I don't want to!" Josh hollered back.

"You never want to do anything I want!" was the angry response. "You're such a baby!"

I sighed and put my head in my hands, at a loss for what to do. This had been going on all day! As many moms do on cold rainy days, I had tried to keep the kids busy with fun activities — board games, scavenger hunts, puzzles, hide and seek, videos.

I'd done activities with the kids; I'd left them alone.

I'd intervened in arguments; I'd left them to work things out themselves.

No matter what I did, it seemed my normally smart, creative, loving kids were determined to fight.

As I took deep breaths, searching for another solution, I realized gratefully that at least my girls were getting along. Happily engrossed in their craft projects, not a cross word had been uttered by either of them for several minutes.

"Well, I can't help it if you just like to do stupid stuff!" the boys' argument waged on.

Lord, I prayed desperately, "What do I do?"

I wasn't sure how much more any of us could take.

Then it happened. The girls started in and I thought I might crumble to pieces.

"See what you did," Ashley screeched. "You broke it!"

"No, I didn't," Dora screeched louder.

Not sure what would come next, I attempted to make myself louder than the rest.

"Alright! Everyone drop what you're doing and get in here now! Family meeting!"

> *It was a day when our family was transformed by two simple words: thank you.*

As I waited a moment for the kids to get settled, the thought occurred to me: THANK YOU! And I knew what I'd do next.

See, I'd recently been trying something new in my own life. Inspired by Oprah Winfrey's book, *What I Know For Sure*, I'd been working to use gratitude to change my attitude and perspective in difficult times. I had seen the simple act of saying thank you make huge changes in myself when I was overwhelmed by negative situations and emotions. Maybe it would work with the kids.

"Okay. What do you want?" my surly preteen asked, flopping into his seat. "What am I in trouble for now?"

"Well," I started, steeling myself for the inevitable resistance. "This isn't working. Everyone's fighting and it's got to stop. So, we're going to try something new. Starting with Dora, I want everyone to just say, 'thank you.'"

"What?" Ashley asked. "What's going on?"

"Just do it."

Naturally, the kids all thought Mom had lost her mind. I wasn't sure they were wrong, but I pressed on.

"Now, we're going to keep going around and everyone tell what they're thankful for."

Clearly doubtful and frustrated, the kids launched in, and I kept them going.

"I'm thankful for our house."

"I'm thankful for my toys."

"I'm thankful for my clothes."

"How long do we have to do this?"

"Just keep going."

The kids grudgingly continued and I started to doubt the process. Their attitudes were not changing and their answers were getting more and more pat, as the kids clearly started competing to find the "right answer."

"I'm thankful for my whole life and everyone in the world."

"What? What am I supposed to say?"

"Keep going."

Then came a break in the storm. Obviously frustrated, Ashley, my somewhat irreverent nine-year-old, searched the room for an answer and zeroed in on the laundry basket.

"I'm grateful for my underwear!"

Instant laughter erupted, music to my ears!

"Great, let it out!" I encouraged. "What else?"

And that was all we needed. The gratitude — great and small, serious and funny — came rolling out.

"My backpack."

"My teachers."

"My toes!"

On and on it went until every face was lit with a new kind of joy and laughter. I could sense a new feeling of peace and comfort in the air, a reminder of not only our blessings, but the love we really did have for each other.

"I'm grateful for being grateful!" Dora declared.

"Me, too!" was the unanimous response.

I don't remember the activities that took place the rest of the day, but the memory lingers of the sense of harmony that prevailed. It was a day when our family was transformed by two simple words: thank you.

Since then, it's become a family motto. Whenever disharmony arises, you can count on someone to say, "Hey, remember your thank-yous!"

~Joy Cook

47

Nine Things We Like About You

*A tree is known by its fruit; a man by his deeds. A
good deed is never lost; he who sows courtesy reaps
friendship, and he who plants kindness gathers love.*
~Saint Basil

For a brief period of time in 2002, my husband Dave and I
moved into our cottage in Wasaga Beach. While the cottage was small, we loved the street it was on and the people
who lived there — especially the two little boys who lived
directly across from us. Their names were Justin and Tyler and they
were nine and ten years old. We had a little black and white Shi Tzu
named Casey Doodle that I took for walks a few times a day and the
boys, and frequently their mother Kelly, would come with us.

Tyler has muscular dystrophy and while he was usually in his
wheelchair it didn't stop him from holding Casey's leash. Casey loved
it whenever he could sit on Tyler's lap and get pushed for part of his
walk. Sometimes another neighbour, Jackie, and her three-year-old
daughter, Anika, would join us. The boys were awesomely good with
Anika and it wasn't unusual for Tyler to have both Anika and Casey
on his lap while we strolled down the road. We never seemed to run
out of things to talk and laugh about.

The boys were funny, intelligent and easy to be with. However, one day when Casey and I were out with them they seemed to be a bit down. All they could talk about was what was wrong with their lives and what apparently important "things" they didn't have. At the end of the first half of our walk I stopped and talked to them about the importance of being grateful for what we *do* have in our lives.

When I told them that I could easily write out fifty different things I appreciated about my life every single day of the year they burst out laughing in disbelief. As we made our way back to our homes I started to point out the things I appreciated around us.

> *They truly didn't believe that there were fifty things to like about themselves.*

First, I appreciated that someone had invented glasses and that I had some, because I needed them to see the glorious trees that lined the street. I could appreciate the sky and the sun and the clouds. I could both see and hear the multitude of birds that nested in the area. I could read books and watch movies.

I told them to pay attention to things when they got home that they simply took for granted, things like flipping a switch and having a light turn on. I pointed out that they had a refrigerator and, more importantly, there was food in it. They had beds and pillows and blankets and their own bedroom to sleep in. They had a mother and father who loved them and they had Casey, Dave, and me living right across the street from them. For goodness' sake, Dave was even teaching them to play cards!

I'll never forget the expressions on their little faces when I promised that I would sit down and write out fifty things I appreciated about them that evening. "No way" and "not possible" were the first words out of their mouths. They were incredulous and doubtful, yet excited that there could actually be fifty things anyone could like about them.

That evening I sat at my computer and typed up fifty things I appreciated about each of them. I made a point of writing "I appreciate" in front of every single item. Tyler had a great laugh and a smile that always made *me* want to smile. He was honest and caring and thoughtful. He loved and took great care with Casey and Anika. He had a great sense of humour and loved to tell really bad jokes. I only stopped writing about the things I appreciated about Tyler because I hit the fifty mark and not because I ran out of things to like about him.

It certainly was not a challenge to come up with fifty things I appreciated about Justin. His favourite food was burnt toast and peanut butter, which I could make really well, as it was also my husband's favorite breakfast meal. Somehow Justin managed to be equally polite and mischievous at the same time. He was creative and artistic and always ready to tell jokes and stories. He was very good about sharing his time and his things with other people.

I printed out the pages I'd written and the next morning I delivered them to the boys. To say they were thrilled would be an understatement. They truly didn't believe that there were fifty things to like about themselves, but there in black and white were fifty items for each of them. Their mother told me later that they read and re-read their lists so many times that it was almost comical.

The next morning there was a knock at our door and when I opened it Justin was standing there with an uncertain look on his face. Tyler, who was behind him, had a grin from ear to ear. Justin thrust a piece of paper toward me and said that it was their list of things they appreciated about me. Then rather apologetically he added that they had only been able to come up with nine things they liked about me and not fifty as I had done for them. "But," Tyler blurted out with pride, "we wrote 'We appreciate' NINE WHOLE TIMES!"

And, they had. In their awkward children's printing they had written "We appreciate" before each of the nine things they liked about me. I was so touched that I almost cried. I told them the truth when I said that these were the most special nine lines I had ever read.

We moved shortly after and over time we lost touch with the boys. I do not know whether their exercise in appreciation stayed with them or made an impact on their lives. Every once in a while I happen across the list of nine things that the boys liked about me.

When I look at it I am reminded that you can never underestimate the power of appreciation and I am forever grateful for the time I had with Justin and Tyler.

~Laura Snell

48

Vanquishing the Dragon

*You cannot tailor-make the situations in life but you
can tailor-make the attitudes to fit those situations.*
~Zig Ziglar

I come from a long line of worriers. My grandmother worried about everything and everyone. My mother did, too. So it wasn't surprising that from an early age I picked up the heavy torch of worry and used it to examine every corner of my life.

If a family member traveled, I fretted over car accidents and plane crashes. If a friend had a health issue, I'd consult the Internet and feel my stomach drop when I read the worst-case scenario, which always popped up first on any search. The evening news became so abysmally hard for me to watch that I limited myself to only fifteen minutes of airtime before changing the channel.

Worry is a natural response in certain situations, but for me the habit had seeped into even everyday events. I rationalized my thoughts as normal and downplayed the fact that I allowed small matters to quickly grow into a fire-breathing dragon of anxiety. But I had no idea my pattern affected anyone else until the day my daughter, Jessica, told me about her plan to make a major purchase.

She and her fiancé had recently graduated from college. They had found a special deal on a small condominium. The condo would be their first home purchase.

"We figure we can live here for a couple of years and then sell it and buy a house."

She couldn't have been more excited and asked me to meet her and take a look before they put in an official offer.

I drove to the address she gave me with my doubts whirling around in my mind. Should they tie themselves down with a mortgage so soon? Could they afford to make the payments? Condos came with fees and often were difficult to re-sell. What if they were stuck with the place when they wanted to move?

> *No matter how hard I had to bite my tongue, I wouldn't voice a single dream-killing comment.*

The building was located in a nice neighborhood and gleamed with a fresh coat of cedar stain. I trudged up the exterior wooden stairs to the third floor and shook my head. Letting the dog out for a potty break and hauling groceries certainly wouldn't be easy. The door to the condo was open so I went in to find Jessica and her fiancé with the real estate agent.

"Hi, Mom! Isn't it cute? The owner just remodeled!"

The condo could have been featured on a television show about tiny spaces. Even a small couch would have trouble fitting in the living room. The kitchen wasn't much larger than a closet. The condo had one bedroom that would easily be swallowed by a full size bed. A queen size would be impossible. I walked through the rooms, looked at my daughter's glowing face, and cleared my throat to speak.

"Have you thought about looking around a little more before making a decision?"

"What do you mean?" she asked, as her eyes narrowed.

"Well, it might be a little too small for you, and being on the third floor could be a challenge. On top of that, I've heard condos can be really hard to sell."

Her brows bunched together.

"Why do you always have to say something negative? Can't you support me at least once in a while?"

Her outburst stunned me into silence. I swallowed and mumbled a feeble, "The condo is cute. If it's what you want, then I'm happy for you."

On the drive home, I thought about what Jessica had said. Maybe she was right. Perhaps I did let my worrying ways color what I said. But, I argued to myself, I only said what I did out of concern for the people I care about. As soon as the thought registered, I realized I wasn't helping the people I loved by taking away their joy.

I decided to change. No matter how hard I had to bite my tongue, I wouldn't voice a single dream-killing comment. Instead I'd strive to be honest, but positive, using only supportive and uplifting words.

When a friend told me she'd be going on a cruise during a time when hurricanes were likely, I only smiled and wished her "Bon voyage." Another friend quit a job without finding a new one first. I assured him he'd secure something better and offered to help any way I could. My son bought a classic automobile to restore, which I privately thought too expensive. I congratulated him on envisioning the car's potential.

The day my daughter and son-in-law announced they were building a large and pricey new home, I looked at the plans and wondered how they'd have time to maintain it. Both of them worked well over forty hours a week. Not to mention how they'd handle the inevitable eye-popping expenses. But when my daughter asked me what I thought, I uttered a simple truth. "It's beautiful."

The beaming smile on her face told me I'd said exactly the right thing.

My children and friends are all adults capable of formulating good decisions. Worrying over every choice they made diminished the magic of celebrating a special moment. I finally realized they weren't coming to me for advice. They were coming to me for my blessing and to share in their excitement.

I still struggle with my desire to be "helpful," but I am getting better at taking a breath and thinking before I speak. With an improved perspective, I've experienced the joy of relationships growing stronger and deeper. I feel happier and less stressed. By vanquishing the dragon of worry, I'm living with a grateful heart in the upside of today, not the theoretical downside of tomorrow.

~Pat Wahler

49

Thank You
for the Reminder

A gentle answer turns away wrath,
but a harsh word stirs up anger.
~Proverbs 15:1

The bus was full and we'd have to wait more than an hour to get to Mount Vernon, George Washington's home. It had already been quite a journey: a long walk from our hotel and a Metro ride with transfers outside of town to this bus station. We didn't want to waste an hour of valuable touring time, nor stand outside on that hot August Sunday.

There were other people at the bus stop in the same predicament. As my husband and I discussed what to do, we noticed a few taxicabs circling. We started chatting with a woman and her teenage daughter who stood nearby. They were also headed to Mount Vernon, so we suggested we share a taxi.

In the cab we exchanged stories: they had traveled to Washington, D.C. from Washington State and we had come from Arizona. We had all attended a patriotic event at the Lincoln Memorial the day before.

As we talked, Deb shared that she was a recent cancer survivor. I could tell that she had been through a lot: she was thin and her hair was short and fine, possibly having just grown back after chemotherapy. She had a kind spirit and she radiated gratitude for life and appreciation for her family. After their D.C. trip, she and her daughter would fly to Europe for a vacation with some girlfriends.

We ended up getting along so well with Deb and her daughter that we spent most of the day with them at Mount Vernon. Deb began calling us their "cousins."

We told Deb that we had a young daughter ourselves, almost two years old at the time, who was at home with her grandparents. As we stood in line to enter George Washington's home, she told us her most important advice for raising a family, which was liberal use of the phrase, "Thank you for the reminder."

She said it's a rule in her house that whenever a reminder is given or a subsequent request for something is made, she and her family must respond with, "Thank you for the reminder." Deb had gotten tired of hearing "I know!" or "You told me already!" from her husband and kids, so she came up with this response instead. It helped everyone speak more calmly and kindly to one another.

> *It's hard to grumble or speak harshly when you're thanking someone, isn't it?*

Her daughter chimed in and said that it wasn't always easy to say those words, but they all tried.

After a great day together, we parted ways with our new "cousins" when the estate closed. I am forever grateful to have met them. Deb's advice, those five little words, "Thank you for the reminder," has stuck with me during the six years since we met.

I just love that phrase. It's hard to grumble or speak harshly when you're thanking someone, isn't it? Even if they *are* reminding you of something you already know. Gratitude changes our attitude.

Our family has chosen to adopt this rule — it was a rule from our "cousin," after all. Our daughter is now seven and we also have a four-year-old son whom we are teaching to know and understand the phrase, "Thank you for the reminder." It takes effort of course, lots of modeling and practice! It's often when I fail to use those words that I'm reminded of the difference it makes. I always regret responding sarcastically or pompously because a relational rift often follows.

I don't know what happened to Deb and her family after our

meeting in 2010. But if I ever see her again, I'll tell her how grateful I am for having met her. Her powerful phrase, "Thank you for the reminder," has had a big impact on our family and friends.

Deb, wherever you are… thank you for the reminder!

~Andrea Fortenberry

50

Trying Destiny

*Inaction breeds doubt and fear. Action breeds
confidence and courage. If you want to conquer
fear, do not sit home and think about it.
Go out and get busy.*
~Dale Carnegie

L isa leaned over the "drop off prescriptions" desk and beamed at me with exuberance. "My birthday is Friday."

I smiled. "Happy Birthday!"

"I'm jumping out of an airplane tomorrow to celebrate," she said.

My smile faded. "Why?" I tend to lose my snappy retorts when caught off guard. Lisa had been filling my prescriptions for almost a year and I liked her.

"I've decided to test my destiny," Lisa said.

I plopped my heavy purse down on the counter. "Can't you find another way to test your faith from the ground?"

"Not my faith," she said. "My destiny. My faith in God is strong! But now, I've decided to let my destiny guide me." She tilted away from the counter and brushed one of her dreadlocks off her shoulder. "Really, I've prayed a lot on this. You have no idea how much I've prayed on this. I'm testing my spiritual limits."

I knew that Lisa worked at the store part-time. She also took night classes at a community college and occasionally attended Buddhist services to explore new experiences. She meditated and practiced yoga.

And up until now, I considered her to be the voice of reason. When she learned that I had owned my own business in my twenties, she shared her idea of a business venture to make herbal oils. She gave me a sample bottle to try, and I loved it.

I leaned in closer. "You're jumping out of a plane?"

She broke into a broad grin. "I think everyone should jump once," she said. "To see what it feels like."

I frowned. "You realize, I've been trusting you with my drugs."

I met Lisa when my former pharmacy screwed up my blood pressure medication — twenty milligrams instead of five milligrams — and I didn't notice the mistake until after the bottle was empty. I had dragged around feeling listless. I reasoned that my exhaustion was a natural side effect of growing old. At sixty-five, it's hard to argue with the "age" card.

> *I was being offered the chance to do something that scared me senseless.*

After I discovered the error, I switched to Lisa's pharmacy. From the beginning, Lisa knew me by name, double-checked my medications in the computer, and even looked up "online savings" coupons for me.

Now, my pharmacy-buddy and confidante was talking about parachuting out of an airplane.

Luckily, there was no one else in line. My voice screeched. "God told you to jump out of an airplane?"

"No, but if the opportunity is there, then I should test my destiny." Lisa smoothed the vest of her blue uniform. "I'm challenging my fears," she said. "I'm tired of being afraid of things."

"I'm afraid of everything," I said. "Fear is good for you."

"I don't believe that. You have no fear. I've seen your website. You've acted in hundreds of commercials and even in movies. You've even written books."

"Only short stories," I said as I searched the bottom of my purse for the prescription that I'd brought in. "I haven't booked a commercial in two years."

In my thirties, I had appeared in national commercials for Levitz,

Popeyes, and Carnival cruise lines. But now, in my sixties, it was difficult to find a category for myself. I don't have white hair. Most TV commercials are geared toward the active, effervescent elderly who are incompetent, incontinent, or impotent.

"That reminds me, I have a casting call for a commercial tomorrow," I said. "I'm a nervous wreck. Terrified."

Lisa's brown eyes twinkled. "What's it for?"

"A car commercial," I said. "I'm not even sure I want to go on. The longer you don't do it, the more frightening it becomes. But can we get back to you jumping out of the airplane?"

Lisa took the pen out from behind her ear. "It's a very reliable company."

"They're not a pop-up business?"

"Nope, made sure of that before I booked my Groupon ticket," she said, rapping the pen on the table a few times.

I groaned and made the sign of the cross. "You're jumping out of an airplane on a Groupon ticket?"

Lisa threw her arms up in the air. "I'm a clerk, not a pharmacist. I'm on a budget."

"Of course," I said. "What was I thinking?"

"No, I checked them out carefully. They've been in business for thirty years."

"Thirty years. I feel so much better now. Lisa, how old are you?"

She looked down for an awkward second. "Twenty-eight."

"Okay," I said. I picked up my purse and slung it over my shoulder. "You have to promise me something. You have to call me the minute you land. Understand? I want a phone call. I'm not going to rest until I get one."

She laughed and pulled out her phone. She tapped in my number as I said it out loud. "I promise. I will call you."

I handed over the prescription to Lisa. Following store procedure, she asked for my birthdate and jotted it on the prescription as verification that it was indeed me. Then, she made one more attempt to win me over. "I think you should try it," she said.

I started to tell Lisa that it was too late for this old broad to do something radical and risky. I was old and fragile. Instead, I just shook my head. "I'll keep that in mind!" I said. I turned to do my weekly grocery shopping for fresh vegetables. Food shopping: Plant-based diet. Wednesday: Prescription drop-off. I realized how organized and predictable my life had become.

The next day, I carefully applied my make-up, rolled my hair in heated rollers, and pulled out my good luck pearls that I only wear for auditions. Then I studied the two different maps that I had Googled the day before. The casting director's office was located in an undesirable part of the city, and I was terrified of getting lost. I obsessed over the maps, trying to figure out the quickest route. I could feel my heart pounding. I stared at a roller sticking out of my hair and yanked it out. It was too much effort. I decided not to go.

Just then my cell phone rang. When I answered I heard Lisa's breathless voice. She was elated, almost singing. "Joyce, I did it. I jumped. It was incredible. Beyond awesome!" Lisa was shouting to be heard over the airport's background noise.

The sound of her happy voice lifted me.

Suddenly, I realized the opportunity I had been given. I was being offered the chance to do something that scared me senseless, challenged me, and raised my blood pressure. I made up my mind: this old broad was going to jump too.

"Lisa, thank you! I'm so glad you called," I said. "But if I want to make it to this casting in time, I have to run. Happy birthday! Now, go celebrate! On the ground, okay?"

No matter what our age, we all have our airplanes that we jump from, everyday fears that we overcome. The airplanes just take different shapes and forms.

First, we have to see them, then be grateful when our destiny appears.

~Joyce Newman Scott

51

The Question

If you are really thankful, what do you do? You share.
~W. Clement Stone

I stood in my tiny apartment kitchen, drinking my coffee and staring at the words I had written on a chalkboard: "My beautiful loving thoughts create my beautiful loving world."

I did this each morning, hoping this quote would help me find my own happiness. My life was stagnant. I was twenty-five and living alone with two cats. I had been mostly single for six years and was working as an underpaid reporter for a local newspaper.

I wondered if I was miserable because I was single. I had watched all three of my sisters and many friends from high school get married, have children, and buy their first homes. I wanted to find a man to marry, so I could "start" my life, too.

I had created a bitter, lonely world for myself — the opposite of the chalkboard quote. One day, I was complaining to my mom about all the things wrong in my life. She was wiping down the kitchen counters when she stopped and looked at me.

"What if you only had today what you thanked God for yesterday?" she asked.

I blinked back the tears her simple question immediately caused. I couldn't reply. I realized that even though I wasn't happy with some aspects of my life, there were many things I wouldn't want to give up. I hadn't taken the time to be grateful for them.

In John Eldredge's book, *Walking with God*, he wrote about keeping a prayer journal as a way to talk with God and organize his prayers. I decided this would be a good way to organize what I was grateful for, so I bought an eighty-nine cent journal on the way home that day.

I began each day by writing down five things I was grateful for in my life. It started out as simple things: my morning cup of coffee, sleeping in on the weekends, and having holidays off from work. After a couple of weeks it became more specific: the first signs of autumn, homegrown pattypan squash, and hearing the birds sing in the morning.

After a month I started being grateful for everything, including: the people in my life, playing games after dinner with my grandparents, my coworker Karen giving me a souvenir from her vacation, and my teenage niece Madison going to a movie with me on a school night. If I ever struggled with something to be grateful for, I would ask myself my mom's question.

> *I can't wait to teach my students the power of gratitude through the same exercise I still use on myself.*

I started feeling joy again, despite my life situation still being the same. Small things I didn't normally notice caught my attention. The air was light, the breeze was refreshing, and my coworkers' jokes were funny.

Feeling joy caused me to pursue my passions again. I started reading and writing for pleasure as opposed to writing for the newspaper. I joined a writers' group and met once a month with other writers and published authors to exchange ideas, receive tips, read each other's work, and offer advice on techniques and style.

I started walking every night after dinner instead of watching TV, and I also joined a Zumba class. I lost weight and now I'm becoming more confident about my physical appearance.

I experienced the most change when I got involved with a fundraising and community involvement program. I would never have done this before. I named the program Smart Cents, after my last name, and used it to raise money for local ministries and to volunteer for community projects. My first fundraiser was for a nonprofit café that fed people who could not afford a meal. My goal was to raise $1,000 in one month, which a few naysayers called too ambitious. In one month, I raised $2,525. Delivering the money to the café and having photos taken of them holding their big check was the most rewarding day of my life. I finally believed I had real purpose and was not put on earth to serve only myself.

My long time friend Aarika called me after reading an article about Smart Cents. "You're such an inspiration. The world needs more Haylie Smarts." Her words touched me deeply. I finally believed I had started my adult life.

With my newfound purpose, I decided to become a teacher in Oklahoma. Teaching had been my first major in college, but I had given it up when I couldn't pass college algebra. I heard about an alternative pathway to certification and worked through the process to become an English teacher.

I can't wait to teach my students the power of gratitude through the same exercise I still use on myself. I want to inspire my students the way I was inspired.

It's amazing how much my life has changed since I started being grateful for all the things I never want to live without. It didn't take a husband, a new house, or a new job to start my life. It took an eighty-nine cent notebook and the question, "What if you only had today what you thanked God for yesterday?"

~Haylie Smart

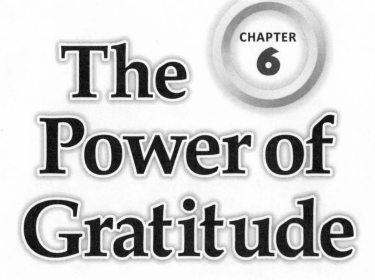

The Power of Gratitude

Grateful for Life

Be glad of life because it gives you the chance to love and to work and to play and to look up at the stars.
~Henry Van Dyke

52

Two Incredible Gifts

*There are only two ways to live your life. One
is as though nothing is a miracle. The other is
as though everything is a miracle.*
~Albert Einstein

Normally, the first question one asks after navigating through the hazy veil of anesthesia back to the bright lights of consciousness is "Am I okay?" That is, unless your twenty-three-year-old son has undergone surgery simultaneously because he is your living kidney donor. The only words that would soothe my soul were the ones my surgeon knew I had to hear before any others: "Your son is fine, he's doing well in recovery, and things could not have gone better. You will see him soon."

This had started when I was thirty-eight and suffered shortness of breath, fatigue, and a low-grade fever, which lasted a few days. I was certain it was just a bug running its course, but when my husband witnessed me having trouble wrangling the overflowing laundry basket up the steps he insisted I see my primary care physician.

The doctor ran some routine blood tests and then called me a few days later to discuss the results in person. I viewed it as yet another annoying appointment to muck up my busy schedule, but since my symptoms had worsened, I went. I was shocked when he said, "I want you to go see a nephrologist. Your kidney function is low." I had no clue what a nephrologist was. I had three young children, a five-bedroom house, several pets, and a busy husband, so if medical care didn't involve the veterinarian or the pediatrician, it wasn't in my universe.

"Okay, I'll make an appointment soon," I reluctantly promised.

"No, you don't understand," said the doctor. "You need to go now. I've made the arrangements. The doctor knows you're coming; he's waiting for you."

The nephrologist got straight to the point. "Your kidneys are only functioning at three percent. You need to start dialysis immediately — tomorrow, as a matter of fact. You will need to fill out these papers and be here at 9 a.m. for your first treatment."

> *No longer am I that impatient, busy woman who fails to appreciate the little things.*

"That's impossible, doctor. I can't do that. I have three…"

And that's where he cut me off mid-sentence: "You don't understand. You are going to need dialysis three times a week. It takes about four hours per session. It cleans your blood so you can live. Without it, you'll die."

In that moment, my life changed forever. People say that all the time — "your life can change in the blink of an eye" — but it meant nothing to me until that very second.

Once my head stopped reeling, I listened. I learned. I cried.

Then I cried some more.

After five long years on dialysis, in May of 1998, the beeper I wore 24/7 started buzzing. A kidney had become available for me.

My transplant was successful and I was granted a new life. It was a bittersweet time. There I was in my hospital room, celebrating my restored health with my incredibly supportive children, husband and family. Yet somewhere out there was a family planning a funeral for their dad, husband, brother, son and friend. He was a music teacher in the public school system who had been killed in a car accident.

Although I treated my new kidney as the incredible and generous gift it was, a mysterious illness took my kidney away from me in 2006. I spent two long months in the hospital trying to save it but nothing worked and I was placed back on dialysis to wait for another kidney.

My youngest son, then twenty-three, insisted on donating one of his kidneys to me. On May 14, 2007, he and I were taken into the operating room that would change both our lives.

Today, we are both healthy and my son's kidney is doing well in its new home inside me.

I am eternally grateful for the sacrifices made by these two incredible men — the schoolteacher who gave me my first kidney transplant, and my son who gave me my second. In fact, I'm grateful for everything in my life. No longer am I that impatient, busy woman who fails to appreciate the little things: the melodious song of a robin, the contagious laughter of a child or the whimsical sound of wind chimes dancing in the breeze before a summer rain.

The word "grateful" hardly seems adequate to describe what my heart holds now. I thank both my donors each day: one sadly gone, and the other here for me to love and cherish for the rest of my happy, healthy and ever so thankful days.

~Mary McLaurine

53

Smiled at the Rising Sun

You never know how strong you are, until
being strong is your only choice.
~Bob Marley

My husband wheeled me to our son's incubator and I peered through the plastic walls at the smallest baby I had ever seen. Our son, who did not have a name yet, weighed barely more than a pound. Tubes and wires overwhelmed his tiny twig-like limbs. I could not see his face; all I saw was the blood pumping through his transparent skin.

An alarm shrilled and I jumped. My son's nurse ran to him and adjusted the ventilator. After he stabilized, the nurse told us we could touch our son for the first time since he was born. I imagined rocking and patting my son, comforting him with my touch and my voice.

When I reached out to touch him, the nurse grabbed my hand. "Stop!" she cautioned. "His skin is very fragile. Touch him gently with one finger. Don't rub; don't move quickly. No patting!" The barrage of restrictions for touching my only child overwhelmed me and I began to cry. I had never imagined that I would be afraid to touch my baby for fear of ripping his skin.

The magnitude of what our little family was facing was sinking in. In the midst of all that, phrases from one of my favorite Bob Marley songs, "Three Little Birds," kept popping into my head. Yes, I would "rise in the morning" but I wasn't sure I would be able to "smile at the rising sun." And even though he sung, "Don't worry (don't worry) 'bout a thing," we *were* worried. And we certainly didn't believe that "every little thing is gonna be all right!"

Later that day, the neonatologist came to check on our baby. His hands were gentle and confident as he examined our son. Even though I could tell he knew what he was doing, I bombarded him with questions.

The doctor finished his examination and stepped aside to show us our son's tiny feet. I burst into tears. I had been so worried about all the tubes and machines and statistics that I had forgotten to look at my son's feet.

The doctor took my hand and gently guided it into the incubator. He placed my hand on my son's foot and looked at me with kindness and patience. "Your son has ten tiny toes on each perfectly formed foot. His kick is strong. He is fighting. Your Prayer Point for right now is that these toes stay nice and pink."

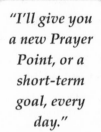

"I'll give you a new Prayer Point, or a short-term goal, every day."

When I first heard the words "Prayer Point," I was a little taken aback. I didn't think doctors were allowed to talk about praying in the hospital. My husband and I weren't religious people, so we weren't sure how to interpret the doctor's comment. We asked him what he meant.

"I know how overwhelming this is right now," the doctor began. "The Prayer Points will allow you to focus your thoughts and worries. I'll give you a new Prayer Point, or a short-term goal, every day. This way, you can focus on that instead of being consumed by all the what-ifs."

At that moment I realized that even if every little thing was not all right, there were still a lot of other things that would be.

Every day, we eagerly looked forward to the doctor's Prayer Point. Some days, it was celebratory: "Today, the baby will open his eyes for the first time." Other days, the Prayer Point was terrifying: "Today, the baby will not need heart surgery."

Prayer Points helped us keep our focus on the positive: a successful feeding, weaning off oxygen, weight gain, and eventually, a smile from our baby.

Most importantly, the Prayer Points gave us hope.

On the days I was struggling, I tried to remember these things:

- I can be grateful for what I have and scared for the future at the same time.
- I can hear statistics that paint a not-so-bright future for my baby and still love him.
- I can be thankful when it feels like there's not much to be thankful for.

I learned a lot during my son's ninety-three-day hospital stay. Mostly, I learned that it's possible to find a silver lining in every situation — and in my experience, the harder it is to find that silver lining, the brighter it will shine once it's discovered.

My husband and I leaned on each other and our support system. We gave ourselves grace. We trusted our guardian angels. We did it: we kept our hope.

We "smiled at the rising sun."

~Andrea Mullenmeister

54

Why I Choose Gratitude

Forgiveness does not change the past,
but it does enlarge the future.
~Paul Boese

n endurance cyclist for many years, I was out cycling on a typical late fall day in central New England. It was one of those days that most likely inspired Robert Frost to write. In fact, I was only a few miles from his birthplace when my life took a bit of an unexpected turn.

Strike that. It was more of an unexpected crash.

No one gets up in the morning wondering if the day will wind down with an ambulance ride and a trip across state lines to the nearest trauma center.

But on November 11, 2010, that was to be my fate.

The local authorities estimated that the teenage driver who broadsided me was moving along between thirty and forty miles per hour when we met. The windshield of his car was pushed right into the passenger's seat. Luckily there was no one sitting there.

My injuries were extensive: broken bones, torn tendons, and head-to-toe bruises.

For the next several days, my wife pulled shards of glass from my head.

And the icing on this accident cake? A traumatic brain injury.

A full year after that November day, a medical professional let me know in no uncertain terms that my life would never be the same. In fact, he labeled me "permanently disabled."

It's been six years since that fated day — the most difficult years, the most glorious years, and the most unexpected years of my life. As predicted, my bruises faded from black to yellow to gone. My bones mended, and the visible signs of my accident faded from the public eye.

But living with a traumatic brain injury, well… to say that life has become a challenge would be an understatement of truly epic proportions.

A hale and hearty case of PTSD only added to the mix.

Many things that I used to take for granted, things like knowing the day of the week, what season we are in, or even how to read, have become challenges.

> *To hold any bitterness or resentment would stop me from moving forward with my own life.*

I hold no bitterness toward the young man who careened into me. To hold any bitterness or resentment would stop me from moving forward with my own life. Everyone has "stuff."

If you have a heartbeat, life has thrown you a curveball or two. It's part of our shared human experience. I've seen close friends lose parents. And children. I know many people who battle life-threatening or life-changing chronic illnesses.

And some of us get hit by cars in the prime of our lives.

The biggest question is this: Will I let this experience, no matter how painful, pull me down or lift me up?

I've seen many who choose to be beaten by life's hardships. They wander around, melancholy at what they've lost, telling their tale of woe to anyone who will listen.

Thanks, but no thanks. I choose to be grateful.

Life is indeed for the living. It has taken me many years to come to grips with the fact that life as I knew it is gone. This was not an overnight process. There were peaks and valleys, wonderful days and then months filled with thoughts of suicide.

My life is vastly different than I ever envisioned. Most of my time these days is spent advocating for those affected by traumatic brain injuries. From working with others who share my fate to multiple keynote presentations at medical conferences, the life that I live today simply astounds me.

I have emerged as a new person with a new mission. My experience as a brain injury survivor has made me uniquely qualified to serve others. I speak to many groups, large and small, about what I have learned. My written work about life as a true survivor has been read around the world, including in *Chicken Soup for the Soul: Recovering from Traumatic Brain Injuries*.

On occasion, I think about the young man who forever changed my life. I wonder how my life might have unfolded had I chosen to hold on to anger, to not forgive him.

Had I chosen that path, misery and discontentment would now define my life. This I know as surely as I breathe. I have seen others who have not been able to let go, to forgive, to move on. They live in constant misery.

And the young man who started me on this new, wondrous path of discovery, what ever happened to him?

I must admit that I tracked him down on Facebook a while ago. If his page is any reflection of his life, he is a student at a local college and moving forward with his life. It is my hope that he rarely thinks about that fall day so many years ago.

And the one time that I did meet him in the weeks following my accident? If you guessed that I gave him a hug, you are correct.

~David A. Grant

55

Doing the Math

*Journaling is like whispering to one's self and
listening at the same time.*
~Mina Murray

"I want you to keep a gratitude journal," said my Alcoholics
Anonymous sponsor. She handed me a book decorated
with bright, neon flowers. "I know you like to write, so
this assignment should be easy for you."

I took the journal and flipped through hundreds of lined blank
pages. The emptiness was daunting.

"What's gratitude got to do with not drinking?"

She laughed her raucous, all-consuming laugh. It was one of
the things that had attracted me to her when I'd asked her to be my
sponsor, but on this day I found it extremely annoying.

"Seriously," I continued, "I just want to stop drinking. I don't need
anything else to do."

"Uh-huh." She tilted her head and waited for the rest of my excuses
to spill forth.

I could feel resentment welling up inside me. I sighed. "Look, I've
got enough on my plate as it is. I don't have time for all this other stuff."

"Uh-huh."

I wanted to wipe that grin right off her face, but I'd chosen her
to help me because I felt she'd be good at holding her ground when
I needed it. At times just like this one.

"Fine. Whatever. So what are we talking about here?"

"Good." She beamed. "You're becoming willing to go to any lengths."

I rolled my eyes. "Enough with all the glib AA slogans. Just tell me what I have to do."

"You don't have to do anything at all. But if you want to stay sober, I invite you to write down ten things you're grateful for every night. Then read me the list during your regular check-in the next morning."

"Just ten?"

"That's it. Just ten."

So the next morning I dutifully called and read her my list. Easy. Then we chatted about a few other things related to the twelve-step program, she asked if I'd be attending a meeting that day, and I went about my business.

Day Two I called and read her my list.

"My memory's not all that sharp," she said. "But I think you read me some of those same things on yesterday's list."

"Yeah? So? I'm still grateful for them."

Several seconds passed and I heard her deep sigh. "Let's try this again," she said. "I want you to write ten different things you're grateful for every single day for the whole month."

> *"If you want to stay sober, I invite you to write down ten things you're grateful for every night."*

"A whole month?"

She laughed. "Yes, a whole month. Then at the end of the month, you'll have 300 different things recorded, and you'll be able to see how much you have to be grateful for. You're really good at seeing all the things wrong with your life; I want you to see what's right."

I considered my answer very carefully. She had a good point. She'd caught me whining and complaining and focusing on negativity quite a bit in the past several weeks.

"I'll try."

"Do or do not; there is no try."

"Spons, you're starting to sound like Yoda."

"May the force be with you," she said, and hung up.

Some time during the next month, a funny thing happened. I took note of it, but said nothing as I continued to call her each morning, recite my list and learn more about the Alcoholics Anonymous program.

Each morning she remained quiet and made no comment on the things I'd written. At times I wondered if she were even listening. But on Day Thirty, I got my answer.

"So how does it feel to have 332 things on your Gratitude List?"

"You noticed."

"Of course I noticed! I'm your sponsor! Every morning I made tally marks as you read me your list. About two weeks ago, you started reading me somewhere between twelve and fifteen things every day."

"Has that ever happened with other sponsees of yours?" I asked.

"It only happens with the ones who stay sober," she replied.

That conversation took place almost two decades ago. I continue to keep a gratitude journal, although I don't call it in to my sponsor anymore, and the restriction "not to repeat" has been lifted.

I am living sober, and that is the first thing on my gratitude list, every single day.

~Sylvia A.

56

An Amazing Gift

He who has a why to live can bear almost any how.
~Friedrich Nietzsche

I t was one of those glorious late summer days when the sun is bright and the colors intense. But I was filled with dread as I pulled my car into the parking garage of the hospital the Tuesday after Labor Day. I was on my way to the oncology department to learn the results of my biopsy. It took all the energy I had to park the car and walk in the door of the hospital.

Within a few minutes I was lying on an examining table. My stomach twisted into a knot as I waited for the verdict from the doctor.

He turned to me and said, "The biopsy showed that you have melanoma, which is the most serious type of skin cancer. There is a seventy-five percent chance it will come back. If it reoccurs around your scar then we can remove it. If it spreads somewhere else… well, there's nothing we can do."

I lay there speechless.

My oncologist continued "Now there's an experimental drug which has been shown to increase the survival rate for people like you by fifteen percent. If you are interested, you can try it. If not, then you can just see what happens."

"Are there any side effects?"

"Well, yes and no. Some people have no side effects at all. But for others, they can be quite severe."

"Well I guess I should try it. If it doesn't go well, then I can stop it."

"Your choice."

"I'll do it."

"Okay. And remember, you must fight this with all you have. If you give up, you'll be defeated before you begin. Don't sell the family farm."

Those words echoed in my mind. I wasn't going to give up no matter what.

As I walked back out into the brilliant sunshine I was numb. I didn't want to talk to anyone. I had to be alone to think so I just drove and drove. Later that day I told my wife and we sat together in shock, silent — there wasn't much to say. We then talked to my two daughters, who were eleven and eight, but they didn't comprehend the significance of the diagnosis or the long-term implications of it all.

> *Overcoming melanoma is a gift I don't deserve and could never have bought.*

Two weeks into taking the anti-cancer drugs the side effects began. At first it was nausea and abdominal pain. Then I lost my appetite and my weight began to drop two or three pounds a week. The headaches were debilitating and my memory began to come and go on me. My deteriorating health caused me to miss more and more days of work.

One night early in December I couldn't sleep because of the pain. I could only toss and turn in bed and I heard our grandfather clock strike every hour. Finally around four in the morning I got up to walk around to see if that would help.

I went into the bedroom of my older daughter Michelle. The light from the hallway traced a golden path across her face as she lay there sleeping. Her long blond hair fell across her pillow and her favorite dolls sat on the floor next to her bed. I thought about how much I loved her and the possibility that very soon I might not be around. I might not see her grow up. I felt a wave of sadness sweep over me. I knew I had to pray but I wasn't going to try bargaining with God. My prayer was simple: "Oh God, please let me see my daughter graduate from elementary school."

I stood there for a few minutes, realizing this might be the last Christmas I would spend with her. That reality hit hard and I could feel tears streaking down my cheeks. When I looked down at my hands I saw they were trembling.

I then walked into the bedroom of my other daughter, Kristen, and prayed the same way. She was so young and peaceful as she lay there with the blankets pulled up around her chin and her favorite teddy bear beside her. As I thought about the end of my life and having to say goodbye to her for good I felt like two giant stones were crushing my heart. My head felt light and I barely had the strength to stand.

I turned to the door and somehow found the strength to walk back to our bedroom. But as I lay in bed I couldn't sleep. I kept thinking how close I could be to the end of my life and how painful it would be to leave my family behind.

A week later my health had seriously deteriorated and finally I put in a call to the doctor.

"I'm feeling really sick from this drug. I can barely get out of bed in the morning, but I don't want to go off it."

"What is your quality of life?" The doctor's question was one I had never considered.

"I have no quality of life," was all I could say.

"Then go off the drug altogether."

"Just like that?"

"Yes, just like that. The benefits you might get are not worth the cost for you. The side effects will not get any better."

"Um, okay. I guess so."

"Call me if you have any more questions."

"Okay, bye." I sat for a few minutes with the phone in my hand listening to the dial tone.

I then had to face the task of dumping the only drug that might help me survive. I took the bottle of pills and looked at it for two or three minutes. Then I opened the bottle and emptied every pill into the garbage. My future was out of my hands.

Within three months, however, I had amazingly recovered from the effects of the medication and a year and a half later I was free of the melanoma. It took time but I was able to see both my daughters graduate from high school and university. And then came the dream that all fathers have for their daughters. I was able to walk each one down the aisle when she got married.

Every day I think about the second chance at life I've been given. I am thankful for surviving cancer and seeing my daughters grow up to become the accomplished women they are. Overcoming melanoma is a gift I don't deserve and could never have bought. And it has become more precious every day.

~Rob Harshman

57

Walking Toward My Dreams

Challenges are what make life interesting. Overcoming them is what makes life meaningful.
~Joshua J. Marine

I'd been waiting to hear these words for years: "Annie, you're a candidate for surgery." Finally, I could get rid of the limp that had been with me since I took my first steps. I was prepared to endure anything to make walking better a reality. My parents, who were in the room with me at the time I received the news, knew that I would go along with whatever operation the doctor recommended. The decision was quickly made to pursue my dream surgery. The doctor would cut and release a few tendons to make my muscles less tight and my gait smoother. I was thrilled!

Cerebral palsy has always been a part of me, both physically and as a part of my soul. I am the person I am today because of my condition. As a result of an injury after my premature birth, the part of my brain that sends messages to control certain muscles in my body isn't wired perfectly. As a result, the left side of my body is weaker than my right. For nineteen years, I had been in and out of doctors' offices and physical therapy sessions, had fallen and scraped my knees countless times, and been fitted for more orthotics than I could count.

But when looking at the entire spectrum of cerebral palsy, I was blessed to be on the very mild end. I was fully functional, with the exception that I was never going to become a track star or prima ballerina. Not because I wasn't determined, but because my body wasn't designed for super speed or graceful leaps. My balance and flexibility were at a minimum, and the muscles in my left lower body were very tight.

In the grand scheme of life, I found ways to accept these things and move on. Sure, I had met my fair share of people who tried to knock me down and say that I wasn't good enough. "Annie's not fast enough" so we won't pick her to be on our team in gym class. "Annie can't balance on her left leg or point her feet" so she won't be able to stay in the dance class. Comments like these were hurtful, but I did my best to not let them break my spirit. It was much easier to enjoy life by focusing on what I could do, and do those things as well as possible.

> *Focusing on the end goal really helped me put the temporary discomfort in perspective.*

The day of my operation arrived in May 2014. I was incredibly blessed to have made it without any surgical interventions until then. Many people with cerebral palsy have at least one corrective surgery by the time they complete a growth spurt in their preteen years; however, I was doing so well that my doctors never saw a reason to intervene. So I was grateful that I had avoided surgery so far, but equally grateful that I could have this elective surgery and make my dream of walking better come true.

As I was being wheeled into the operating room I was more excited than worried! As I felt myself go under on the operating table there was a sense of comfort in knowing that one chapter of my life was closing, and when I opened my eyes a few hours later, another would begin.

The beginning of that next chapter was most certainly a rough one. My first day in recovery was a bit hazy and plenty uncomfortable. But I remember telling myself, "It's not so bad, you can get through this!" Focusing on the end goal really helped me put the temporary discomfort in perspective.

When I woke the next day, a physical therapist was standing near my bedside. It was time to attempt walking! I was groggy and I slowly stood up. My legs suddenly felt extremely sore and unfamiliar. I couldn't imagine how I was going to make it to the door, much less the end of the bed. I shakily took two tiny steps forward, unable to fully extend my legs. Pain shot up through my calves and hamstrings. Wincing, I plopped back down. I wasn't expecting my trek to end so quickly and was somewhat frightened by how my muscles felt different than they had for the previous nineteen years of my life. "Can I please go back to sleep?" I asked.

"We'll try again tomorrow" she replied. "Take another day to rest." Relieved to be back in bed, I said a quick prayer that I'd be able to walk well the next morning, received another push of medication in my IV, and slept for most of the day.

Something must have magically occurred overnight because the next morning I felt like I could conquer the world. When the therapist gave me the okay to walk, I was able to make it across the room, out the door, and across the main floor! As I turned around I heard the nurses behind me laugh, saying, "Whoa, she's on the move!" My legs told me I was walking, but my heart felt like I was flying. It was as if I was literally leaving all of my previous struggles behind me. In that moment, I knew this was the beginning of me living my dream. It was the most beautiful feeling in the world.

Today, I continue to walk better than I ever have before. But limp or no limp, I am forever grateful to live life with cerebral palsy, because it has taught me more about gratitude, courage, and compassion than having two "equal" legs ever could.

Since my surgery, I have become the best version of the person I was always meant to be. And as I venture forward, I know that the strength and happiness that I've gained from living my best life possible makes the process of putting one foot in front of the other infinitely more fulfilling.

~Annie Nason

58

Whatever Comes

We acquire the strength we have overcome.
~Ralph Waldo Emerson

W e weren't far out when a wave swept in and carried us to deep water. Then the riptide took us further out. My husband is nine inches taller than I, but he couldn't touch bottom either, nor could he make headway against the surf.

I'd never feared drowning before, because I knew I could breaststroke for a good fifteen minutes. But after a thirty-minute struggle, I told my husband I couldn't stay afloat. He began screaming for someone, waving his arms, crossing them as he frantically sought help. It was 6 p.m. and no one was left on the beach.

I imagined headlines in the local paper noting our deaths: "Caught in a Riptide." I wondered if they'd say whether our bodies had been recovered. I didn't want our kids to wonder if we had been ripped apart by sharks. I wondered if they knew where our important papers were stored so they wouldn't have trouble settling our estates. Then, I sent up a prayer that they would live happy lives despite the way they lost their parents.

The water hit my eyes again. "Hold onto me!" I yelled as I felt myself grabbed by the sea. My husband turned and reached back. With the tips of his fingers, he took hold of the skirt on my bathing suit. "Don't let go!" I whispered, probably inaudible to him as the crash of the surf drowned out our words. The howling wind and the pounding of the swells on the beach were all I heard. My body bobbed like a rag doll. The skirt on my suit stretched taut as the ocean played tug of war with my husband.

"My toe touched!" he said. I felt a glimmer of hope. My husband pushed on, and I floated nearer to him. We proceeded like that until he had my hand; we waited for each wave to move us in a little and then he tried to hold the ground gained. Finally, he yanked me, and we collapsed at the end of the water, below a high ridge of sand. When he let go of my fingers, I feared I'd wash back into the ocean. So with all my might I crawled up the hollowed out embankment. I flopped lifeless on the sloped edge. The tide wouldn't snatch me back.

Then I felt something in my head burst. It felt like a firecracker exploded on the right side of my skull. I turned back toward my husband, who still hadn't made it up the embankment, and saw his face buried in the sand. I felt grains of sand in my nose and felt my bathing suit edge up high on my legs, but I was too weak to adjust anything. I just lay there.

> *As I mused on this "life after life," I accepted the idea of being confined to a wheelchair.*

I don't know how long my husband and I slept. I seemed to go in and out of dreams. Now our kids would have bodies to bury, and they wouldn't wake in the middle of the night to terrors wondering where their folks' parts washed up. I felt gratitude. I heard a distant dune buggy and raised my chin slightly to see a lifeguard fly by up top, close to the dunes and houses, not near us. Could folks even spot us here lying below the cliff of sand, like debris swept in by the tide?

At some point, I asked my husband if he could get up. "Let me lie. My heart is racing," he murmured. Then, we fell back unconscious.

Later that evening, when the sun sank, we climbed up the slope and retrieved our flip-flops and the towels we'd left on the beach a long time before. As we mounted the steps leading to the boardwalk, we ran into a couple with cocktails in hand who asked us if we were all right. I told them we nearly drowned but my husband saved me. The man said a surfer had drowned that very day and another man the week before. "Riptides are frequent on this beach," he told us.

In the ensuing days, my headache didn't get better, and my balance worsened. I started having trouble typing on the computer. I seemed to be stuck in a perpetual fog.

We went to the hospital and a CAT scan showed that a pool of blood had collected on one of my brain's lobes, caused by burst capillaries. The capillaries broke because of an adrenaline surge that erupted when I clawed my way up the bank.

An MRI was scheduled for two days later, but before that test happened, I had a seizure in which I dropped to the floor. My left side went numb, and my left hand curled unnaturally over my chest. En route to the hospital, I accepted my fate — that I'd be paralyzed forever. As I mused on this "life after life," I accepted the idea of being confined to a wheelchair. I surmised I could become a Wal-Mart greeter in this next stage of my mortal journey. I pictured myself at the entrance to a mammoth store waving at folks with my right hand, and in my mind's eye, I was smiling as I said hello to shoppers.

As it turned out, my paralysis was temporary. The blood absorbed within months, and I was back to my old self.

What I learned en route to the emergency room was that I would survive whatever setback I encountered. I'd survived drowning; I'd survive this stroke. I'd make the best of any situation that came my way.

Now when some unforeseen event happens that might seem like a major upheaval to another woman, I think how lucky I am — lucky to be alive. It might sound corny or sappy, but once you survive something that could have ended your life, you find an inner strength and a knowledge that you will go on.

~Erika Hoffman

My First Date
with Nelson

*I learned that courage was not the absence of fear, but
the triumph over it. The brave man is not he who does
not feel afraid, but he who conquers that fear.*
~Nelson Mandela

N elson stared at me with his well-lit face as if to say,
"It's you and me, baby!" It was our first night together,
the first of many nights we would be attached to each
other for ten hours. I examined his square body with
the nervous anticipation of a newlywed. I had practiced for weeks
and knew if tonight went smoothly this would be the start of a steady
relationship.

I confidently rolled the mid-sized cart where Nelson was perched
closer to my bed. I reached around him and briskly pushed his "on/
off" switch. I relaxed when he turned on readily and I watched as he
glowed and hummed his introduction. I scampered into the bathroom,
put on my facemask, and washed my hands eagerly with antibacterial
soap. I neatly assembled my supplies next to Nelson and waited as he
rhythmically groaned and whirred, his face giving instructions each
step of the way until it was time to hook my surgically implanted
abdominal catheter to the line coming out of him. I had practiced this
countless times with my nurse. I pushed down my pajama pants to
expose my tummy and carefully attached myself to Nelson and waited

wide-eyed for my first fill of dialysate fluid. My tingling belly bulged as the 2,000 milliliters filled my abdomen. I tensed my standing legs, waiting for pain, but none came.

Nelson is my peritoneal dialysis cycler; he keeps me alive each day by cleaning the toxins out of my body because my kidneys up and quit. Diagnosed with end-stage renal disease six months prior, I had been doing in-center hemodialysis. "Dialysis" was already part of my vocabulary because my father was on it prior to his death, but in relation to me it was daunting. I was only forty. But my inner strength quickly surfaced after diagnosis and I knew I had to "get busy living or get busy dying." When I heard about peritoneal dialysis, dialysis that I could do at home while asleep, I knew it was for me. It would give me more freedom in my schedule, diet and life overall.

> *I knew I had to "get busy living or get busy dying."*

Apprehensive, I gingerly sat on the bed and watched TV while Nelson began his work, which consisted of five two-hour cycles of cleaning the toxins out of my body. Though the TV was on, I stared earnestly at Nelson's expressionless face and studied his random soft noises, one of which sounded like the faint bellow of a distant foghorn. I had yet to find out what all the noises meant, but my nurse and other experienced PD patients told me I would quickly attune to Nelson's sounds. After what seemed like an eternity but was only a few minutes, I stopped watching Nelson's neon countdown and let my muscles relax as I enjoyed my favorite sitcom.

I jumped when I heard a loud steady "beeeep" as Nelson announced, "Patient line blocked." I grabbed my trusty user's guide and anxiously flipped to the troubleshooting pages while concurrently hitting "stop" to silence the aggravating alarm. I found the error code on page three and was instructed to make sure the line was properly connected, with no kinks. I hit "OK" and after a few R2-D2 noises Nelson went back to his countdown. I had survived my first alarm — only forty-two other error codes to look forward to.

I tried various positions in the bed, awkwardly contorting my protruding belly until comfortable, finally understanding why women use pregnancy pillows. I lay stiffly, afraid to sleep but eventually lulled into slumber. I awoke six hours later and drowsily rolled over to Nelson, who announced the cycle was finished and he'd see me that night. Success! I had made it through my first home dialysis session. Bleary-eyed, I unhooked myself from Nelson and affectionately turned him off. "Nelson" I uttered. I named him "Nelson" because, like Nelson Mandela, he was going to work tirelessly for my freedom. No more driving to the center three days a week and spending four hours each time — a more normal schedule, a more normal life, was within reach. I was enthusiastic about all the freedom I could once again have with Nelson as my partner.

After a short disconnection ritual I walked into the kitchen to make coffee and took note of how I felt. "Not too shabby," I thought to myself. None of the dizziness or drowsiness I often felt after hemo sessions. There was a little discomfort where my catheter met my body, but that was nothing in the grand scheme of things.

That was 622 treatments ago and Nelson remains my Taupe Knight — our relationship is easy and we're closer than ever. As in all unions, there've been bumps in the road — a few 3 a.m. customer service calls and nights of repeated alarms, but I've grown to understand Nelson's messages and intonation, and I've become much more comfortable sleeping in his company. Granted, he forces me to be home by my nightly curfew so we don't miss any of our time together, but it's a small price to pay. Relationships are all about compromise, right? Nelson has allowed me to lead a healthy and productive life leading up to transplant.

Today I walked into my sunny apartment post-hike, kicked off my dusty sneakers, and headed into my bedroom to take a shower. There was Nelson, waiting patiently next to my queen-sized sanctuary, as he always is. I smiled broadly, patted Nelson warmly, and mused to him, "You complete me." Then I hopped in the shower — because I had a lot more to accomplish.

~Sasha Couch

My Open Heart

It is only with the heart that one can see rightly;
what is essential is invisible to the eye.
~Antoine de Saint-Exupéry, The Little Prince

bout two years ago, I was chatting with a plastic surgeon in San Francisco when she noticed this little line peeking out of my sweater. "What is that?" she asked me.

"Oh that's my scar," I replied, lifting up my top to reveal what looks like a second belly button and my actual belly button. "It goes all the way down."

"You know," she said to me, looking closely at the line, "I could easily do a little procedure so you don't have to see it anymore."

"Absolutely not," I tell her, "My scar is my favorite thing about me."

When I was a baby, I had a very dramatic open-heart surgery that I was not supposed to survive. I weighed only six pounds at six months. None of the doctors thought I was going to make it. Growing up, the Winnie the Pooh and Babar stories were intermingled with the stories about how my mother had to feed me with an eyedropper and track the ounces in a little notebook. I wasn't allowed to crawl since the doctors had to saw my ribs to get to my heart and they didn't want the risk of me falling on my chest while the ribs were healing. My favorite part of the story was that they put a little patch on my baby heart to protect it while the muscle grew over it.

When you are born with something that is supposed to kill you, and you survive, there is a great amount of pressure to lead a fulfilling life. You start to wonder why you were kept on this planet — what is your purpose? I know we all face these questions on a daily basis, but for anyone who has lived through something this drastic, it becomes especially important to find the meaning. Every morning when I get dressed and look in the mirror, I see my huge battle scar and, in a way, I relive the battle.

> *That's the thing about surviving — once you've done it, nothing really scares you.*

Every birthday, I reflect on whether I am doing justice to my second chance. It doesn't help that my amazing mother always writes something in my birthday card to remind me: "The child who fought so hard to be here" or "The one who has been proving them wrong since day one." I know she re-lives it too on each of my birthdays.

As I get older, like most girls in their twenties, I re-evaluate my life. I wonder if I am on the right path. I think that my gratitude for being alive translates into an extra self-imposed pressure to find my life's purpose.

Recently, in the quest to find my life's mission, I had a thought: maybe my mission in life is to help patch the hole in the world's heart. I know it sounds corny, but to me this means being kind to strangers, forgiving mistakes, because we all make them, and most importantly, giving a second chance to people who were told they would never get one.

That's the thing about surviving — once you've done it, nothing really scares you. While others may misinterpret kindness for weakness, I believe the doctors did something more then just fix my heart — they opened my heart to the idea that despite the front many put up, as Anne Frank said, "In spite of everything I still believe that people are really good at heart."

Most people don't have a scar on their stomachs to remind them, but many people have had to, in a figurative sense, patch up their own hearts, and survive whatever created the hole. I've learned that the minute you open your heart that hole will close.

~Davina Adjani

61

A Gift of Time

If you don't ask, you don't get!
~Stevie Wonder

January 20, 1965

Dr. Michael DeBakey
Methodist Hospital
Houston, Texas

Dear Dr. DeBakey,

I am a widow of 52. My husband died three years ago after an illness of almost ten years, which kept him at home and under the care of many doctors. I have supported my family for the last 12 years and with additional odd jobs on the weekends. With the aid of scholarships given to my two fine sons, 18 and 21, who have always worked during high school and college and summers, they have been attending the University of Connecticut, one in pre-med and one in pre-law — high aspirations out of very difficult youth.

Life is very dear to me, at least until my sons have completed their education and can stand on their own feet in this world, particularly since they have lived the greater part of their lives in the dark shadow of their father's illness.

There may be other surgeons who can perform the operation I have been told I must have to survive (removal of a blockage in my main aorta) but to my mind there would be no other who could give me the gift of life. I *ask you to do this operation although logic tells me that there may be others who may be almost as competent as you, and I have no right to expect that you will grant my request.*

The trip to Houston can be managed, and hopefully, if your fee can be within the realm of possibility for me, my prayers would be answered. You are, I am certain, besieged with the same request from people all over the world but I shall continue to hope that you will find it possible to help me.

Sincerely,

Mrs. Edith Sherman

I knew Mom was sick but only my nine-year-older sister knew how serious it was. My brother and I were away at college and they thought it wise not to share it with us until there was a plan. Mom had been diagnosed with a very dangerous aorta-blocking aneurism. Her internist explained there was only one doctor who had successfully performed the needed procedure and his most recent patient had been the Duke of Windsor. Not a lot of hope for Edith Sherman. But this was my mother, after all. She demanded more time to be there for us and for herself after decades of a really difficult marriage.

She went to the library and researched her heart out. There was no Google back then. Research of this nature was tedious, but she read about Houston's suddenly famous Dr. Michael DeBakey and his groundbreaking "bypass" surgery. The Duke had called Dr. DeBakey who was, at the time, in the White House conferring with President Lyndon Johnson about the findings of the President's Committee on Heart Disease, which Dr. Debakey chaired.

So my mother wrote that letter.

Six days later, she received a reply.

Dear Mrs. Sherman,

Thank you for your letter of January 20, 1965.
I shall be very happy to take care of you, particularly in light of what

you have accomplished under obviously adverse conditions to make it possible for your children to obtain a good education.

The least I can do will be to offer my professional services at no charge to you. I am sure my colleagues here would also be pleased to offer their professional services to one who is of such admirable character.

With all good wishes, I am
Sincerely yours,
M. E. DeBakey, M.D.

My mother and sister went to Houston. The life-saving Dr. DeBakey could not have been kinder. There were lots of painful, "iffy" days in ICU but she fought hard and recovered. Aortic plaque buildup would lead to four more bypass operations by the good Dr. DeBakey over thirty years. Dr. DeBakey always greeted her like family and bragged that she was his oldest living patient.

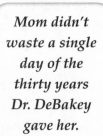

Mom didn't waste a single day of the thirty years Dr. DeBakey gave her.

My mother lived for thirty more years and during that time she gave back with gusto. She became very active in the community and she soon was elected to the legislative body of Stamford, the Board of Representatives. The city of Stamford was undergoing great change in the downtown area. My mother was appointed to the Urban Renewal Commission and soon she became Chairman of that Commission. In ten years as Chair, she moved mountains, mayors, governors, congressmen and senators in her tireless efforts to rebuild this city of 110,000. My words cannot do justice to the praise that covered the front page and editorial pages of the local papers when she died at eighty-two.

Front-page headline: *Edith Sherman, driving force behind downtown revitalization, dead at 82.*

Another front-page headline: *Edith Sherman really had the drive to make the city better.*

Editorial: *Stamford yesterday bid a final farewell to a woman whose leadership and vision have left an indelible imprint on this city.*

My mother sat on every charity board within ten miles. Her walls were covered with "Citizen of the Year" awards and other such honors.

She spoke her mind. She was famous for her candor and her chutzpah. The local media editor said it best:

Edith Sherman and the Politics of the Possible

Here is the thing to remember about Edith Sherman. She liked politics not in spite of the fact that it was complicated and contentious, but because of that fact.

Mom didn't waste a single day of the thirty years Dr. DeBakey gave her. She traveled the world in her own style. While most women her age would be content to cruise to the Caribbean, my mother was ballooning over the Serengeti. All she wanted for her seventieth birthday was to have the entire family share a craps table at Bally's in Atlantic City. We did it and, as if scripted by Frank Capra, the whole family won a boatload of money on my mom's roll of the dice.

Mom and a close friend of hers, Lillian, decided to go to India. My mother wound up sitting next to a very pleasant woman who happened to be India's Minister of something. More amazing, the woman was the college roommate of Prime Minister Indira Gandhi. By the time the plane touched down in India, my mother and the Minister — now an expert in all things urban renewal — were best friends. Her new friend arranged lunch with the Prime Minister. The photo of Mom, her friend and Indira Gandhi was hung prominently on her "good job" certificates wall. She went back to India a couple of years later and hooked up again with Prime Minister Gandhi. Not long after that, the legendary leader was assassinated.

My mother made the best possible use of her thirty extra years until she passed away at eighty-two. Dr. DeBakey, who died at ninety-nine, had an impact on my family that cannot be measured. And without knowing it, he had a huge impact on our small city as well.

A couple of years after my mother died, they named the street that leads into the mall "Edith Sherman Drive." She had basically built that mall and the mayor wanted to acknowledge her great contributions to the revitalization of the downtown area. The local cable news crew was there. "So Mickey," the mayor proudly said, "Do you think your mom would have liked this?"

I paused, wanting to say something appropriate. "Y'know Mayor, it's really nice. But you knew my mom pretty well. I think she would have preferred I-95 or a major bridge."

~Mickey Sherman

The Power of Gratitude

CHAPTER 7

Simple Pleasures

The best things in life are nearest: Breath in your nostrils, light in your eyes, flowers at your feet, duties at your hand, the path of right just before you. Then do not grasp at the stars, but do life's plain, common work as it comes, certain that daily duties and daily bread are the sweetest things in life.
~Robert Louis Stevenson

62

Next Exit: Happiness

Look at everything as though you are seeing it
either for the first time or last time. Then your
time on earth will be filled with glory.
~Betty Smith, A Tree Grows in Brooklyn

My son's obsession with roads was driving me crazy. "I've been interested in Interstate 83 since Mother's Day 2014!" he told me. Really? It had only been a little over a year? It felt a lot longer.

James is thirteen, and over the years his autism has been responsible for perseverations on shapes, numbers, time, music and maps. The interests come on suddenly, last anywhere from a week to a few years, and get pretty intense. Sometimes the fixations are cool, sometimes mind-boggling, and sometimes just plain irritating. Eventually, no matter what the topic, I get to a point where I JUST WANT TO TALK ABOUT SOMETHING ELSE!

But my exasperation flew out the window during a recent drive — an excursion to indulge James's burning desire to glimpse his favorite skyline view of our city from his favorite stretch of his favorite highway. As we sped down the road, James could not contain his gleeful bursts of laughter. I internally shook my head, baffled and yes, slightly annoyed, at the intensity of his pleasure.

"I must be the luckiest boy in the world, because I like so many things!" he exclaimed.

My perspective shifted at sixty miles per hour.

How do I get to where he is?

My son, who needs help understanding so many things, perfectly comprehends what it means to live in the moment and appreciate. Great music, gorgeous sunny days, bike rides (and of course highway drives), family, and HIMSELF. I spend so much time trying to teach my son so many things, but I need to learn this important lesson from him. To see the positive, not the negative. And not just to see it, but to revel in it. And be grateful for it.

> *"I must be the luckiest boy in the world, because I like so many things!"*

Many people say kids with autism see only the concrete. This is a myth my son dispels almost daily. Last year, on my Mother's Day card, he wrote, "I love the spirit of you." I love the spirit of you too, James. Sometimes that gets lost in the clatter of therapists, tutors, protocols, and criticisms that crowd our days. But even though James is, in so many ways, a work in progress, his spirit is a masterpiece.

One recent Saturday afternoon, we were running some errands together. At one point during this ordinary day, James turned to me and said something extraordinary.

"Mom?"

"Hmmm?" I absentmindedly replied, bracing myself for another comment about Interstate 83 or a local road.

"I'm thinking about how I feel about my life."

Astonished, and trying to remain blasé, I asked "Yeah? How do you feel, buddy?"

"Content."

And in that moment, right there in a nondescript parking lot, so did I.

Thank you, buddy, for showing me how to sit back and enjoy the ride.

~Nancy Burrows

The Grocery Store

There is a calmness to a life lived in
gratitude, a quiet joy.
~Ralph H. Blum

Grocery shopping was the chore I hated most. I could always find plenty to complain about on any shopping trip. What did I forget to put on the list? Why did they have to keep moving things around? Who ever thought that self-checkouts were a good idea? And how come these plastic bags last 500 years in a landfill, but won't make it to my car without breaking?

On the worst grocery-shopping day of the entire year, the day before Thanksgiving, I stood with a full cart waiting to check out. I counted eleven carts ahead of mine as I stood in a line that backed down the frozen food aisle. Every line was filled with grumpy shoppers in a big hurry. And I was no exception. My in-laws were coming for Thanksgiving and everything had to be perfect. Every moment I was captive in the store put my schedule in jeopardy. There were pies to make, dressing to assemble, and my cranberry–Jell-O salad, which absolutely had to be made the night before.

As I stood there feeling sorry for myself, the ladies in front of me began talking.

"I feel almost guilty standing here in all this abundance," one said. I don't know who she was talking about, but she went on to say, "You wouldn't believe how poor they are. They labor all week, and the food they can buy with their wages fits in their two hands."

The ladies moved on to other topics but I started thinking. I'd never spent a week's wages on groceries. I only used a fraction of our weekly income even when I planned a feast like Thanksgiving. I bought treats routinely and splurged on luxuries whenever I wanted. Also, I couldn't possibly carry all of the groceries I bought every week. The store gave us shopping carts to push around because we were buying so much. And then there were even employees to bag our groceries and help put them in our cars if we bought more than we could handle alone.

How had I never noticed all this before? The shelves were jammed with food from around the world. Anything we wanted was trucked in or even flown in for us. The store was comfortable, safe and well lit. The food was monitored for freshness and inspected. If I didn't have time to cook, I could buy my whole Thanksgiving dinner pre-made, and there was a bank, a pharmacy and a flower shop in the store, too, just to make life even more convenient.

> *Going to the grocery store is no longer a chore.*

Everywhere I looked — amazing. By the time I got to the register, I was about to burst. How wonderful my life was! The cashier was frazzled, so I told her she was doing a great job and she relaxed a little. I thanked her and the bagger, telling them what a pleasure it was to have their help. I wished them a happy Thanksgiving. People stared at me, and then I heard others doing the same thing. On my way out, I told the store manager how efficient his employees were and how much I appreciated his store. He smiled and stood straighter, thanking me for saying that. He'd probably heard a lot of complaints that day.

In the parking lot, tears of gratitude stung my face in the November cold as I loaded my car. I rode to my comfortable, warm house and cooked a fine dinner that night. Compliments abounded from my family the next day, and I responded that it was my pleasure.

Going to the grocery store is no longer a chore. Ever since that day, I have seen it as a gift that many people in the world don't have. Whenever I enter a store, I'm reminded of all I have to be thankful for in my life. Gratitude — it's contagious. I caught it from a couple of ladies standing in front of me at the grocery store.

~Susan Boltz

64

The Simple Life

*As you simplify your life, the laws of the universe will
be simpler; solitude will not be solitude, poverty will
not be poverty, nor weakness weakness.*
~Henry David Thoreau

I t was 2 a.m. and I had to use the restroom — badly. I gently nudged my sleeping husband. He made a grunting noise so I whispered, "I have to go to the bathroom." There was silence for a second, then a simple, "Okay. Let me get dressed."

He slid on his jeans and moved to the front seat. As I slipped on my jacket and shoes our van's engine roared to life. We began to move and I saw the store lights filtering in through the curtains that separated the back part of the van from the cabin. When he stopped I slid out the side door, and went inside.

He never grumbled when I needed to use the restroom in the middle of the night, no matter how tired he was or how cold it was outside. He would patiently move to the front of the van and drive me right to the door.

We didn't choose the simple life; the simple life chose us.

In early 2013 I was working in Washington, D.C. as a federal analyst and my husband was in pest control. We had a nice apartment and lots of stuff. Then one day in March, while I was recovering from surgery on my ankle, I received a letter from the agency where I worked informing me that they would not be renewing my position. Two weeks later my husband lost his job.

Our savings didn't last long and by mid-May we were homeless. We saw it coming so we outfitted our van with extra storage and a bed. We decided that getting an apartment would be an unwise move since neither of us was having much luck finding another job. "It's only temporary," we kept telling each other — but temporary was much longer than either of us anticipated.

Days before we had to be out of our apartment we put an ad on Craigslist and opened our home for strangers to sift through our belongings and buy what they wanted. There is something strange about having strangers go through your possessions and put prices on your memories. I still wasn't getting around well so I mostly sat on the sofa — until we sold it. We slept on our bed that night and the next day crawled into the van with the few things we kept and drove away.

And there isn't much I'd do differently except maybe do it all sooner!

I've realized that sometimes we have stuff, but sometimes our stuff has us. There was something liberating about not having things all around. For the first time ever I could really think. I stepped outside my comfort zone of work, commuting, lunches, and shopping, and I really started to live.

There were days when we didn't know where our next meal was coming from, but somehow it worked out. We both learned to trust God for our provision, for our very existence. We both felt freer even though things seemed uncertain.

As July approached, the heat was becoming unbearable during the day. We decided to head down to South Carolina where my husband's mother lived. When he told her we were living in our van she cried.

For the next two years we were in and out of the van. My husband found a job and I began doing some freelance writing, but we couldn't get to a point where we could afford to get an apartment. After one late night discussion in the comfort, coziness, and privacy of our van we decided that we really didn't want a house or apartment.

In April 2015 we purchased a travel trailer and haven't looked back. We are the happiest we've ever been. We pay for Internet but we don't have cable — or television at all. We read, do things on our laptops, and we talk. Our marriage has grown stronger.

Many people don't understand, but I have come to realize that it is all about perception. When someone asks me how I survive without cable television I say that it gives me more time to read and write. When they don't see how I can live without an attic, large closets, and 1,000 square feet of living area, I tell them that I don't need all that space because I don't have all that stuff.

Don't get me wrong. At first downsizing was extremely painful. I did it three times in two years. I got rid of a lot of stuff, but that's all it was — stuff. My life is so much simpler now. I get up in the morning and have coffee with my husband. There's no rush to be on a commuter bus at 5 a.m. When he leaves for work I sit down to write. My little dog sits with me and we take breaks during the day so he can go outside. We walk around and I enjoy the world that I am now a part of as opposed to just trying to survive it.

> *I've realized that sometimes we have stuff, but sometimes our stuff has us.*

I cook dinner, go shopping with my mother-in-law (who still grapples with my limited storage space and lack of desire to acquire stuff), and I spend time with my husband.

I had long craved simplifying my life. For so long I had wanted to just get rid of the clutter and live a freer, more relaxed lifestyle, but I was never brave enough to step outside of my comfort zone and make it happen. When the simple life chose us we were afraid at first. Now, we embrace it and wouldn't have it any other way.

The world may see two quirky people who live in a travel trailer and own virtually nothing, but I see a husband and wife who have chosen to simplify and escape the prison of stuff. We wouldn't have things any other way.

~Stephanie A. Mayberry

65

Nigerian Boys' Village

*The willingness to share does not make one
charitable; it makes one free.*
~Robert Brault

The hot African sun beat down on our vans as we bounced over deeply rutted roads on the outskirts of the city of Kagoro, Nigeria. The sky was a hazy blue and I could feel sweat trickling down my back as we drove.

The road was lined with small plots of land, each home made from mud and concrete blocks. Chickens scurried across the road and goats wandered around the farmyards. Young children played tag on the edge of the road while some of the women pounded yams for the evening meal.

We were on our way to a boys' orphanage to hand out clothes, hats and personal items. Eventually, we slowed down and turned into a narrow entranceway framed by tall bushes. The driveway led to a compound of a dozen cement-block buildings, with corrugated steel roofs that sparkled silver in the bright sunlight.

Several groups of boys gathered as we drove in and parked under a large mango tree for shade. They looked at us curiously because visitors like us — Canadians — never came to this boys' village.

The director of the orphanage came over and greeted us warmly with a handshake. He suggested we sit in the shade where it was marginally cooler. He then had all the boys come over to join us. Somewhat reluctantly, they left their dorms and came toward us, not knowing what to expect.

The director started off. "We want to welcome all of you to our boys' village. We are so pleased you have come. Each of these boys is here because he had nowhere else to go. They all have stories and we're going to tell you some of them."

He called one of the boys to come forward. As he put his hand on this boy's shoulder he said, "Joseph is seven years old and he struggled living with his parents." He then had Joseph turn around. As he lifted up the back of Joseph's shirt we all gasped. There were deep cuts all over his back. "His parents thought he was full of demons so they used a knife to cut his back to let the demons out. Clearly this was very dangerous. Arriving here saved his life." Joseph then rejoined the other boys.

> *Many of them had never even owned a tooth-brush before.*

The director motioned for Jakob to come forward. With his hand on Jakob's shoulder the director spoke. "After his father died, he began to get into trouble. Jakob would steal things from the market to help his family. He got caught three times. After the third time one of the men from the market came to his mother. He told her that if he caught him again he would kill him. He was serious. So Jakob's mother searched all over and finally brought him to this place. He is safe here and he feels it's his home." Jakob smiled as he looked at the director and then us.

One after another the boys shared their stories. It was hard to wrap our heads around everything they had been through before getting to the safety of this village.

When the boys had finished talking, we went back to our two vans and unloaded two large cardboard transport boxes, each about six feet long. The boys still had no idea what we were up to. We lined up the boxes so that we would be sure each boy received the exact same items. We started by giving each one a T-shirt, a baseball hat and a tie. After that we handed out toothbrushes, nail clippers, hairbrushes and other personal items. Most of the boys had only the clothes on their backs so we were giving them something very special. Many of them had never even owned a toothbrush before. The boys were excited and immediately put on their new T-shirts and baseball hats.

We had also brought along several soccer balls. The boys posed for photos with these balls before they headed off to play a pickup game.

A couple of the teenagers took me on a tour of the compound. We saw the new pump that went deep enough to bring up clean water for the first time. We walked through the dorms where every boy had his own bed with a net over it to protect against malarial mosquitoes.

They had their own little garden where they grew vegetables and yams. The village also had a few goats that provided milk, and sometimes, meat. Every once in a while a neighbor would give a small donation of food to the boys.

As the sun began to slide down in the afternoon sky and color it orange we knew it was time to leave. We had to get back to where we were staying before dark, when the highways would become dangerous due to bandits.

All the boys came together to say goodbye. Many shook our hands and thanked us.

Then Jakob stepped forward to speak. "Thank you for coming here to our village. Thank you for all your gifts. We are the thankful ones for what you have brought to us."

But Jakob didn't know the larger truth. We were the ones who were thankful for the opportunity to give gifts to these boys. They appreciated everything we gave them. We were the ones who saw the excitement in their eyes as we handed out the T-shirts, hats and towels. And the excited sound of the boys playing soccer with the balls we brought was the greatest reward we could receive.

~Rob Harshman

Uno, Popcorn, and Laughter

*Children will not remember you for the material
things you provided, but for the feeling
that you cherished them.*
~Richard L. Evans

O ur eight-year-old son could barely hold the handful of cards. "I'm hungry," Zack said as he laid down a "Skip" card.

"Nice play," I said, looking at my teenaged daughter, Mia, over his head. She grimaced back.

Times had been tough since their father, Barry, had been laid off. He wouldn't get his unemployment for another two days, so heading to the refrigerator wouldn't really help.

Barry came upstairs from checking the oil in the car.

"It needs a quart," he said.

"Can it wait until Wednesday?" I asked.

He shook his head. "I guess it will have to."

Our landlady had already been to the door earlier in the day. She certainly didn't want to wait two more days. I was still sick to my stomach that even though I had sent them to their rooms our children had overheard her wrath and threats, her inability to understand that we were doing the best we could. We had sold everything we could; eBay was my near constant employer as I got rid of anything we could spare.

Now we had just enough in the cupboard so that it looked like we had food, but it was mainly boxes of tea, old bottles of herbs and spices, and an expired box of powdered milk that I was hanging onto just in case.

The refrigerator was even more of a mirage because of all the condiments inside: bottles of soy and teriyaki sauce, my son's favorite peppers, mustard, and such.

"I'm hungry," Zack repeated. He wasn't the only one.

I rummaged among the pantry shelves, pushing things aside, standing on tiptoe, and looking inside containers. Suddenly I came across a lumpy package of something tucked at the back of the cupboard: popcorn.

"Popcorn," I said, holding the bag aloft as if I were holding a prize. I was! My heart sank just as quickly as I wondered if we had any oil. A search revealed that we did have a bit of vegetable oil, enough to make a big pot full of the fluffy white stuff. We'd have to hold the butter, because we were fresh out. I didn't care. It wasn't a fancy dinner, but it was something.

Within no time the house smelled like a movie theater. Mia and I put out dishes of various sauces and a selection of salts and spices. I knew how much she liked popcorn, so I hoped she would enjoy it.

"It's popcorn buffet night!" I said jollily, hoping the pot would fill everyone. We'd worry about tomorrow when the time came. Maybe we could find a few overlooked CDs to sell to the local music shop. For tonight, we were okay. I couldn't help but look upward and utter silent thanks.

Our characteristic humor soon erupted over bowlfuls of the fluffy corn. We joked about all of the permutations possible: deadly hot teriyaki, so salty soy, popcorn a la pickle juice. Barry, Mia and I burst into laughter, but Zack didn't quite understand the rules of the naming game.

"Say something so I can laugh," Zack said, setting us off again. Whenever things get too serious we still use that phrase.

By the end of the night we'd created so many different kinds of popcorn we could have started our own company selling specialty snacks.

When our turns came to play *Uno* we wiped our hands and laid down a card, grateful that we were inside, together, protected from the autumn wind that whipped the leaves around the yard.

We made blueberry tea, though we didn't have sugar. This was not deprivation, I thought, as I gradually relaxed at seeing how the food brought us together; this was happiness. And everyone went away if not full, then satisfied.

> *Even after Barry found a job, popcorn buffets remained a tradition in our family.*

The next day a friend brought over an extra pan of lasagna she "just happened to have." I thanked her profusely.

"Does this mean we can't have a popcorn buffet again tonight?" Zack asked. We all laughed as I quickly explained our impromptu dinner of the night before to our neighbor. I tried not to notice the pity in her eyes. She'd endured her own tough times.

Even after Barry found a job, popcorn buffets remained a tradition in our family, a kind of communion, a way to remember tough times that have come before.

Nowadays when we get together as a family someone is always watching calories, pushing away dessert. We have more than enough. And we did then, too: we had *Uno*, popcorn, laughter, and each other.

~Drema Sizemore Drudge

The Joy of Dirty Dishes

I would maintain that thanks are the highest
form of thought, and that gratitude is
happiness doubled by wonder.
~G.K. Chesterton

Almost all the silverware in the house is heaped like a haystack and it's sprouting the odd cheese plane, ice-cream scoop, and bread knife. Plates are stacked on cookie sheets, and bowls on the plates. Child-sized mugs lean against the adults' teacups.

So many dirty dishes.

And they're mine, all mine.

I'll admit it: It used to be hard for me to find joy in an overwhelming chore like this, but I remember the day it all changed.

It was the day when I went to the doctor to learn if my third child was going to be a boy or a girl. "Jane or Elijah?" I wondered. "Which will it be?"

But the ultrasound tech had different news for me: "I need to tell you something," she said, as she moved the screen so I could see it.

Two. Two little bodies floating there, facing each other, fully formed, beautiful, perfect.

Perfect. I swear to you: they were perfect.

But they were not safe. The tech couldn't find any barrier between our twins. And neither could the first specialist. And neither could the second.

"Monoamniotic," they told us. "High risk. You need to check into the hospital."

It was the only way to give our new little girls a chance. With no barrier between them in the womb, they were in danger of tangling their cords. Once that happened, more movement could pull those cords tight, cutting off their oxygen, killing them.

And these two little girls were already such dancers. I could feel them spinning around inside me.

There was no cure: only a way of upping the odds. If I stayed in the hospital, the babies could be on monitors that tracked their heartbeats. I'd stay right next to the OR, and if the heartbeat faltered in one of them, the doctors could perform a crash C-section and maybe pull them out in time. Maybe. If, on the other hand, they made it safely in utero to two months before their due date, the C-section could just be an early one, because at that point, their odds would be better in the NICU than inside of me.

> *It sounds bizarre, but in those moments I wanted nothing more than to wash dishes.*

It was the best chance, and so of course we took it.

I checked into the hospital. I sobbed after I kissed my two toddlers goodbye for the long separation... because it was the only way I could save their new siblings.

It was then, lying on that hospital bed week after week, watching the constant, reassuring heartbeats of my twins on the monitors, that I began to be grateful for doing the dishes.

You see, in those moments, there was nothing I wanted more. I know it sounds strange, but I think anyone who has been seriously ill or injured will understand what I mean: When you are isolated from normal life, there's nothing you long for more than that normality.

I couldn't do anything. I couldn't take care of my toddlers, I couldn't even see them. I couldn't help anyone — except by lying still enough that the doctors could monitor by babies. Week after week after week.

It sounds bizarre, but in those moments I wanted nothing more than to wash dishes.

Because washing the dishes would mean that I was home. It would mean that I was with my family again. And so I wanted to wash my husband's dinner plate, I wanted to wash Brie's plastic silverware, I wanted to wash Sam's sippy cup… and I wanted to wash my twins' tiny bottles.

I wanted to be with my family — all six of us together — and I wanted to be allowed to care for them again.

But in that moment I didn't even know if that dream would come true. I didn't know if it would be all six of us. What if I left the hospital and… I shudder even to think it… what if I left the hospital… and it was just me? What if we did all this to save them and it didn't work?

I learned to pray there, on that maternity floor, during those long weeks.

And so today I am grateful for dirty dishes. Because that enormous pile of dishes in front of me today? The plates and cups, the silverware and bowls, the sticky peanut-butter knives and the gloppy cereal bowls? They are there, and they are so numerous, because they are used by all four of my children. By God's grace, those dishes are used by my husband and me, and by Sam and Brie, certainly… but also by Jane and Kate: our identical twins who arrived early… but alive. And who now are healthy, bright-eyed second graders, rivaling their older siblings for noise and joy and messiness.

~Jessica Snell

68

Dinner with the Kids

A successful marriage requires falling in love many
times, always with the same person.
~Mignon McLaughlin

My husband, two sons, and I are in town doing our regular Tuesday night shopping when we decide to get pizza. We arrive at the parking lot at the same time as a newlywed couple. Painted in white shoe polish, proudly displayed on the rear window of their car are the words, "Ignore us, we're on our honeymoon!" Well, that immediately gets my attention. I notice that he gets out of the car, goes around and opens her door. He takes her hand in his as they walk inside.

My husband gets out of the car, opens the back door on his side, and takes our five-year-old son's hand in his. I get out of the car, open the back door on my side, and take the hand of our three-year-old. We all walk inside.

Once inside, we are seated across the room from the couple, but in full view. As they sit side-by-side, arm-in-arm, smiling and talking, with the occasional kiss on the cheek, I think back to our honeymoon. I wonder, "Will we ever have that kind of time for each other again?"

My thoughts are interrupted. "Mom! What kind of pizza do you want?" asks my older son. The four of us discuss the matter... a major decision, you know. We decide on one medium deep pan supreme and one medium hand tossed meat lovers.

I think back... Ten years ago this Friday night was our wedding night. For the next five years, we had each other's undivided attention as friends and lovers. I smile. Then, I remember how empty we sometimes felt with no children. I thought of the nights I had cried myself to sleep, with my husband holding me in his arms, as there were medical complications, and we didn't think I would ever be able to have children. My thoughts are once again interrupted.

"Mommy, will you take us to have our faces painted?" asks my younger son. Face painting was a regular Tuesday night ritual at this pizza place. I take the boys over, and we are faced with yet another major decision: which picture? My husband comes over to help one of them decide, while I help the other. Finally, one chooses the American Flag and the other chooses an eagle. As their faces are being painted, they flinch and giggle. My husband and I laugh with them. They finish up and we return to the table just as the pizzas arrive. After my husband gives the blessing over the food, we eat, talk, and laugh as we enjoy each other.

"I hope you, too, will some- day know the joy and love that children bring into your life."

I don't notice the newlyweds again until they are on their way out the door. As they glance our way, I give them a smile and think, "I hope you, too, will someday know the joy and love that children bring into your life."

As the boys and I are finishing up, my husband pays the check and gets a box for the leftover pizza, tomorrow's lunch. I pack up the pizza as he puts the boys' jackets on them. With the pizza in one hand, I take our older son's hand with the other. My husband takes the hand of our younger son, and opens the door with his other hand. Once we're outside, he puts his arm around me and kisses my cheek. I smile, and think to myself, "He noticed them, too."

~Ronda Nobles Nuñez

69

The Man Who Had Nothing

We can only be said to be alive in those moments when
our hearts are conscious of our treasures.
~Thornton Wilder

I loved visiting Granny and Papa when I was a little girl. I thought their little house in the country was wonderful. Papa had a couple of hens that laid blue eggs. I don't know if he ever ate the blue eggs but he was proud of the funny looking hens. Granny and Papa also had a gentle old hound dog that let me dress him in my doll clothes and push him in my doll carriage. The dog seemed to have taken on their patience and gentleness, and he tolerated me with confused brown eyes.

We had a ritual that I came to love. Papa always kept peppermint candy in his overalls pocket and when I was small I thought it was the best candy in the world. At odd moments, always unexpected, he would reach into his pocket and take out a peppermint for me.

Papa also had an old school bus parked in the back yard that he was always tinkering with. His plan was to fix it up and take Granny on a road trip one day. He let me sit behind the wheel and pretend I was driving while he worked on the engine.

Papa was the most satisfied, content man I ever knew. I grew up hearing him speak often of how blessed he was. He adored Granny and she was at the top of the list of the things he was grateful for. She was a tiny woman and he could never walk past her without putting one of his huge hands on top of her head or gently touching her shoulder.

One evening, as we sat on the porch after supper, he went inside and brought out a photograph and handed it to me. It was a picture of a petite dark haired woman striking a saucy pose in red high heels. "This is your granny when she was young. Wasn't she a beauty?" He then glanced at Granny with loving eyes. "She still is."

Confused, I look at Granny in her shapeless dress and apron, her curly gray hair in disarray, her small face stitched in fine wrinkles. I was too young to know that he saw her with his heart and not with his eyes.

As I grew older I visited Papa and Granny less and less. Their small crowded house seemed run down and poorly furnished to my critical eyes. I was inwardly disdainful when I heard Papa speak of how blessed he was when I knew he could barely put food on the table. He was

> *I was too young to know that he saw her with his heart and not with his eyes.*

good with his hands and he made a meager living as a handyman but that old school bus was rusted now and sitting on flat tires. It would never get road worthy to go on that road trip with Granny.

I had started to view my grandfather's life as a failure. Oh, I still loved Papa and Granny and I would always have fond memories of my childhood days spent with them and the funny hens and the sweet old hound dog. But I had lost the admiration I had for him when I was a child. I thought he was poor, and not smart enough to know it.

Papa died of a heart attack when I was in my second year of college. When I walked into the chapel for his funeral I was shocked at the people who packed that little church. There wasn't even standing room and people spilled out into the vestibule. I pushed my way through the crowd and passed doctors, lawyers, teachers, bankers, and clergy among the factory workers, farmers, and clerks. It seemed as if every one in the town, from every walk of life, was represented.

Standing at the casket was Bill Fletcher, a wealthy landowner who often hired Papa to do odd jobs. With tears in his eyes, he turned to me. "Your grandfather was the most honest, kindest, gentlest man I have ever known. No matter what was going wrong in my life I always felt better after a little chat with him. He always helped me keep things in proper prospective. He always found life wonderful. He got more pleasure out of his simple lifestyle than I could ever muster from mine even though I probably had more money in my wallet than he had in the bank."

Mr. Fletcher shook his head and rubbed tears from his cheeks. "He never lost the wonder of a child. He used to talk about those hens that laid blue eggs as if he had a rare treasure. And how he loved Annie. A woman has never been loved more than she."

He put his arm around my waist. "You are lucky to have grown up around such a wonderful man. He never had much money, but oh, what priceless treasures he did possess! I wish I was half the man he was." He glanced around at the people in the crowded chapel. "Everybody who knew him loved him. How many people can you say that about?"

Papa, who, in my eyes, had nothing, was envied by some who had everything that the world could offer. But I learned that day that the world is very limited in what it can offer. And what it does offer can be easily lost, such as money, fame, and worldly goods. I realized that the blessings that Papa often spoke of were not tangible things that could easily slip from your grasp. He was speaking of love, friendship, a stellar reputation, respect, and a good woman by his side for seventy-two years.

I found Granny and hugged her tight. "I am a lucky woman," she said. "I had the love of a good man for seventy-two years. I am blessed."

I kissed her wet cheeks. "Yes, you are." I said firmly. I could honestly say it now that I finally know what real blessings were.

~Elizabeth Atwater

70

Looking for Rainbows

Rainbows apologize for angry skies.
~Sylvia Voirol

"What is that sound, Mommy?" My sweet, three-year-old daughter Ashley sat in her car seat in the back of the van as we bumped along the road toward town from our home in rural Idaho. As I glanced in the mirror and saw her worried face looking back at me, I had to admit I was wondering the same thing. Did that knocking sound mean that our old van was dying?

"Oh, it's just the van bouncing, honey. It's okay. Hey, look over there at that baby lamb!" I said, as I pointed out the window to distract her. She didn't need to worry about this. I silently wished I could find something to distract myself as more worries surfaced. What would my husband and I do if this van died? Brandon had quit his job a few months before to start his own cabinet business. It had been a goal of ours that we had been working toward for years and, although we felt it was the right time, things were very tight for our little family. I had put off this trip to the store for as long as I could, knowing that we didn't have money for much more than the bare essentials. The only reason I was finally shopping was that we had run out of toilet paper.

"Just get me to the store and back," I thought. I was nearing the end of my pregnancy with our third child and my oversized tummy seemed to always be in the way. At that moment, I felt beaten down. I was tired, I was huge and I was on the verge of tears. Just when I felt like I could not handle one more thing, it started to rain.

"Mommy, look! There's the store!" Ashley's enthusiastic giggle brought me back to the task at hand and I turned into the parking lot.

I was happy to spy a parking space right near the front of the store. We wouldn't have to walk far in the rain. Just then, a car came from nowhere and pulled in front of me to get the space. The stress and worry that I had felt moments before turned instantly to anger. What was wrong with that guy? Couldn't he tell that I wanted that parking spot? I simmered as I looked around for another space that was close to the store. My attitude got worse when I pulled into the only open parking space and there on the ground next to us was a puddle of oil. The rainwater was adding to its size by the second. I knew this was going to be a problem. My little Ashley loved to splash in puddles no matter what was in them.

> *"Somehow we will make it. We have done harder things."*

Getting her out of her car seat, I said, "Ashley, you need to hold my hand. Mommy can't carry you because my big tummy is in the way. So hold on tight to my hand, okay?" She nodded and her short brown pigtails bounced. She was very compliant until she saw that puddle. She shook free of my hand and ran toward it before I could stop her.

In that instant, I visualized oily shoes, oily little pants and socks, and if I was not able to move any faster than I was currently going, oily handprints on her pink ruffle shirt by the time I got to her. Could this day get any worse? First the van, then the rain, then the parking space, and now I was looking at having ruined clothes that I could not afford to replace.

Then, suddenly, Ashley stopped short of the puddle and in a quiet voice, said, "Look, Mommy! Rainbows!" Her fat little finger pointed out the oil mixing with the rainwater and creating swirls of color. She was enthralled with what she knew was the most beautiful thing she had ever seen.

That is when it all changed for me. A moment before, I had been unable to focus on more than the puddle of oil on the ground and the many other things that were making my life hard. I was worried about so much that I couldn't see anything good anywhere around me.

I stood in the parking lot, with tiny drops of rain coming down on my head and I watched my daughter teach me that we don't have to look far to find beauty. Life is full of it, even in the most unusual circumstances. Where moments before, I saw an oily mess waiting to happen, she had seen beautiful rainbows.

I stood for a minute and thought about what a wonderful shift had just taken place in my way of thinking. The baby inside me kicked and I rubbed my overgrown stomach, excited to meet this new little child. I wasn't even worried about the van. "Somehow we will make it. We have done harder things," I thought, as Ashley pointed out a particularly bright circle of color.

I held her hand and after a minute we jumped the tiny puddle of rainbows together and walked into the store. Ashley squeezed my hand and with a happy little bouncy giggle, she said, "Mommy, we were so lucky to see those rainbows, weren't we?"

"Yes, honey, we were indeed."

~Tina Grover

71

What I Learned from My First Thanksgiving

Thanksgiving Day is a jewel, to set in the hearts of
honest men; but be careful that you do not take the day,
and leave out the gratitude.

~E.P. Powell

I remember growing up in Malaysia, dreaming about taking my first bite of a huge turkey leg and wondering how it would taste. All the American TV shows I had seen about Thanksgiving always featured the succulent bird as the main dish.

The opportunity to eat turkey finally occurred for me at age nineteen. I was in the U.S., attending Louisiana State University, and my host family in Baton Rouge invited me to join them for their Thanksgiving dinner. Although I did not get a chance to hold a huge turkey leg in my hand and devour it as I had dreamed about, I did consume all the delicious dark meat I could eat that day. After the excitement of feasting on a turkey for the first time subsided, I came to realize the significance of gathering for this special American holiday.

Thanksgiving quickly became personal for me. Why was I thankful? How had I been blessed? Who in my life was I most grateful for this year? All these questions became the ideal opening lines for a wonderful story-telling session. I found myself answering each question as if I was taking a test. However, instead of feeling the usual test anxiety, I was experiencing joy and love.

I thought about the past year. I tried to imagine how my parents must have felt in Malaysia when they made the difficult decision to send their only son halfway around the world to seek a future they could only envision. Although they had heard a few horror stories as well as joyful ones from parents whose children were studying abroad, ultimately my parents chose faith and hope over fear.

My mom, Nyah, and my father, Baba, grew up during World War II. They were both teenagers when Japan invaded our homeland on December 8, 1941. Living with fear was second nature for my parents during the Japanese occupation. I remember my mom and dad sharing war stories with my sister and me. The atrocities inflicted upon the country's citizens were intended to incite fear and obedience in the population.

What kept my parents focused on the future were faith and hope. My mom and dad taught my sister and me that having faith is believing something better is right around the corner. Their love led to trust, and trust became the foundation for my being in the United States.

I clearly recall my mom and dad standing at the edge of the departure lounge, anxiously watching me disappear into the crowd as I headed to my gate. My dad smiled at me as I looked back to wave goodbye one last time. Months earlier, we had sat down to discuss this life changing event for the Tan family. My dad had been ill for the last two years with recurring pneumonia. Despite my dad's deteriorating health, he concurred with my mom's decision to send me to America. My parents were grateful their prayers for a better future for their children were answered. No emotional sacrifice or financial burden would deter them from sending me abroad.

A soft tap on my shoulder drew my attention back to the present. With a big smile Ms. Eleanora offered me a cup of her aromatic home-made apple cider. She and her husband, Nick Carter, were my hosts. Ms. Eleanora was born and raised in New Orleans, and a graduate of Newcomb College. A Southern belle, she was always attentive to my needs when I visited her family.

I met Mr. Carter, a retired LSU professor, three days after arriving in Baton Rouge. He picked me up from my dormitory and took me to his home for lunch. Ms. Eleanora's southern charm and hospitality made me feel at home immediately. The Carters were excited to assist me in getting acclimated to my new community. Since it was the middle of winter, they took me shopping for warm clothing. Weekly Sunday dinners with the Carters were a wonderful substitute for meal times with my family back in Malaysia, whom I longed for quite frequently. Spending time with Ms. Eleanora was fun and educational as well.

> *"I am thankful my parents trusted me and believed in my potential enough to send me to the United States."*

She taught me American slang to help me assimilate with my peers. She also provided emotional support when I shared news about my ailing father.

While sipping my first taste of the warm and delicious apple cider, I was reminded of the time I spent with Ms. Eleanora in her kitchen a couple of days earlier. I had invited myself over to help her with the preparations for the big Thanksgiving dinner. I wanted to learn how to cook a turkey with her special oyster and French bread stuffing.

Watching Ms. Eleanora cook had rekindled my memories of my mom in her kitchen in Malaysia. During the days leading up to the Chinese New Year celebration, my mom practically lived in the kitchen. Both ladies shared a tremendous focus, yet a peaceful and loving demeanor, as they performed the tasks of prepping and cooking for their families and guests. In many ways, the kitchen became their private stage where they planned and orchestrated their holiday culinary delights. I felt privileged to see them in action and contributed whenever invited.

My reverie was suddenly interrupted when Mr. Wiley Poole called out my name. "Johnny, it's your turn now to share your story. What are you thankful for this year, young man?" Mr. and Mrs. Poole were longtime friends of the Carters. In an instant, the lively living room went silent. The Stevens, other longtime friends of the family, the Carter's son, twin daughters, daughter and sons-in-law, and grandchildren, all turned their attention to me.

My initial nervousness about being in the spotlight gave way to calm as I spoke. "I am thankful my parents trusted me and believed in my potential enough to send me to the United States. I am thankful to have Mr. and Mrs. Carter as my host family. And finally, I am thankful that all of you gave me the first dibs on the dark meat." With that everyone started laughing at my use of the words "first dibs." Today was the first time I heard those words. They were spoken by Ms. Eleanora after her husband said grace over the gathering. She made it clear to everyone that since I was a first-time guest I had the honor of filling my plate with anything I wanted from the dinner table. Her gesture not only nourished my appetite, but my homesick heart as well.

The magical day, filled with a bountiful feast and the generosity of new friends, gave birth to my understanding of the true essence of Thanksgiving. Once a year, this uniquely American holiday reminds me to reflect on those blessings for which I am grateful, including the people, situations and events that have enriched my life. There were years when I was able to gather with my family; years when I experienced the holiday spirit thanks to the generosity of friends; and still other times when I found myself counting my blessings in solitude. Regardless of the situation, I have always focused on appreciation, and that has brought joy and love to my heart.

~Johnny Tan

The Power of Gratitude

Silver Linings

*If you concentrate on finding whatever is good in every
situation, you will discover that your life will suddenly be
filled with gratitude, a feeling that nurtures the soul.*
~Rabbi Harold Kushner

72

What a Difference One Point Can Make

*Gratitude is an art of painting an adversity
into a lovely picture.*
~Kak Sri

I am visiting my mother in the hospital while she recovers from pneumonia and other complications from triple bypass surgery. She complains about the food to my brother, my father, my boyfriend, and me. My boyfriend and I have just returned to Houston from a Christmas visit to his parents' home in Ohio, where I plan to go to law school in the fall.

If she is complaining, I reason, it means she is getting better. My brother motions for me to step outside and join him in the hall. He leads me to a stairwell, far beyond the hearing of my mom and dad. I prepare for the worst.

"You cannot go to law school," he says. "Dad has cancer."

My father, who never gets sick, who never missed a day of work in thirty years as a public school principal due to illness, has cancer.

"You can't tell Mom," he says.

So we walk back into her room, attempting poker faces. "What's wrong?" she says, reading mine immediately. I change the subject.

My father is the calm in the storm to my mother's "Chicken Little." Recently he was on the news, calming a cafeteria full of students after a school shooting. He attends church and teaches Sunday school. He helps disadvantaged and at-risk students. He is my pillar of strength, the guy I called when I first moved to Houston and felt lost and hopeless in the Big City. He can't have cancer. Not my dad.

He is planning his retirement with a brand new RV. He is ready to enjoy his golden years traveling the country with my mom once she recovers. But now he has cancer.

Once my mother learns of Dad's diagnosis, she rouses herself in recovery far faster than she would have without a purpose. She eats healthier, exercises and mends her heart so she can take care of Dad. Neither she nor my father will hear of me staying in Houston or skipping law school.

> *One point more and I'd be a lawyer in Ohio, rather than Texas.*

I stay through Dad's surgery to remove the tumor from his colon. His prognosis is good. So off to Ohio, and law school, I go.

Law school at age thirty-eight is not easy. Even for me, who made good grades in graduate school. Even in the most conducive environment it is tough. Add a new city, a boyfriend with two children who visit on weekends, two dogs and two cats in a tiny house and it gets tougher. The first year is a wake-up call. My grades slip. I lose my scholarship. But I begin to get the hang of it. I take on an internship, then a job. I switch to night classes. My grades improve.

I monitor Dad's progress through phone calls and holiday visits. His cancer is in remission.

I have one semester of law school to complete. Suddenly the tiny house — with two dogs, two cats, and two children on weekends — gets even smaller. The children's mother goes missing and emergency custody ensues. They move in with us. It is an adjustment for them and an adjustment for me. I am no longer "Dad's Cool Girlfriend" who takes them shopping or to get ice cream. Now I am the lady who tells them to please play more quietly because I need to study.

In the meantime Dad's cancer is back. Stage IV: a prognosis of six to eighteen months. We are back in Houston for Christmas and to tell my parents of our engagement. Ten days with my parents and no one says a word. I find out on the way to the airport to return to

Ohio and law school.

"Why didn't you tell me sooner?" I ask.

"I didn't want you to mess up your grades again worrying," Dad says. He is determined to beat it.

The last semester is tough but I manage it. My parents arrive in Ohio for my graduation in May.

I am in shock. My formerly portly father is gaunt. His pants are cinched at the waist. Fifty pounds lighter, he looks thirty years older. In a moment alone, I ask him how he is.

"Well, Sissy," he says, "I'm not dead yet!"

They return to Houston and I concentrate on passing the Ohio bar exam. I use flash cards. I take prep classes. The three-day exam is grueling. I wait four months for the results.

Only to find out I have missed passing by one point.

All that time away from Dad while he was healthy and then while he is ill. For what? A law degree with no license. What good is that?

My employer is not impressed and I am let go. I feel like a failure.

I take a job as a freelance writer and photographer for the local independent newspaper while I consider my options.

"Why don't you take the bar exam in Texas?" my mother says. "You can stay with us and study."

No dogs, no cats, no kids. No distractions.

A former colleague has a job opening with flexible hours at his company. I will have plenty of time to study.

So I move back to my parents' home in Houston, with whom I have not lived for nearly twenty years. It is another adjustment. I set up a schedule. Study before work. Bar prep on tapes in the car on my one-hour-each-way commute. Eat dinner with Mom and Dad. Study in the evenings and in bed by 10:00 p.m.

I spend free time with Dad. He will not talk about leaving, but it is only a matter of time. Whenever I ask how he is, I get the same answer: "Well, Sissy, I'm not dead yet!"

This time the exam is not so grueling. I am prepared. It is not easy but I know I have passed. In August I drive back to Ohio to help my fiancé pack the house. He has agreed to move himself and his children to Texas so I can be near my father.

We find a house to rent in my parents' neighborhood — just across the street. In September Dad gets weaker. By November he rarely leaves the house, although he does manage to vote in the election. But there is pride in his eyes when I return from the licensing ceremony with a copy of the State Bar program for him. By Thanksgiving he cannot walk across the street to join us for dinner.

Two days before Christmas my father leaves this world for the next. Nearly eighteen months from his diagnosis.

That was 2005. Just one point kept me from passing the Bar in Ohio. Just one point almost dashed my dreams of being a lawyer.

What a difference one point can make. One point more and I'd be a lawyer in Ohio, rather than Texas. But that one point gave me eight more months with my dad.

~Amy Corron Power

73

Blessing in Disguise

What seem to us bitter trials are often
blessings in disguise.
~Oscar Wilde

Friday had finally arrived and with it the week off my sister always took with us during our family's annual trip back home. We eagerly awaited our time with her, but late Friday evening, when she arrived home from work, she announced her boss had given her an unexpected surprise. "I've lost my job. They've closed down the school and asked that I clear out my teaching materials by the end of the weekend. They sold the building."

Our mouths hung open in disbelief. She had worked at that school for more than fifteen years.

I started to worry immediately. My sister was sixty years old. She had a college degree and years of continuing education classes, not to mention thirty-eight years of teaching under her belt. Who would hire an older teacher and one so obviously over-qualified? The new school year had already started so who would even be hiring anyway?

I'd always claimed my sister was the happiest person I knew, but I figured her happiness came from fulfilling her passion: working with children. And if she couldn't find a teaching job, would her continuously bubbling fountain of joy run dry?

I was angry and sad as well as worried. Not only was my sister one of the happiest people in the world, but also one of the sweetest.

She had a special gift when it came to working with children and had always excelled at her job. After all the years of devoted service, how could my sister's boss not give her or the other teachers any warning?

My family's usual excitement about our vacation was tempered. How could we enjoy our vacation now that we were worried for my sister? And how could *she* enjoy her vacation?

We gathered around the dinner table, a glum bunch, picking at our food. My eyes grew misty as I reached over and hugged my sister. "I am so sorry," I said. "What a nightmare for you. Finding a job at your age is difficult enough — and your boss stinks."

> *As my sister explained her positive attitude to us, her words reminded me that gratitude is a choice.*

While my sister admitted the shock hadn't quite settled in, she calmly looked at the rest of us. "I'm not going to worry about it," she announced. "I intend to enjoy my vacation, and I'll tackle finding a new job when it's over and you leave."

We spent the remainder of our dinner venting our anger at what had taken place, while my sister listened quietly, not adding much to the conversation. Then, an amazing thing happened.

As my sister explained her positive attitude to us, her words reminded me that gratitude is a choice. Instead of moping around feeling sorry for herself, she saw potential for good. "This isn't the first time I've lost my job," she stated. "Yet throughout my life, I've never been unemployed. I've always been taken care of and watched over. I have no doubt a job will come along and besides, change is good — it brings the opportunity for growth."

With a thankful heart she acknowledged the blessings she'd had in her life so far, and stood steadfast in her faith that those blessings would continue. I knew from my own life experiences that she spoke the truth and she'd be okay, even if the path ahead took her in a different direction.

And she was right. Several weeks after we got home from vacation she called and said that she'd found a wonderful teaching job. In truth, she's never felt happier, more fulfilled, or more appreciated. In fact, the change was a positive, wonderful step forward for her, one she would not have taken if she hadn't lost her job.

Like a security blanket of warmth and reassurance, my sister's gratitude had wrapped her in comfort. It alleviated her fears and allowed her to focus on beginning another phase of her life. Gratitude helped her embrace change with open arms.

~Jill Burns

74

Out of the Rubble

*Caring about others, running the risk of feeling, and
leaving an impact on people, brings happiness.*
~Rabbi Harold Kushner

It was a frigid night. I had worked all day and picked up my eleven-month-old son from a friend's house on the way home. I gave only a passing thought to the cop sitting in a patrol car parked across the street. I pulled off my mittens with my teeth and fumbled with the keys. It was already nine o'clock, and I was tired and hungry.

Four months had passed since my husband Paul boarded American Airlines Flight 11 on the morning of Sept 11th. To the casual observer, it probably seemed as if I was doing pretty well. A closer look would have revealed that I was barely holding it together.

My town had taken my small, broken family under its protective wing. Friends offered to watch my son for a few hours on weekends, hoping to alleviate the stress of my new role as a widowed mom. My garbage pails were magically transported from the curb back to my garage on pickup days. Dinners appeared regularly on my doorstep, sometimes with a signed card and sometimes with no clue as to the angel's identity. Once, an acquaintance who knew I was Jewish drove four towns over to a kosher restaurant to bring us a chicken dinner. We don't keep kosher and I am a vegetarian, so the poignancy of the effort was especially keen.

I tossed a bowl of frozen vegetables into the microwave. The doorbell rang. It was the police officer. He asked if he could come in. Not knowing when I got home from work, he said he had been waiting for me since five.

Before 9/11, an officer at the door might have been cause for alarm. But in recent months I had become accustomed to a blur of people stopping by unannounced. I was too numb to care that this one just happened to be in uniform.

The cop was young, maybe in his late twenties. He sat at the kitchen table. I made tea; he made small talk: Did I always work such late hours? How long had we lived in town?

"Forgive me," I finally said, "would you please just tell me why you're here?"

My question seemed to catch him off guard. His body stiffened as he shifted in the chair. "I came to tell you the New York Police Department found something that belonged to your husband."

My town had taken my small, broken family under its protective wing.

At that time, none of Paul's remains or belongings had been recovered. I had provided DNA samples to the medical examiner's office but I wasn't expecting much. The terrorists had used my husband's body as part of their bomb to bring down the Twin Towers. The best I could wish for him was instant and complete obliteration.

"They found his wedding ring," the policeman said. "It's being held for you in New York."

I immediately had a sense that I should feel something big. Relief. Joy. Anger. I should scream. Or at least cry. But in the months since 9/11, my emotions had been wrung out, left numb and brittle like the lifeless twigs on the winter streets. It hurt too much to feel. I was too tired. Nausea rose in my gut. A sudden sweat sent a shuddering chill through my body. Deep breaths — in through the nose and out through the mouth.

"Could you please watch my son for a few minutes?" The officer said yes.

I walked into the kitchen and picked up the phone. I don't remember who I called first. My mother? My sister? In the few minutes that passed between receiving this news and sharing it with someone else, I had filled in all the blanks — woven a complete story from one, five-word sentence: "They found his wedding ring."

The images developed like a Polaroid. The first thing I saw was the already iconic yellow raincoat. Some firefighter or city worker was at the end of his shift clearing the rubble of the World Trade Center. Buried beneath the twisted metal and burnt debris, he spied something shiny. He was exhausted and his back hurt, but he bent down and picked it up. Maybe when he saw what it was, he choked up. Or maybe it was the tenth ring he'd found that day and had no more tears for this one.

At the end of the shift, he emptied his pockets onto a supervisor's desk. The supervisor took the ring to someone who made out the dates engraved inside, and she gave it to someone else who checked the DNA. Chancing no mistake, the information was confirmed with the FBI unit that had visited me the week after 9/11 and taken information about Paul, including our wedding date. And tonight, in what now seemed like the ultimate kindness, a local police officer had waited outside my door for four hours in twenty-degree weather to deliver this news in person, and now sat on my carpet playing with my son while I spun out this tale to my family and Paul's.

I have no idea who that cop was but I think about him. And I think about the person who found Paul's ring and the person with the magnifying glass who read the wedding dates and the initials carved inside. I think about my sister-in-law and brother-in-law who had the mangled band reshaped and cleaned before driving four hours to bring it to me.

But I also think about the dinners and the garbage pails and all the people who stopped by just to see if I was "all right." Over the years, these gifts of outreach and support have shaped my memories of that time. Yes, there was searing pain. But there was also goodness that has left an indelible imprint on my heart and given me a depth of gratitude that guides me every day of my life.

~Audrey Ades

75

A Super Hero

*As we work to create light for others, we naturally
light our own way.*
~Mary Anne Radmacher

The very young doctor stood with my husband and me in
the corridor of a big city hospital's trauma unit. He nervously told us our fourteen-year-old son, Andy, was brain
dead and would not recover from the head injury he had
sustained when he was hit by a drunk driver. My life ended too, at
least my life as I knew it. I stood still… waiting… my heart breaking
and my mind going numb and then I asked, "What do we do now?"

"Have you ever thought of organ donation?" he offered.

It was as though he had thrown me a life preserver in an angry sea.
It was my chance to keep the child to whom I'd given birth alive, in a
way I'd never even thought about while he lived. His heart would go
on beating, his eyes seeing, his organs thriving and pumping in others.
I knew it wouldn't be Andy, that his hands would never hold mine
again, that the body I had nurtured and cared for would be laid in a
grave and that I would have to leave him there, that I would never see
him again. But part of him would still live, and I was grateful for that.

The letter we received from the organ procurement organization
told us Andy's heart was received by a man who had been sick for
years, his liver by a widowed father of teenagers who was in a coma,
his kidneys by people for whom they were perfect matches, his corneas
by a fifteen-year-old boy and a grandmother who, until the transplant,

had never seen her grandchildren. They were all doing well, and even though I was weeping into my pillow every night, visiting the cemetery every day, poring through my precious boy's things and answering sympathy cards, I was grateful that my son had given them second chances at life. "Andy, you're a super hero," I whispered.

After a few years, I started wondering about the recipients. Andy was extraordinary in life, happy and caring and bubbling over with enthusiasm for everything the world offered to him. On the day he was hit, at the end of the driveway of the only home he'd ever known,

> *Thank God that organ donation is possible and viable.*

he was doing what he loved most, riding his three-wheeler to our pasture to care for Max, the horse he loved. Were they happy too, these people in whom my boy lived on? Were they grateful for their lives? I decided to try to find out.

After contacting the organ procurement organization, I wrote letters to each of the recipients, anonymously, according to procedure. I wished them all well, told them what a wonderful kid their donor was, and invited them to contact me if they wished. Then I waited.

Finally, I received a letter from a woman in Nebraska, halfway across the country, near the place where I was born and raised. She was the recipient of Andy's kidney, a perfect match, a gift that had literally given her back her life, her health and her sanity. Kathy was hesitant and shy, bothered by feelings that are common to transplant recipients, that she lived only because someone else died, someone young and innocent. She told me she had been told little about Andy and even thought he was a girl but that she prayed for her donor every day.

We wrote letters, we e-mailed and talked on the phone, and finally we arranged a face-to-face meeting. There was so much to say, so many emotions to examine and sort out, so many good things, so many tears and fears to share. I explained to her that I didn't see the transplant the way she did, that I knew Andy didn't die so that she could live. "Andy died because someone got drunk and got behind the wheel of his van," I said. "No one wanted Andy to die, not the doctors, certainly not us, not even the drunk driver, but he died anyway, and then we were faced with a choice to allow others to live, a choice we were grateful to have."

I believe Kathy has been able to let go of some of the typical transplant recipient guilt that results from regaining your life with another's organ donation. Over these years, we've shared something I never expected: great fun! She has a wonderful sense of humor, just like Andy did. She thinks her kidney brought some baggage with it, and one of the first things she told me was that prior to the transplant she was repulsed by the idea of Reese's Peanut Butter Cups. The idea of peanut butter paired with chocolate was disgusting to her, even as a child. After the transplant, they were her favorite. What was Andy's favorite candy? "All of them," I said, "but especially Reese's Peanut Butter Cups."

"I was almost a health nut," she said of her struggle with dialysis and her failing kidney. "I never ate fast food and was always careful. After the transplant, I found myself sitting in the drive-thru all the time." I was delighted, wondering if my Big Mac–addicted son's preferences had somehow transferred with the kidney. It was a joyous thing to ponder, a gift.

Over the years, Kathy has truly become part of the family, sending me the most beautiful Christmas floral arrangements every year and honoring Andy's memory in many ways every day. We share each other's families, and we agree that Facebook is a special blessing.

I have met her mother, who said something that I will hold in my heart forever. "Thank God there are people like you in the world."

Thank God Andy was in the world, and that I got to be his mother. Thank God that organ donation is possible and viable and actually can save people's lives. Thank God for Kathy and for her willingness to conquer her fear and angst and reach out to me.

I know now that even in the depths of sadness and pain and sorrow, there are blessings, small and barely discernible at first, greater as time goes on. While I miss my sweet, wonderful son every day, I am grateful for these blessings, the little ones and the bigger ones and the ones that continue to grow. I'm especially grateful for that nervous young doctor who had the courage to suggest organ donation.

Most of all, I'm grateful that when Kathy went for her last check-up, now twenty years since the transplant, her doctor pronounced that the kidney is "working like a super hero."

~Luanne Tovey Zuccari

The Wakeup Call

This world was made for you too. Enjoy it, explore it,
experience it. Don't hold back. It is God's gift to you.
Don't be a wallflower in the dance of life.
~Author Unknown

My stylist stood behind me with her hands on my shoulders and I watched her reflection in the salon mirror as she spoke. "I am so sorry that this happened to you, my friend." I had just shared the latest development in my life — five days earlier, I'd been fired from my job.

"Don't be sorry, Julie." I said. "Sometimes bad things happen for good reasons. I'm glad they let me go."

She looked back at me. It felt strange making eye contact in the mirror with someone who was standing behind me. "I've never seen someone so happy about getting fired. You should be upset for what they did to you."

"Think of it as something that happened *for* me, not *to* me."

She smiled and shook her head as she reached for a sheet of foil. "I still say you were awesome at your job."

I smiled back. "I *was* awesome at my job. But I sucked at living my life." She finished applying the foil, set the timer, and as the color processed, I talked more about my job.

"Seven years ago, taking a field manager position with a global corporation was a great fit for me. I enjoyed the work, travel, and the

Silver Linings | 281

people. But, four years in, several hundred managers were terminated as the company announced a restructuring. Everything changed — including upper management, job descriptions and employee morale.

"The restructuring wasn't short-lived. It spanned a period of three years and the company continued to struggle. Policies changed more often than the seasons and managers nationwide worked tirelessly to save the company and their jobs. In the process, I ignored the fact that I wasn't enjoying my life.

"During those three years, my nose was never far from the grindstone. Working from a home office was supposed to be a benefit, but with the stress and fear of job loss, it simply meant that I never left work."

Julie interrupted. "Oh my word. Why didn't you just quit?"

"Because I'd convinced myself that I couldn't afford to leave my job. Realistically, I couldn't afford to stay. Not only was my career on a collision course, my whole world was spinning out of control. I lived each day in excess: too much work, stress, drinking, eating and spending.

> *"I was awesome at my job. But I sucked at living my life."*

"I spent most of my time sitting in front of a computer and had replaced self-worth with work. It had been months since I'd exercised, had a meaningful conversation with my husband, read a book, taken a walk or eaten a healthy meal. Ending the day with a glass of wine became routine. One glass led to a couple and I worried that my habit was teetering on the edge of addiction. I longed for a good night's sleep. My nights consisted of waking in a panic every forty-five minutes, then lying in the dark thinking about work.

"A month ago, another wave of employees was terminated. Those who still had jobs were under more pressure than ever. We struggled to meet corporate goals but suspected that it didn't matter what our results were. The effort to turn around the company was only resulting in more downsizing.

"A month later, last Thursday, actually, I received an e-mail from my boss, requesting that I call her at 11:45. As the call connected, she was the first to speak — her voice was emotionless. 'Hi Ann. Thank you for adjusting your schedule to call. Please know that a member of HR is also on the line.'

"It was the moment I'd feared. I sat, frozen, as she followed her script.

"'The reason for today's call is to let you know that effective immediately, you are no longer employed by our company. Unfortunately the goals that were set for you were not met.' (I didn't know any managers within a nine-state radius who'd met their goals.)

"I disconnected and stared down at my phone. For three years, I had been part of the turnaround effort. But in the end, it didn't include me. It didn't matter how hard I'd worked, how many hours I'd dedicated or the sacrifices I'd made. A two-minute phone call ended my career.

"I had turned my life inside out for this company and had nothing to show for it. Then reality crept in. I had plenty to show for it. I was twenty-five pounds heavier than the day I was hired. My spending habits had crowded my home with enough stuff to fill a moving van. The recycle bin was brimming with wine bottles. And the face that greeted me in the mirror each morning was unhappy. That person in the mirror is not the person I want to be.

"As I look back at the choices I made along the way, I don't regret any of them. They were lessons that will lead me closer to the life I want to live. I'm thankful that I had the job, and will be forever grateful for the wakeup call that ended it."

The timer buzzed and Julie reached to shut it off. "You're amazing," she said as she led me to the shampoo sink.

"Not amazing. Just enlightened. My employment status wasn't the only thing that needed to change."

It's been a year since that day in my stylist's chair. A year since I was fired from a job that I thought I'd retire from. Fired. My husband hates the word, but I claim it proudly; it saved me. I had put happiness on hold for a long time, and it took a wakeup call to reconnect me to the life that had been right here waiting for me all along.

~Ann Morrow

A Healing Trio

*Gratitude is one of the sweet shortcuts to finding peace
of mind and happiness inside. No matter what is
going on outside of us, there's always something
we could be grateful for.*
~Barry Neil Kaufman

My daughter's first year away at college didn't turn out the way I imagined it. High school had been emotionally challenging for her so she eagerly embraced the opportunity for a fresh start. On move-in day I happily helped her set up her room. I hugged her goodbye and walked toward the door of her dorm room.

Then I turned back to take one last look at her in her new home. I flashed back to my dorm room from freshman year and nostalgically noted how similar they were — the institutional furniture combined with touches from the girls' childhood — their stuffed animals and tattered pieces of "blankies." Even the posters on the wall hadn't changed much. Her roommate had hung the same Jimi Hendrix poster so many kids displayed in 1970 when I left for college.

As I stood there I recalled how much I loved my college years. I was simultaneously thrilled for her and a tad frightened, knowing all the things that can go wrong when a freshman has that first taste of freedom. I managed to hold back the tears until I was safely in my car. I sat there and took a deep and calming breath.

During those first few weeks, when we spoke on the phone she sounded pretty happy. Her voice had that perfect balance of excitement, curiosity, and cautious optimism. Her classes were inspirational. She was making friends and learning to balance school and fun.

As time passed, it seemed the cautious optimism was turning into pessimism. My daughter was doing fine academically but personally she was struggling. She began to suffer some significant physical challenges. With those came emotional issues and those were heartbreaking to hear about. Each conversation seemed just a bit worse than the one before. My formerly positive child was turning toward a dark side. I worried the darkness would become more pervasive than the light in her life.

> *At the end of each day we would take the time to identify three things worth noting for their goodness.*

I searched for ways to help her with the physical struggles. I began doing research online to learn about what she was describing in order to find a doctor to help her, but in the meantime I wanted a more immediate fix, something to help her get through each day without being despondent. When we spoke I tried to turn the conversation to something positive for her to think about. I talked about the good in her life. But I realized this was not something I could effectively do for her — to make her turn her mind toward the light. This was something she had to do for herself.

I suggested a nightly ritual. The last thing each of us did before bedtime was to e-mail the other a list of three things for which we were grateful. There was no item too small or too trivial or too big or too corny. The goal was simple — at the end of each day we would take the time to identify three things worth noting for their goodness. We agreed not to be judgmental about each other's list. It could be anything from "My oatmeal at breakfast was especially delicious," to "My best friend called just to say hi," to "I got an A- on an English paper I worked hard on," or "My project at work is finally finished." One day it might be, "Saw a gorgeous sunset," and on that same day it could include, "Passed a homeless person sleeping on the street and thought about how fortunate we are to have a safe place to sleep." One day in February it might be "I saw my first crocus," or "So happy to have sisters."

The only thing that mattered was that we did it every day. In this daily routine one thing became clear. In each day, from the gloomiest to the most resplendent, there are myriad things for which anyone can be grateful… if we seek them out. Some days the list of three poured forth freely while other days it was a stretch to find three. But find three we did, each of us, every single day.

I launched this routine to help my daughter, but, as so much of parenting turns out, I learned valuable lessons too. I found myself looking forward to making the daily list. Throughout the day I'd make a mental note of small things, random acts of gratitude so to speak, in order to remember them later. It's surprising just how many I could find some days. Although we agreed on three, occasionally I'd throw in a bonus item, just because it was that kind of day.

Ultimately we did find the answer to the mystery of my daughter's physical struggles and she is happy and healthy now. We stopped doing our nightly list together because we had both found our way back to a place with more light than dark.

But I didn't stop making the list. I found it so uplifting and so soothing as a way to wrap up each day that now I do it in solitude, like a nocturnal meditation. Every night as I place my head on the pillow and close my eyes I make a mental list of three things for which I am thankful. That trio of gratitude makes for a peaceful finale of every day.

~Deborah Drezon Carroll

Gratitude in Crisis

However motherhood comes to you, it's a miracle.
~Valerie Harper

'd just finished my grocery list and was about to leave our small apartment when the cold air at the door sent me back for a sweater. That was when the phone rang. I froze when I heard a woman from the county child welfare department say, "We have a newborn little boy that needs immediate placement. Are you interested?"

My heart raced. Tubal pregnancies and multiple surgeries had closed the door to having biological children. My husband Jack and I were in the certification process with a foster and adoption program in Santa Barbara County, but were not yet approved. Thrilled at the offer of a newborn directly from the child welfare department, I said, "Yes!"

Jack rushed home from work.

We enthusiastically scrambled to get everything ready to receive this precious gift. We were at the end of the fostering and adopting certification process, so our home was already equipped with the basic necessities to care for a child. Even with nine months to prepare, having a baby is awe-inspiring and intimidating, and now we had only a few hours.

Michael was only one day old when the social worker placed him gently into my arms. He had been born to a teenage girl who had walked into the hospital emergency room complaining of stomach pains. She'd denied she was pregnant, then proceeded to give birth to a beautiful seven-pound boy she hadn't realized she was carrying. After refusing to name the infant, or tell anyone who the father was, she simply left.

The next few days flew by as I adjusted to an altered rhythm of life. I'd spend hours holding Michael, marveling at the way he'd coo softly when content. His long slender fingers stretched and flexed as I hummed a tune, and Jack thought he might be a budding musician one day. I'd place little kisses on his soft neck, reveling in his sweet scent. He was perfect.

> *I couldn't be incapacitated by fear and anxiety and be thankful at the same time.*

"Once the mother signs the paperwork we can move forward," the social worker informed us a few days later. "These type of cases normally go straight to adoption."

Cautiously optimistic, Jack reminded me Michael wasn't ours yet, and to be careful how invested I became. True, but as more of our friends and family heard what happened and met Michael, they assured me this must be God's answer to a long standing desire for children. I was exhorted not to doubt. So, as more days passed, I relaxed.

A week later, the alarm blared at 3:30 a.m. and Jack crawled out of bed to leave for his weekly fifteen hour delivery route to the central valley. I fed Michael, settled him back in his crib, and then tried to catch a little more sleep. A few hours later I was startled awake by the phone.

It was the social worker, with bad news. "Hi, Jenny. The baby's teenage mother finally told her parents about him," she stated quickly. "It seems the parents have friends that are interested in adopting him." She hurried on without emotion, "Please get him ready to go. I'll be there in an hour to pick him up." She paused before adding, "The baby's grandmother will be with me."

My world stopped!

I mumbled something vague about having him ready. I hung up the phone in slow motion, then crumpled to the floor, sobbing. All I could think was, "I'm losing another child."

I stumbled into the shower, where I sobbed uncontrollably. I was going to have a panic attack or hyperventilate, so I decided to start thanking God for anything I could think of... the shower, the bathroom, the hot water. As my breath started to slow down, I continued — and as I concentrated on being grateful for the baby, for my time with him, for his mother, and family — my breathing returned to normal and my mind finally cleared. As long as I stayed focused on being thankful, the hysteria ceased, and a supernatural calm took its place. I even told myself it would be a privilege to introduce this precious little one to his grandmother for the first time.

I stepped out of the shower, dressed the baby, and was packing a little bag of things to send with him when I heard a tentative knock at the door.

"Everything ready?" The social worker glanced quickly around the apartment. She was obviously concerned about the delicate situation and how I was going to react.

His grandmother's eyes widened with joy as I placed Michael in her arms. Smiling, I told them about his eating and sleeping schedule, and gave them his things. When they left, the social worker looked hugely relieved.

It was evening when Jack finally returned. His worried eyes scanned the apartment until he found my listless form on the couch.

"He's gone," I cried, reaching out.

Jack knelt, took me in his arms and said, "I know." He told me he'd had strong feelings all day that the baby would not be here when he returned home.

I'd cared for, prayed over, and loved that little boy for only ten days — but losing him tapped into a hidden reservoir of grief from previous miscarriages and threw me into a potentially dangerous melt-down. The act of giving thanks was the life preserver that popped me back above the emotional water line and enabled me to complete the difficult task of giving Michael up graciously.

When God said, "Give thanks for everything," he wasn't kidding. I couldn't be incapacitated by fear and anxiety and be thankful at the same time. The simple act of giving thanks threw a switch in my brain that gave me the ability and strength I needed to do the impossible with grace.

After Michael left, I was able to fully grieve all the little ones that had passed through my life up to that point. Continuing to be thankful enabled me to love and care for several more foster children on their way to permanent placements with family members.

Then, on Labor Day, 1990, the phone rang... "We have a newborn little girl that needs immediate placement."

We named her Zoe. Two years later we finalized the adoption — but she was ours from the very beginning. She was absolutely perfect.

~Jenny Estes

Taketh and Giveth

All misfortune is but a stepping stone to fortune.
~Henry David Thoreau

Aaron, our three-year old, was snug in his bed. Although it was late on a weeknight, Aaron's father, Todd, and I had just retired for the night. I was drifting in that place right before deep sleep when I heard someone banging on the front door. In my half-sleep stupor, I thought someone had broken into the apartment. Todd was also having trouble comprehending why someone was pounding on the door at one in the morning and he stormed to the front room in a fury.

I stayed in the bedroom but noticed a peculiar orange-colored light spilling down the hall. I peered into the hallway just in time to see Todd open the front door. Our neighbors' apartment was directly across from ours. Their front door was also open and I saw their living room was completely engulfed in flames.

I ran into the living room and saw that the orange-colored light was coming from the patio. The flames had already spread across the roof of the apartment building and now burning embers were raining onto the patio. The neighbor charged in with a fire extinguisher and we all ran out to the patio in a futile attempt to save the apartment. When we opened the sliding glass doors, we could see that the awning over the patio was completely ablaze.

I ran to the room where Aaron was still sound asleep, grabbed his winter coat out of the closet, picked him up from his bed, and ran outside. I stood just outside the apartment in disbelief, in bare feet and wearing only a T-shirt. It was late October and cold. Todd had the foresight (and ignorance) to run back into the apartment to grab his car keys and wallet, my purse, a robe, a pair of jeans, and some tennis shoes for me. As he ran back out of the apartment he was already coughing and a trail of smoke followed behind him. Still in a daze, I handed him our son to hold while I dressed solemnly in front of our neighbors.

Two minutes later the entire roof of the building was engulfed in flames. The five families that lived there were all standing outside absorbing the shocking reality of the situation. Without neighbors to rescue or belongings to grab, there was nothing to do but watch our homes go up in flames. The night was cold but the fire was so intense that it was too hot to stand close to the building. My son, however, began to shiver. There was another neighbor with a little boy a few months younger than my own. I motioned to her and we put both of our boys in Todd's truck, turned on the heat and turned on some music to drown out the noises outside. I found a few toys lying on the floorboard and got the boys interested in playing before I gently closed the door and turned back to what used to be my home.

> *In order to be blessed with my sincerest desires, I had to be stripped of the things that made me too comfortable.*

This was the first place that I actually called "home" since I left my parents' house. Before that I had a dingy apartment with rude neighbors and bills I could barely manage. This apartment, however, was full of sunlight and cheer, with friendly neighbors. I loved coming home each day. I had managed my finances and was living well. My son had a room full of toys, I had a gorgeously furnished living room and dining room, my kitchen was fully stocked, and there was a patio that I had made quite cozy.

But now my home was burning, with thick black curls of smoke rising from the tall flames. I knew my neighbors felt the same way because most of us, even the men, were in tears at some point during the night. It wasn't just the loss of material possessions that made us weep, it was the loss of a sense of self—of home. Everything we owned, everything we had worked so hard for, everything we knew to be ours was being destroyed before our very eyes. Our throats closed up, our eyes watered, and our hearts ached.

Eventually, the fire trucks arrived. The sirens and commotion seemed dizzying at first but then the chaos became comforting as it took our attention away from the flames. I tried to talk to my neighbors, but it was too much to take in at once. I stood off by myself near the truck that held our son and the neighbor's boy, away from the firefighters and other neighbors. Todd followed and comforted me. Standing there, I remember it as if I had taken a picture. He put his arm around me and I held on to him, partly because I was so cold and partly because I was so sad. I cried a lot.

We left the scene shortly after the firefighters arrived and took shelter at Todd's apartment. I couldn't sleep that night and I got up to go for a walk and clear my head. As the fog of grief lifted, I was overwhelmed by a sense of gratitude. I was thankful for my family, thankful for my neighbors, thankful that everyone had escaped the building uninjured, thankful for my faith. I had a talk with God that night and I said, "I don't know what I'm supposed to do next but I trust that you'll show me."

Over the next few days I received many well wishes, many condolences, many donations of clothing and toys. But the conversation that changed my life was with my best friend's husband, a mortgage loan officer. He asked me if I had considered buying a house. I explained that I couldn't afford one. He asked if he could run my information to see what I could afford. I agreed but quickly dismissed the idea and went back to grieving my loss.

When my son had been born, I knew that I wanted him to grow up in a house. I set a goal for myself to own a home within four years. The weekend of the fire, I came to terms with the fact that my finances wouldn't allow me to achieve my dream. The realization was crushing to my morale and I hesitantly accepted the fact that I would have to live in my apartment for another few years.

A few hours after my phone call with the loan officer the phone rang and I received news that I never expected. My credit was good enough for a substantial home loan. I'm not usually an animated person, but that day I screamed into the phone and thanked him profusely. By the end of that week I found a buyer's agent and was looking at houses.

It took three months of searching for the perfect home in the perfect neighborhood at the perfect price — but I found it. A mile down the road from the home where I had grown up, my son would grow up in his own house.

I purchased my first home a few months before the original deadline I set for myself when my son was born. In order to be blessed with my sincerest desires, I had to be stripped of the things that made me too comfortable. I lost my apartment and found my dream.

~Simone Adams

80

A Journey to Myself

When you are compassionate with yourself, you trust
your soul, which you let guide your life. Your
soul knows the geography of your destiny
better than you do.
~John O'Donohue

L ife is a very curious thing. With all its "busyness", its ups and downs and its both beautiful and sorrowful moments, we rarely seem to have time to stop and think. Yet, we are supposed to be here on a journey of self-awareness, seeking to find comfort in our own skins and to fully know our most authentic selves. Sometimes it takes a mishap, an unfortunate situation or even life-threatening illness to force us to take the time away from the hustle and bustle to focus on this journey.

I always say that every hardship I have experienced in this life came with a silver lining. In this particular case, nearly succumbing to HIV in its latest stage with an AIDS diagnosis, I was finally granted the gift of time. It was time to step back, or in my case, spend a few months in bed recovering, to re-evaluate my life and everything in it. Surviving a close brush with death has a way of truly affecting you on so many levels and turns all that you thought you knew into nonsense.

Having to fight my way back from near death was no easy feat. I had a rare form of pneumonia and had lost a dramatic amount of weight. Wracked with fevers as high as 104 degrees and suffering from allergic reactions to all my medications, things looked very bleak.

Every day was touch and go, and every day I gave thanks when I woke up. I tried to wrap my head around how all this could be happening to me and realized that deep down inside, if I were to survive, that something beautiful must come from this.

I was determined to fight for my life and swore that if I were granted a second chance, I would give my all to make a difference in any way I could. Months of bed rest gave me plenty of time to re-evaluate my life. I read as much as I could and I stumbled upon a beautiful saying from the gorgeous actress Audrey Hepburn. She once said, "As you grow older, you will discover that you have two hands, one for helping yourself, the other for helping others." This resonated deeply within me, and while recovering and growing stronger I suddenly knew my reason for surviving.

> *By looking upon my illness with gratitude for its gift of time and focus, I ended up finding myself.*

I decided to volunteer as soon as I was able with a local nonprofit that did work in the field of HIV/AIDS. It dealt with the integrative process of wellness, dealing with the mind, body and spirit of those infected/affected by HIV/AIDS. By participating in their programs I learned so very much. In a world that had deemed those of us infected as unworthy, tainted and untouchable, I began to see the opposite in the reflection of my fellow "family" members. I worked with people from all walks of life, learning quickly that this virus did not discriminate. Stereotypes fell quickly by the wayside.

As my strength grew so did my capacity for volunteer tasks. Speaking to classrooms of children and young adults, heading various fundraising events, and working one on one with the newly diagnosed I saw so much beauty in a world that wanted to forget us! Each person, from a sixty-eight-year-old grandmother who lost her husband and learned she had AIDS in the same day, to a twelve-year-old boy who was born with HIV — I was able to see myself in each of them. In them I saw that I was still very much worthy of love, that I had many gifts to offer the world, and that I would overcome the stigma and prejudice that this virus breeds.

Working with others, I allowed myself to find self-forgiveness, to be vulnerable, and to open up to others. I realized that I was merely existing prior to my diagnosis, and that through my service to others I had finally found my most authentic self! Life suddenly made so much sense.

In the nine years since my diagnosis and my fight back from the brink of death, my life has changed dramatically. I have never felt more comfortable in my own skin. The simple act of giving back to others brought me home to myself. I now am a tester, counselor, and linkage to care specialists in the field of HIV/AIDS and have gone on to receive titles such as Activist of the Year several years in a row and Volunteer of the Year. These awards mean the world to me, but more than that, I have received gifts that cannot be measured by any earthly means. By looking upon my illness with gratitude for its gift of time and focus, I ended up finding myself, the very flawed but beautiful loving spirit that I am at my core.

~Daniel J. Mangini

81

When Life's a Puzzle

*We can complain because rose bushes have thorns, or
rejoice because thorn bushes have roses.*
~President Abraham Lincoln

For months we'd been thinking about how to celebrate two very special events: our wedding anniversary and the birthdays of two of our grandchildren — which were all on the same date. In the past, we'd always gotten together for a big celebration here in sunny Southern California. But this year my oldest son and his family had moved to the northern part of the state. So my husband Don and I decided to drive up to their new home and celebrate together with them on our first real vacation in years.

My head whirled as I imagined all the fun things we could do on the trip north — plus all the fun things we'd get to do with our grandchildren when we arrived there. After all, now that Don and I were both finally retired, we could take all the time we wanted on this trip and enjoy it to the fullest!

Then, just two days before we were to leave, great storms swooped across our state. Soon, between mudslides and flooding, all roads north were closed between us and our destination. There went our trip. But at least, I told myself, Don and I could celebrate our anniversary together at a nice restaurant here in our own town.

Then those pounding storms hit our area as well. In just a few hours our normally quiet back yard had turned into a lake — with the water level reaching all to way to our back door!

Just like that, we were in emergency mode.

Now, instead of dressing up in our finest for an evening out, we slopped around in muddy boots and heavy rain slickers. Instead of visiting amusement parks and museums with our grandsons, we were desperately digging drainage ditches. Cold sandwiches replaced gala dinners. In place of gaily-wrapped presents, we carried concrete blocks and sacks of sand.

And then our long-awaited anniversary arrived. What a bummer! Don was out braving the pounding rain and flooded streets to look for more emergency supplies at our local stores. I was down on my knees scrubbing mud, sand, and who-knows-what-else off our kitchen floor.

After a while, Don returned. Dripping all over the just-scrubbed floor, he set down the emergency supplies he had just purchased. Then he pulled a crumpled bag out from under his slicker. Grinning, he announced, "Happy anniversary, dear!" and handed me a box of chocolates, a card, a rose, and a jigsaw puzzle!

> *Until, piece-by-piece, they all came together to form a glorious mosaic of love.*

I stared at the picture on the cover of the puzzle box: a wild assortment of candy hearts. You know — the kind that say "Kiss me quick" and "Be my Valentine."

He grinned. "I thought we could do the puzzle together. Something just for fun."

With storms raging all around us, threatening to flood our home? When for the very first time in our grandchildren's lives we couldn't be with them on their birthdays?

That evening my husband cleared off our coffee table and began sorting the puzzle pieces. I joined in just to be polite. After all, it was our anniversary. And before we went to bed that night, the border was complete, and the box of chocolates half-empty.

For three days our coffee table was strewn with those tiny pieces of cardboard. Until, piece-by-piece, they all came together to form a glorious mosaic of love.

And other puzzles solved, as well.

After all, if we had made the trip north when we first planned, and had been gone when the storm hit here, our home would have been ruined. Instead, by being forced to stay here, we were able to save it. Now that the danger was over, we could safely make new travel plans.

Indeed, when we finally did make that trip north, not only were the roads open and the sun shining again — but we took along a little bag of candy hearts with us to celebrate. And our grandchildren loved them.

~Bonnie Compton Hanson

The Power of Gratitude

Paying It Forward

No kind action ever stops with itself. One kind action leads to another. Good example is followed. A single act of kindness throws out roots in all directions, and the roots spring up and make new trees. The greatest work that kindness does to others is that it makes them kind themselves.
~Amelia Earhart

82

The Waver

Let us be grateful to people who make us happy,
they are the charming gardeners who make
our souls blossom.
~Marcel Proust

My husband, son and I had recently moved to a small coastal community in Washington State. One cold, rainy morning after my husband left for work at the dental office I decided to go into town to shop. I packed up my toddling son, placed him in his car seat, slipped a DVD into the player for him, got in the driver's seat and away we went.

A few minutes later, I noticed a person in a big overcoat walking a large black Lab down the side of the road. As I got closer, I raised my hand and waved at the nameless person. A little surprised, the person waved back. I smiled. He smiled. It happened in a split second, but it was a moment of clear communication.

Coming back from town, I came upon a bearded older gent who was ambling down the road with a small driftwood log in each hand. I raised my hand and he raised a log. Smiles crossed both our faces.

Over the next five years, I waved at everyone. I'm not sure what they thought of me. They might have been calling me that "crazy lady who waves at everybody," but it didn't matter. It was fun, and it made me feel more connected to my new community.

Then, one November afternoon, my beloved husband died. That

Paying It Forward |

day I stopped waving at people. On the drives to town I focused on the road in front of me. I kept my hands to myself and listened to my son talking in the back seat. I had to deal with the reality of being a widow.

Many weeks later, a dark stranger raised his or her hand and beckoned to me. I waved weakly back and then I smiled. The person smiled. I couldn't tell you if it was a man or a woman, an old person or a young one, but I realized in that moment that I had to start reaching out again. I had a seven-year-old to bring up. He needed a mom who was connected and awake and living in the present moment.

> *What I realized was that the more people I waved at, the better I felt.*

On the next trip, I started waving again. I initiated the waves. I had to force myself to do it, to crawl out of my depression and loneliness, but I did it. That was an immense step forward.

I didn't know most of the people I waved to. Some became regulars. Others were people I'd met along my treks. What I realized was that the more people I waved at, the better I felt. Within weeks, I had returned to living a life full of zest.

One day at the grocery store I heard, "You're the one." I ignored the voice and continued to locate the perfect bag of tiny red apples. "It's you, isn't it?" the voice continued.

I couldn't figure out if I was the one being addressed. I placed a sack of apples in my basket.

"You're the waver, aren't you?"

A hand came to rest on my shoulder. I turned to acknowledge the voice. "What?"

"You're the one who waves at me in the mornings, aren't you?"

"I don't know. Am I?"

"You drive a silver van. You must take a child to school in the morning. You always seem to drive by about the same time each day."

I took a quick look at the lady. I didn't know her.

"I'm the lady that works in the flower garden. You know, on I street?"

I didn't recognize her or remember waving at her, but I said, "Oh, yeah."

"I have to tell you a story."

I whispered, "Okay."

"A few weeks ago, I was standing in my garden allowing my rake to hold me up. I'd just been told that my baby sister was dying of cancer. I didn't want to work my garden anymore. I didn't see any reason to. Ella was the reason I had the garden. She bought the lot for me so that I'd have something to do when my husband went golfing. After my husband died, gardening became my passion."

My mind jumped to my dead husband. It hadn't been that long ago that he'd come home with two large rhododendrons for my birthday. He planted them in the front yard and said, "They're deep red. They'll be so pretty when spring comes." I sighed. He never got to see them bloom.

"Anyway," she said, as she dropped her hand to her side. "I was ready to call it quits. I didn't have any reason to tend my garden. With my sister dying, who would I give flowers to? Then you drove by. You waved at me and smiled. I let go of the rake with my right hand and waved back. Then I smiled."

"Thanks for waving," I said, as I started to push my cart away.

She placed her hand on the handle of the basket and stopped me from moving. "The next day you did the same thing. By the third day, I was expecting your intrusion. On the fourth day, I got the call that my sister had died, and you weren't there."

This time I took a close look at her face. Her immensely beautiful foggy blue eyes, her tawny, craggy cheeks, her pursed and tinted lips. I did know this lady, but from where?

"A week later," she went on, "I was out in the garden ripping out my just bloomed plants and throwing them on a small fire. I didn't have the gumption to till the land anymore. It felt like everyone in my life was gone. I'd worked the land long enough."

Tears welled in the corners of her eyes. "Then you drove by and waved. I stood up and waved back. As I started to bend down and grab another plant, you backed up, stopped and rolled down your window. You said, 'I just wanted to tell you how much it means to me to see your flowers in bloom. You're out here rain or shine. It lets me know that no matter what changes in my life, your flowers will always be there to brighten my day.'"

She paused for a moment. "I needed to hear that my passion made a difference."

I reached over and touched her slender shoulder. "I needed to hear your story."

Tears filled both of our eyes as we bowed our heads in understanding.

I still wave at strangers, but now I'm more likely to stop and say, "Hi," and make a friend.

~Candace Carteen

83

Possibility and Promise

In helping others, we shall help ourselves, for
whatever good we give out completes the circle
and comes back to us.
~Flora Edwards

I looked at the bronze plaque on the scholarship wall. I ran my fingers across the surface and touched the raised letters. My promise to pay it forward was now a reality. It was all made possible because of an incredible act of kindness with extraordinary consequences.

How was this even possible? College was never in the picture for my family. We struggled financially. It was a task just to get through one day at a time. But a miraculous detour forever changed my life....

It began on a Sunday evening in the summer of 1970. I was fifteen, the oldest of five boys and three girls. Dad was off somewhere with our car. Mom had to catch the bus to work the night shift. I was upstairs helping my siblings get ready for bed while we danced around enjoying our favorite rock and roll music.

We didn't hear the car pull up. Dad charged in and slammed the front door. The house shook. We jumped in terror.

"Lawrence, turn that crap off. Get down here... now!"

"Just a minute," I answered.

"Now!" he yelled.

"As soon as we finish praying," I shouted.

More doors slammed. I did my best to shut out his swearing.

Something shattered.

We knelt and prayed. "Now I lay me… God bless Mommy, Daddy… Please make Dad stop."

I hugged my brothers and sisters good night.

"Be careful," Jimmy said.

I crept down the stairs.

"What the hell did you do all day? You worthless punk," Dad yelled.

"I cut grass and went to Norm's Studio and cleaned. At least I'm working." Anger clouded my judgment. My blood boiled. I did everything I could to help Mom with the bills, while Dad got drunk.

"Don't talk to me that way." He slapped me across the face and slammed me into the wall. Once again, I was the target of his rage. Once again, I was beaten. Once again, I ran out of the house. In a way, I felt fortunate that I was the only one he seemed to hate. He never hit any of my siblings. At least I knew they'd be safe.

I ran through the woods to the park. In the mid-summer evening there was still some daylight. Back then Mt. Lebanon Park was the place to be. Every night hundreds of kids from all over Pittsburgh hung out there.

The park, my friends, and rock and roll music were my safe havens.

I sat on a swing at the park's edge. I tried to hide my tears when I saw Reverend Bill walking up the hill toward me. I hadn't met him before but I'd heard he was some kind of minister who helped the kids at the park. Everyone liked him and trusted him.

"What's the matter?"

I opened my heart and sobbed my way through the details. "My dad lost his job years ago and spends all day watching TV. My mom and I work hard to pay the bills. He steals our money and gets drunk at night. He comes home smashed and destroys everything we own… and whales on me.

"Mom struggles to keep the house and put food on the table. She works nights as a keypunch operator so she can take care of us during the day. She retouches photos and keeps books at home, to earn what she can.

"Me, and the next few siblings in age, have worked from our earliest years. We give our money to Mom to help in any way. We wake every day at 5 a.m. to deliver papers, go to school, then work additional jobs into the evening." I resented the fact that we worked while Dad did nothing. He was supposed to be the male breadwinner, not me.

Bill broke in. "Why don't you come down and have something to eat?"

He led me to a picnic pavilion where about twenty adults congregated. They did their best to make me feel comfortable. They invited me to come back any Sunday.

Over time I learned that they were a group of people who shared a deep concern for doing good. They broke away from conventional churches and used their donations to improve the quality of life for the community. They called themselves the No Church Church.

> *"Just do the same for someone else someday,"* Mr. Miller said.

One of their chief concerns was youth. They even paid Reverend Bill's salary so he could be there for the kids in the park, many of whom were troubled.

Next to my mom, the folks in the NCC had the biggest hearts of anyone I ever knew. They took me under their wings and encouraged me to believe in good and do for others. I learned to love those people and looked forward to Sundays.

During my senior year they insisted I apply for college. I kept making excuses not to because I knew we couldn't afford it. I was too embarrassed to share my plight with anyone but Bill. My mom juggled bills every month. Our heat got shut off during the coldest winter nights. We lit the house by candlelight when the electricity got disconnected. We scraped by with whatever food we could afford. When our house would go up for sheriff's sale, we would sneak out at night and tear down the signs that showed our address. Mom didn't want our family to be shamed through the neighborhood. Somehow, we managed to keep the house.

Finally, in May, Bill sat me down and made me apply to college. A few weeks later I got a letter from the University of Pittsburgh at Bradford. They accepted me into their "Trial by Fire Program," which was starting on July 5, 1972, just a few weeks away.

We couldn't afford college so I tossed the letter.

Bill asked me if I'd heard anything yet.

"Yeah. What's it matter? I can't afford college."

At the next NCC supper, Mr. and Mrs. Miller asked me to stop by their house on Monday.

Monday night, I walked to the Miller's house. After a few minutes of conversation they handed me a check for tuition, books, room, and board for my first semester.

Tears filled my eyes. I couldn't believe it.

"Thank you! How can I ever repay you?"

"Just do the same for someone else someday," Mr. Miller said.

With the help of loans, grants, and many supplemental jobs, I graduated in 1980. I started a wonderful career and went on to teach at the University of Pittsburgh and Penn State. I took evening classes and earned a Ph.D. in 2000.

My dad and I became friends. He pulled himself out of his depression and got a job.

And now, on the scholarship wall at the University of Pittsburgh at Bradford, the plaque reads "Larry Rock 'n' Roll!!! Schardt Scholarship Fund — In appreciation for those dedicated to helping others — Paying it forward. Peace, Love, & Happiness."

~Larry Schardt

84

The Gratefuls

When one is thankful for the blessings in their life, they
are choosing to attract more positivity and abundance.
~Michael Austin Jacobs

T he nippy autumn air crept through the walls of the mountain cabin. I stood looking at the lone bag of pasta and the jar of mustard in the pantry. My stomach was rumbling and I wondered how long I could make the pasta last. I started to cry. I couldn't believe my life had spiraled so far out of control.

My husband had died and then I had been fleeced by two con artists, a shifty banker, and my own bad decisions. I lost everything and landed in a tiny, isolated summer cottage, unemployed, and 150 miles from my remaining friends. In the space of two years I had lost my husband, my Solara convertible, my art deco condo, two storage units holding all of my belongings, and most of my self-esteem. Even the red Chevy Cavalier I drove was on loan from the new boyfriend I met on Craigslist. My boyfriend was supportive, but he declined to get involved financially, on the basis that it would be empowering if I dug myself out of this hole.

The phone rang. I swallowed my tears and answered it. My food stamp application had been approved, and I could pick up my electronic benefits card the next day. I would have $200 every four weeks for food. $7.14 a day. A king's bounty. A miracle. I hung up the phone and sobbed, relief mixing with self-recrimination. I finally allowed myself to hope that I just might make it through.

It was time for me to make a change. As I drove the fifty miles to civilization, shifting in and out of neutral to save gas by coasting down the hills, I remembered Oprah talking about gratitude. Every night she'd list ten things that she was grateful for, and it was having a positive impact on her thoughts. On the drive home, with $98.65 worth of groceries from Grocery Outlet, I decided that my thoughts were pretty much the only thing I had control over at this point.

> *The Gratefuls made me feel my life wasn't all bad, and with that came hope for the future.*

And so it began, my lists of "Gratefuls." Every night when I crawled into bed under the green silk of the down comforter that somehow had stayed with me, I would search my day for ten things to be grateful for.

Those first weeks were challenging. My life had been stripped bare. My prospects seemed dismal because I couldn't afford to refill my Prozac prescription and was going through unsupervised withdrawal. So I began with the basics.

"I'm glad I can see." I was, I realized, surprised to feel something positive. "I am grateful I can speak. I am grateful I can hear." Really basic.

Stuck, I looked at the overflowing bookshelves. "I'm grateful I have so many books to read."

"I'm grateful for my dog." Always for my dog.

My boyfriend helped with the Grateful lists and he used precious cell phone minutes to ask, "So, what are you grateful for today?" I started looking for things to add to my nightly list.

"I watched the autumn leaves fall today," I told him. "I sat on the porch, breathing the fresh cedar air and I realized how beautiful it is up here."

"Is that one grateful, or two?" he asked.

"Three," I answered. "A yellow-rumped warbler perched on the railing and watched me for a bit, then gave me a song and flew away."

"Yellow-rumped warbler?" He was amused.

"Oh, wait, that's four. I found a book on birds."

"How wonderful," he said, far away but getting closer to my heart.

Slowly, I began feeling again. The Gratefuls made me feel my life wasn't all bad, and with that came hope for the future. There were more trials to come and it would be another full year before I was employed again. But I was on the right path at last.

A few months later, my boyfriend came with movers to rescue me from the snow and drama that arrived with the cabin's owner. We moved into an apartment together in a new town, a fresh start for both of us. One day I actually put more than ten items on the Grateful List. Visits to a therapist cleared my head; then there were job interviews, and then a job offer! It was in a small town another 100 miles away, but I was grateful to be working in the software industry again, grateful to have a steady income, grateful to get off food stamps. I misted up the first time I was able to pay for all the groceries I wanted.

There were setbacks to be sure, like going to the grocery store and finding out that the IRS had frozen my account. Leaving the store without being able to pay for the food brought back the shame and despair that I thought I had left behind. Although a phone call sorted it all out, that night the Gratefuls went back to basics. Eyesight, my dog, my hearing. But in making my list I noticed I was far from my last bag of pasta.

Time passed. The economy rebounded. I quit the job I hated in the small town that didn't accept me. Thrilled to be heading home, we went for a celebratory Starbucks. As I sipped my $5 double vanilla latte, I overheard a social worker filling out an intake form with a woman in crisis. As the woman detailed her difficulties with a quiet despair, I realized that just one year ago I had been as desperate as she was now. Stunned, I pulled all the twenties out of my wallet and went over to her table.

"I'm sorry, I couldn't help overhearing. A year ago I was in your situation, but today my life has turned around. I want to tell you there is hope for your future. I want to give this to you because, well, because I can."

She stammered out "thank you," staring at the money in her hand as I walked away. We both had tears in our eyes. That night, my list of Gratefuls was very, very long.

Today I am financially secure, and still with the same boyfriend, who routinely shows up on my Gratefuls list. He was right, by the way, about giving me room to find my own way out of the mess. I now believe I can conquer anything. I am more than grateful—I am content.

I don't talk much about that dark night of my soul, unless someone who is depressed or struggling asks for advice. I tell them a bit of my story and about the power of being grateful, even when the way looks dark. I'm surprised at how quickly people dismiss gratitude, as if it couldn't possibly work. There were other factors in my recovery, of course. The economy turned around. Therapy helped. I am back home, surrounded by people I love in a city I understand. But there is no doubt in my mind that it is the Gratefuls that changed my life from a destitute widow to a happy woman living her dream of being a full-time writer.

Tonight, the Gratefuls themselves will top my list.

~TC Currie

85

Facing My Fears

In about the same degree as you are helpful,
you will be happy.
~Karl Reiland

"NO WAY! There is no way. I can't do that. Actually, I CAN do it but I don't WANT to do it. Never!" That was my first response to an assignment given to me by my boss. I am the senior editor at Chicken Soup for the Soul and my boss was asking me to be in charge of a future *Chicken Soup for the Soul* book. To oversee all aspects of it and come up with a complete manuscript that would be turned into a book. That is not an unusual request. My boss is Amy Newmark, the publisher of Chicken Soup for the Soul and she had asked that of me many times before. But this time, the book title she was putting me in charge of was *Chicken Soup for the Soul: Living with Alzheimer's & Other Dementias*.

The reason I had such a strong reaction to Amy's request was that my mother had died a little more than a year before we started production on the book and she had suffered from Alzheimer's disease for seven years before that. While we did have caregivers to help us out, my family and I had taken care of her all that time. It was a very long time. Alzheimer's is a hideous disease. Hideous! It takes the person you love away from you a little bit at a time, one day at a time, until there is no one left. No one at all! It is very emotional, stressful and difficult taking care of someone who suffers from Alzheimer's, watching them disappear. My mom and I were very close and for the last few years of her life, she didn't know me. She didn't know any of us. She didn't even know who she was. It was a terrible time in my life. And now I was being asked to relive all those years, all those memories, all the phases of the disease, all over again. No way!

I talked to D'ette Corona, the associate publisher of Chicken Soup for the Soul and my very close friend, and told her how I felt. She spoke to Amy on my behalf and offered to take over the project. She wanted to protect me. Even though D'ette would have done an amazing job, Amy said she wanted me to do it. Somehow Amy knew that even though it would be extremely difficult for me, I was the right person to be in charge and oversee the project. Who, on our staff, knew more about the disease than I did? Who would know if a story submitted for the title was accurate about the stages and symptoms of the disease? Who would be able to relate to the stories better than I could? If not me… then who?

> *I am grateful that I could take my family's pain and help the families coming up behind us as they travel the same road that we did.*

And so I took a deep breath, jumped in, and got to work. We started collecting stories for the title and they flooded in — literally thousands and thousands of stories. They covered each and every stage of the disease, from questioning what was wrong with someone, to diagnosis, to the end of life. There were stories from family members and friends of people who had Alzheimer's; stories from caregivers; and heart wrenching stories from people who actually suffer from the disease and were still able to write about how they felt. How powerful all those stories were.

I read all of the stories that were submitted… all of them. What a difficult job that was. The stories were so personal. I cried a lot. Those stories brought back so many painful memories of what my family and I had gone through. But I laughed too. Not *at* the people but *with* the people. You have to keep your sense of humor in order to keep your sanity and there really are some funny moments. I was working closely with the people at the Alzheimer's Association since the royalties from the book go directly to them. Together we narrowed the submissions down to less than 200. Then Amy selected the final 101 stories that were included in the book.

Alzheimer's disease is such an important topic and a book topic that had been requested by *Chicken Soup for the Soul* readers over and over again. After almost a year in production, *Chicken Soup for the Soul: Living with Alzheimer's & Other Dementias* was released on April 22, 2014. On April 23, 2014, only one day after its release, the book had sold out on Amazon and a second printing, as large as the initial print run, was ordered! What a terrific response. The feedback was truly amazing. Over and over again we heard people say that they had felt so alone before they read the book and now they felt like they were part of a community. They were comforted to know that others were going through the same things, and they were learning valuable advice from the people who were "ahead" of them in the progression of the disease.

Looking back at the experience, I know Amy was right to put me in charge of the book. While it was very emotional and very difficult for me to relive everything that we went through, it was also cathartic. It helped me heal. It helped take away my pain. I feel that my contribution to that book and my work on that book was a tribute to my mom. I was even asked to give a few speeches about the book at Alzheimer's Association events. What an honor. I know my mom, a university professor and therapist, would have been so proud of me for helping other people with this disease. So thank you, Amy. I am forever grateful to you for doing what you thought, and knew, would be right. I am grateful that I could take my family's pain and help the families coming up behind us as they travel the same road that we did.

~Barbara LoMonaco

86

Not Just a Cup of Coffee

People never forget that helping hand especially
when times are tough.
~Catherine Pulsifer

My husband and I were out picking up candy, chips and some cold drinks — all the things that we would need for snuggling under warm blankets and watching movies while the temperature outside dropped below zero. On the way out of the parking lot, we noticed a man standing on a patch of grass, holding a sign. The sign didn't say anything about needing money for gas or food. It didn't say anything about trying to get anywhere. It simply said, "Help would be appreciated."

We didn't have any cash on us, so my husband rolled down his window, picked up the bag of snacks and handed it out the window. I shivered as the wind blew cold air into the car.

Knowing what we handed over wouldn't be enough, my husband and I pulled across the street into a fast food parking lot. We parked, walked back through the cold and approached the man with the sign. He looked at us for a moment as if we were crazy, but he followed us to the restaurant.

The man told us that he was trying to save his money for some gloves and candles rather than buying food that day. My heart broke. We explained that we wanted to buy him a meal and he should pick out anything he wanted from the menu. It was our treat. He said he always wanted to try a double cheeseburger, but had never gotten the chance. So we bought him a double cheeseburger, large fries, large soda and a hot coffee.

The total was around nine dollars. It was a drop in the bucket for us, but the world to him. He even offered to share his coffee with us because "it had to be cold walking over." He was worried about *us* being cold.

After he finished eating, we went back to the store and bought him hand warmers, blankets and a few candles. He said he was a veteran who had come home to find his wife with someone else. He had lost his apartment after losing his job. Since then he'd lived in a tent because the shelters were full and he wanted to leave room for the women and children. I couldn't help but give him a hug as he thanked us and headed away.

What he didn't know was that my husband had been without a job for six months.

I think we saw that man in passing a couple more times. We would wave or hand over a couple of dollars if we had any cash on us. Then one day, he just wasn't there. A year passed and we didn't see him again.

One day I went grocery shopping with my husband. We decided that we should treat ourselves on the way back and headed to the fast food place. We heard a voice say "hi" while we were looking up at the menu. It sounded familiar.

There, behind the counter, was that man. He had been working there for eight months and was soon going to be promoted. He was preparing to get an apartment nearby, too.

We talked about the weather and about how his life was going before a line began forming behind us. I said we should probably pick something and get out of the way. He said, "I already took care of it."

He set down a tray in front of us, with two of everything: double cheeseburgers, large fries, large drinks and coffees. I picked it up, thanked him and walked away before I started crying. What he didn't know was that my husband had been without a job for six months and it would be another two weeks before he received any money from his new job. We were down to our last twenty-five dollars. Money was tight and that fast food was going to be a treat. Those nine-dollar meals may not have meant much to him anymore, but they meant a lot to me. I sat down at the table, looked at the food and smiled. I normally don't like coffee. I never drink the stuff. However, this was not just another cup of coffee.

~Charlotte Triplett

87

The Sewing Club

*One can never pay in gratitude: one can only pay "in
kind" somewhere else in life.*
~Anne Morrow Lindbergh

I was raised in a multi-generational matriarchal home, steeped
in poverty. Once a month, we went with Mom to the local dis-
tribution center and stood in line for our allotment of "surplus
commodities" — flour, canned meat, peanut butter, lard, and
powdered non-fat milk. There was never enough money for basics,
so asking for anything extra, such as movies or school activities, was
out of the question.

We knew we were poor, but we had never known any other way
of life, so it didn't seem to bother us. My brothers each got two new
T-shirts and two pairs of jeans every school year, which they would
share so it seemed like twice as many clothes. As the only girl, my
clothing would be fashioned from hand-me-downs or by tearing apart
a shirtwaist dress with several yards of fabric in the skirt, and sewing
it into a couple of new dresses. I learned to sew on my grandmother's
treadle Singer sewing machine at a very young age and was quite
proficient at making my own clothes.

In junior high, all the girls took Home Economics classes, but
the sewing classes bored me. We would spend weeks on an apron, or
putting a zipper in a simple A-line skirt. I could knock out an entire
outfit in an evening if I wanted! Additionally, it was a real strain for
my mother to provide the necessary fabric for the Home Economics

projects, and it was always of lesser quality than most of the other girls' fabric. I never tried out for any of the teams or clubs, such as cheerleading or band, because uniforms and instruments were too expensive, so I felt excluded from most activities and had little in common with other students.

In seventh grade, however, that all changed due to the kindness and generosity of some mothers of the "rich kids." These women formed an after-school Sewing Club, to which one had to be invited. Unbeknownst to the dozen or so members, you wouldn't be invited unless you were poor! These women made it seem like an honor to belong, and the only requirement was a desire to sew. We could make as much clothing as we wanted and it was all free! The women took us to a real fabric store — my mom could only afford the cheap fabric at the local TG&Y five and dime store — and taught us about fabric selection and how to use a pattern that wasn't cut from newspaper. They taught us how to tweak a design to make it not look like a cookie-cutter dress. They fed our creative minds as well as our tummies, making sure we took a sumptuous snack break while they taught since dinner was often pretty sparse at home.

> *We could make as much clothing as we wanted, and it was all free!*

We held a fashion show, attended by teachers, but no other students, so we wouldn't feel intimidated. I won recognition for a dress I created in this club, and it fueled my passion for sewing.

My family made yet another move and I went to yet another school, but I never forgot those women and their many gifts.

Fast-forward four decades, and I finally had the chance to pay it forward. As a volunteer, I started teaching sewing to foster teens through a local foster agency, and then through the Child Welfare Services. I bought a few more sewing machines and moved on to a family resources center, teaching impoverished women how to alter or re-purpose used clothing from thrift stores, just as I had done so many years ago.

I have taught sewing to men and women from every walk of life, and children as young as four years old, as I continue to seek more ways to make a difference in my little corner of the world. I have taught in public schools, senior centers, homeless shelters, after-school programs, and community assistance programs for the poor. Along the way, I have shared my story of the Sewing Club hundreds of times, paying tribute to those kind women of so long ago. I wish they could know the huge impact they had on the life of a lonely, impoverished seventh grader at West Mesa Junior High School so many years ago.

~Conni Delinger

88

Trifle or Treasure?

*Nothing exalts the soul or gives it a sheer sense of
buoyancy and victory so much as being used to change
the lives of other people.*
~E. Stanley Jones, Victorious Living

Since 1997, I have traveled to Bolivia every year as a member of my church's Volunteers in Mission team. My first trip was the life-changer — the one that opened my eyes and my heart to the world beyond the self-centered one where I lived. The experience changed my values and my lifestyle.

I return each year for a refresher course in what is really important in life, taught by people who live a simple, hard, but thankful life. Every year is another lesson that deepens my faith and makes the scriptures a reality. Quiet moments with gentle people reveal lessons I need to learn and are a reminder to live what I have learned.

In April 2012, our team traveled to Capayqui, a remote village at 11,000 feet on top of a mountain in the Andes. In our many years of work in Bolivia, Capayqui was the most difficult village to reach and the poorest we visited. Even though it was only 110 miles from La Paz, it took twelve long hours to get there.

I served as an interpreter for the team, using my Spanish language skills in ways I had never imagined. I also managed the pharmacy and dispensed basic medicines to our patients. I explained how and when to take them in Spanish, which was often translated to Aymara, the native language.

The pharmacy in Capayqui was in an old adobe brick structure with a leaky thatched roof. The warped wood floor was sagging. There was no electricity and therefore no heat or light. A patchwork of broken windowpanes let in the light — and also the cold air. A small, scarred table and two rustic benches displayed our inventory of medicines. The pharmacy doubled as our dining and meeting area, too.

Capayqui was lucky — they had a resident nurse, Bacilio, who would be similar to a physician's assistant in the U.S. He served seven other villages in the district, traveling by foot or motorcycle to see his patients.

Little things mean a lot when you don't have the big things in life.

Bacilio stood outside the pharmacy window as we worked. As I explained the prescriptions, he wrote each patient's name, age, diagnosis and prescription in a lined notebook for future reference. He wrote in small, labored penmanship with a pencil stub that he sharpened with a knife.

I watched how he struggled to write. I went to the bag of school supplies we had brought to leave with the local school. I found a small, plastic pencil sharpener — a trifle that we often throw away in our sophisticated, high-tech culture — and several pencils.

I returned to the window and said, "*Para ti, Bacilio.*"

His eyes grew huge when he saw the pencil sharpener and new pencils. "*Para mi?*" he asked.

"*Sí, para ayudarte con tu trabajo,*" (Yes, to help you with your work.)

"*Gracias, señora!*" he whispered, as he accepted my simple gift. He smiled as he slowly sharpened a new pencil. He was like a child enjoying the magic of a new toy.

Have you ever looked into someone's eyes and seen how deep his gratitude is? Little things mean a lot when you don't have the big things in life.

Bacilio was careful and meticulous with his new treasures. He placed the pencils and sharpener carefully in a small box at the end of each day and kept his pencil sharpened to a fine point. Writing became easier and faster for him. Our trifle had become a treasured tool.

The gift of an inexpensive, plastic pencil sharpener opened the door for a new friendship. Bacilio and I enjoyed conversations about our cultures, our lives and our God high in the Andes Mountains. When I left, I made sure Bacilio had his own personal stash of sharpeners, pencils and notebooks.

The experience of sharing something so simple and yet so valuable gave personal meaning to Saint Francis's eloquent words: "For it is in giving that we receive."

~Linda E. Allen

89

A Fan of Kindness

Not what we say about our blessings, but how we use
them, is the true measure of our thanksgiving.
~W.T. Purkiser

There aren't many things that faze teenage boys. They aren't shocked by television violence, video sex, or movie car crashes. They don't flinch at people eating live insects, wrestlers throwing chairs at each other, or characters exploding in blood-and-guts video games. Most young people I know aren't easily impressed by many things — an attitude that frustrates those who teach them. We educators have a lot of competition in getting the attention of our students.

That's especially true in a foreign language class. Most of the students are there because they have to be, and the majority of them never expect to use the language again. "Isn't this kinda like algebra?" one student asked me. "Do adults really use this stuff?"

That cynicism and lack of interest is one of the reasons I have enjoyed taking groups of high school students to Spain during summer vacations. I wanted the students who studied Spanish with me to be able to use their skills in Spain — reading street signs, watching TV, ordering lunch, talking to Spaniards. I hoped it would make their classroom lessons real and, in miraculous cases, encourage a few of them to take more Spanish.

One year I organized a trip to Toledo and Madrid; four colleagues and eighteen students from our all-boys school registered for our adventure. I'm certain the students were planning to get good looks at Spanish *chicas*, sneak tastes of sangria, and try McDonald's Big Macs in a foreign country. My plan, of course, was to show them all the things we had discussed in class.

They did meet some *señoritas*, try some sangria, and walk away unimpressed by Spanish Big Macs, but it was the history that kept their attention. They saw a Roman aqueduct in Segovia, one held together not by mortar but by the precise cutting of the stones. They climbed the narrow streets of Toledo, learning firsthand why this city on a hill would have made a safe capital city for Rome and for Spain. They admired the cathedrals and castles of Spain, marveling at the handiwork of people who never lived to see the fruits of their labors.

> *We saw the building of a friendship with no mortar save kindness.*

I knew the students had realized that the world is a bigger place than Toledo, Ohio, when one of them sat next to me and mumbled, "I feel so small." We were looking at the vast view from the door of the church at The Valley of the Fallen. The student mused, "All of these important things going on here — before I was even born. Castles and kings and explorers, and I never knew anything about them." His "wow" was soft and heartfelt.

That was quite a realization for a teenage boy! I knew then that the big attractions had impressed them, and that the trip had served its educational purpose. But we learned a more important lesson in a hospital in Toledo when we found ourselves watching one of our students being admitted. Ryan's discomfort had lasted for several hours, and we decided to take him to the hospital as a precaution, just in case he had eaten bad food or suffered from the heat.

We had permission to okay any medical procedure, but the Spanish physician preferred to talk to Ryan's parents, especially his dad, who was a physician. The diagnosis — after a long conversation made longer by the need for translation — was an inflamed appendix that needed to come out immediately. Ryan's middle-of-the-night surgery put us in contact with hospital personnel, from clerks to nurses to surgeons, almost none of whom spoke English. Their patience and kindness made a stressful situation easier to handle.

In the face of this emergency situation, we were especially touched by the actions of an older Spanish woman. Her husband was a patient in the other bed in Ryan's room, and she sat quietly as her husband slept after his own surgery.

The room was not air-conditioned despite temperatures of more than 100 degrees, and Ryan was confined to his bed, not permitted to eat or drink anything for the first twenty-four hours after surgery. He was clearly uncomfortable—hot, sick, and unable to communicate well with those who were taking care of him. We did our best to make him comfortable, applying cold compresses to his forehead and promising him that we would bring the coldest water we could find as soon as the doctor gave his okay.

The sweet Spanish *señora* watched as we took turns trying to entertain Ryan and take his mind off his situation. She saw us struggle with the coin-operated television on the wall, and probably didn't understand why Ryan wasn't too excited to watch a very old episode of *Bonanza* with English subtitles. She certainly didn't understand our attempts at jokes or appreciate our concern about how Ryan could feel comfortable on a bed that was a foot too short for his lanky frame.

But she knew what to do and her action was wonderfully soothing and reassuring. Watching us struggle with the wet compresses, she walked to Ryan's bedside with a shy smile. She opened her purse, took out an ornate Spanish fan, and used it to cool him. She encouraged me to sit down, then stood at Ryan's bedside for nearly thirty minutes, moving that fan back and forth over him, singly softly to him until he fell asleep. Then she handed the fan to me, saying I should keep it as a gift. "You have a new friend in Toledo," she told me.

What a lesson my students and I received! We were humbled to see how pleased she was to offer comfort to a stranger. We saw the building of a friendship with no mortar save kindness. We learned that the present (and the future) may well depend on the actions and attitudes of people who will never have palaces or parks named after them. No textbook or classroom lecture could ever make that point as strongly as that little Spanish *señora* with a fan.

Ryan is a doctor now, ten years after his week in a Spanish hospital. He was a student who did study more Spanish, and he took his language skills and that memory with him to medical school and beyond. "I remember how it feels to be sick when you cannot explain what is wrong," he told me. "I haven't forgotten how frightened I was and how grateful I was for what she did. She wasn't a doctor or a nurse, but she was kind and thoughtful to me. That's how I want to interact with my patients."

I keep the fan from my Spanish *amiga* in a prominent spot in my classroom these days. When the students ask, I tell them the story of Ryan's shortened vacation to Spain and the lifelong education we all got that day in a hospital room in Toledo. "There's no chapter in our textbook for lessons like that," I tell the students. "But how lucky we all were to learn it!"

~Christine A. Holliday

90

The Water Holds No Scars

There is certainly something in angling that tends to produce a serenity of the mind.
~Washington Irving

I have fly fished for over fifteen years in Big Thompson Canyon. Wading in the waters of the river of the canyon's namesake, I have made countless casts, caught thousands of fish, and experienced life in a realm where I felt like a stranger at first. Now, after so many hours alone in the canyon, I feel at home, having grown to know myself in ways undiscovered until I immersed myself in this watery world of fish, aquatic bugs, and their seemingly magical empire.

The focus required to complete the task of enticing wild trout to take an artificial bug draws one deep inside, leaving the hectic outside world far behind. Rhythmic casting, balancing on moss-covered rocks, and staring intently at the dry fly drifting on the river's surface is more therapeutic than lying on a leather couch in some psychologist's office.

All decisions made on the river are mine alone: where to fish, what flies to use, when to move upstream. The normal benchmarks of success and failure do not apply in this environment. As I've fished the eighteen miles of publicly accessible water, I've faced wildly varying emotions: elation, sadness, joy, disappointment, and deep, personal satisfaction. I've come to grips with the deaths of family members, made new friends, openly wept, and experienced an out-of-body, all-knowing, stretch of time that still shakes and soothes me to my core.

Somehow I needed to share what the river, the fish, and the act of fly fishing had to offer. Then, in 2010, I saw a TV show about Project Healing Waters Fly Fishing, I knew I had found my answer. The nonprofit organization is dedicated to the physical and emotional rehabilitation of disabled active duty service personnel through fly fishing and associated activities including education, rod building, fly tying, and outings.

Six months later, in April of 2011, I hosted a daylong fly fishing trip on Big Thompson River for a dozen military members from the Fort Carson Warrior Transition Unit. Each soldier fished with his or her own personal guide and lunch was served by a local family with food donated by neighbors along the river. Many veterans caught their first fish on a fly that day. I was so grateful for all the support and volunteers who made that day a possibility.

> *Somehow I needed to share what the river, the fish, and the act of fly fishing had to offer.*

With the support of more volunteers and their generosity, I hosted a second trip for another dozen soldiers from Fort Carson in the fall of 2011. This time, lodging, dinner and breakfast were donated by the owners of the River Forks Inn. Additionally, fishing fees were waived at a local dude ranch that offers outstanding fly fishing. The soldiers enjoyed two full days of fishing, food, camaraderie, laughter, healing, and great fishing, again all thanks to the fishing guides, fly shops that loaned gear free of charge, and other volunteers who donated their time and energy to make the two-day event a great success. All of this was accomplished at no cost to the military members.

Shortly after this trip was complete, I met with Duane Cook, a Vietnam veteran who lived in Cheyenne, Wyoming. With him, we charted the course of what became the Platte Rivers Chapter of PHWFF. Our first trip took place in September of 2012, with a dozen veterans, some of whom fought in World War II. These veterans were our first members to fish with the chapter, all living in northern Colorado and southern Wyoming, the areas we served.

Our good fortune continued as more veterans and active duty members joined our organization. Fly shops donated fly tying materials and vises for fly tying classes, churches donated space for fly rod building classes, and volunteers continued to raise money and donate their time so the veterans could participate free of charge. Through the generosity of the National Office of PHWFF, we were able to nominate and send two members on weeklong fly fishing trips to outstanding destinations in the U.S.

Thankful for each day that we could offer healing and hope on the water, we continued to work to build our chapter. Three years later we are one of the largest PWHFF programs in the United States and in 2015 we logged over 16,000 miles on the road, taking our members fly fishing.

I am continually stunned at the level of generosity afforded to our chapter by fishing lodges, guides, local businesses that donate services, and financial backing. There is no way to express my gratitude to those who help, except to keep taking our deserving service men and women out fly fishing so they can experience and enjoy the healing properties while on the water.

The Platte Rivers Chapter motto is, "The water holds no scars." I found that to be true during my time spent fly fishing on Big Thompson River. I continue to see the same in our members when they catch a trout with a fly they tied and a rod they constructed. I am grateful for the opportunity to serve our military service members, for their willingness to participate in our programs, and the chance to witness firsthand the positive changes they experience when sharing a day fly fishing together.

In the end, I am also grateful to Big Thompson River for teaching me about myself with great patience and understanding, and for washing away my scars so that I can be strong enough to provide the opportunity for others to achieve the same healing in their lives.

~Dean K. Miller

91

From a Job to a Privilege

We are shaped and fashioned by what we love.
~Johann Wolfgang von Goethe

I love my job! Over the past sixteen years I have had the privilege of reading every book published in the *Chicken Soup for the Soul* series. What began as just a job has become so much more. I feel as if I've gotten to know each and every contributor personally, and I feel as if I've experienced the most important events in their lives side by side with them through their heartfelt stories.

Reading tens of thousands of Chicken Soup for the Soul stories has made me the person I am today. I believe I am a better mother, wife, daughter, sister and friend because of each lesson that I've learned. I am truly grateful for the selfless sharing of our writers.

As a new mother, I loved *Chicken Soup for the Expectant Mother's Soul* and often cited the story, "It Will Change Your Life," in which Dale Hanson Bourke wrote about how becoming a mother changes everything in the most amazing ways. As my son Bailey grew and was ready to start school, *Chicken Soup for the Teacher's Soul* was released. I can't tell you how many teachers received a copy with a Post-it marking a selection that I thought described my feelings perfectly. It was a letter that a father, Richard F. Abrahamson, had written to a teacher, telling the teacher how hard it was to let his child go off to school and how much faith and trust he had that his child was in the right hands. I learned I was not the only one who was hesitant to send her child off to school!

And then once I was comfortable sending him off, what was I supposed to do if *he* missed *me*? Barbara LoMonaco's story, "The Last First Day," provided the solution. I gave my son a penny to keep in his pocket. He could put his hand in and touch it and be reminded that I was there with him. He welcomed the connection and he took that penny with him every day for the first month of school.

A few years later, my best friend's seven-year-old son died suddenly. To this day, years later, this is possibly the worst event in my life. I wasn't sure how to help my friend or her family through such a horrible time. So I opened my copy of *Chicken Soup for the Grieving Soul* and read Jo Coudert's "What You Can Do for a Grieving Friend." I got the advice that I needed, which was that it was enough for me to just listen to my friend and say, "I'm here for you."

As the years rolled by, like all parents, I questioned my parenting. I was never sure as a working mother that I was there enough. I read "The Damn Cape" in *Chicken Soup for the Working Woman's Soul* and could relate to how Colleen Eastman wanted to make costumes, be room mom and do anything else the school requested. Boy, was I worn thin. I got the advice I needed from Cheryl Kirking's story, "Gotta Watch the Fish Eat," in *Chicken Soup for the Soul: Moms Know Best*. Cheryl explained how she finally put her foot down and said "no" to a Thursday night meeting. In her story she shares, "We feed the fish every night, of course. But on Thursdays we make an effort to sit together as a family and watch them." Although I have not met Cheryl personally, I want to thank her for giving me permission to say "no" and reminding me how important a family evening is.

The years have flown by…. When Bailey was a teenager, I was happy I took the advice shared in "A Worthy Investment" in *Chicken Soup for the Mother's Soul 2*. While Allison Yates Gaskin converted her garage into a place for her kids and their friends to hang out, I took it one step further and converted the formal living room… ping pong table and all. It worked… the teenagers were always here.

Because Chicken Soup for the Soul stories have always had such an impact on me, it wasn't a surprise that when my dad passed away

I ran straight to my *Chicken Soup for the Soul* collection for comfort. Again I was able to use the stories shared to write my portion of his eulogy. There were heads nodding as I related the lessons I have learned through my job. I shared that we should all stop and light the candles we were saving for a special occasion, wipe our hands on the towels we hung for decoration in the guest bathroom, and open the sunroof without worrying about our hair. I learned the importance of enjoying the moments we have.

People have asked if I ever get tired of reading Chicken Soup for the Soul stories. My answer is always, "Let me tell you about a story I just read." As my twentieth wedding anniversary approached we had just finished editing *Chicken Soup for the Soul: Married Life!* Reading the story "The Gold Ring Club" by Dana Martin had a huge impact on me. When we got married, yellow gold was the fashion, but now it seems everyone is wearing white gold or platinum. Dana shares in her story that while a yellow gold ring may be dated, it is the fact that it is dated that is so important. She says, "I'll stick to the gold wedding band and cherish its symbol of triumph over adversity, good decisions over bad, and for love conquering all."

> *How lucky I am to have a job that provides for my family while at the same time teaching me to count my blessings.*

When Bailey was in high school, I was so excited to read our stories about new drivers, first dates and high school sports. In *Chicken Soup for the Soul: Parenthood* the story "Perspective" taught me a lesson I needed. My son was a high school soccer player and while I loved to watch him play I have to admit I was one of those parents who "coached" from the stands even though I had never played a day of soccer in my life. Rosemary Smiarowski explained how at her son's final game she decided to just "be there" in the moment. She wrote, "My self-imposed 'tunnel vision perspective' allowed me to selfishly focus on my eighteen-year-old son who had been playing basketball since he was old enough to bounce a ball. What I saw was a confident young man playing a team sport and having the time of his life." At our next game I couldn't get the story out of my mind and I focused on just my son. I was amazed to see at the end of the game that he walked up to each coach and thanked him. Wow! It is funny what you learn when you do just "stop and smell the roses."

As my son headed off to college I was grateful for the creative gift idea shared in the story "Not Just a Medical Kit" in *Chicken Soup for the Soul: Campus Chronicles*. For her high school graduation, Jaclyn S. Miller received a bag containing medicines she might need while away from home. While at first Jaclyn thought it was an odd gift, she became the "go to" girl on her dorm floor. What a wonderful idea! I had so much fun putting together a tackle box containing medicines I knew Bailey might need should he get sick when I couldn't be there.

We all have regrets and have made mistakes along the way but it wasn't until this past Christmas that I came face to face with one of mine. For some reason it is not my favorite holiday. Maybe it is the added stress of the decorating, the shopping, the five family birthdays that fall during the same week, and of course the mess. I have been teased over the years about how quickly the tree hits the curb for trash pickup, usually by the 26th! This year was different. As the mother of an only child away for his first year of college you can imagine how excited I was when Christmas break came around. Our publisher Amy Newmark's story "A Happy Mess" in *Chicken Soup for the Soul: Merry Christmas!* hit home. As she shared in her story, "There's actually nothing sadder than a completely clean house after Christmas, because then I know it's all over, and we have to wait a whole year to do it again!" I focused on that message and enjoyed Bailey's entire Christmas break without even thinking about taking that tree down until he left.

As a new empty nester, and the wife of a firefighter, I have many evenings all to myself. So I became the youngest member of a crochet group and learned how to make blankets and beanies. After reading the wonderful stories in *Chicken Soup for the Soul: Volunteering & Giving Back* our small group got inspired and began making beanies for breast cancer patients undergoing chemo at our local hospital.

Last night I was talking to an old friend and she shared the heartache she is going through dealing with both of her parents suffering from dementia. Because of the wonderful stories I have read in *Chicken Soup for the Soul: Living with Alzheimer's & Other Dementias* and *Chicken Soup for the Soul: Family Caregivers* I was able to provide her with the insight that she is not alone and the importance of not taking personally the things her parents do and say now. She laughed and cried as I read her stories from both books.

There are so many more stories that have improved my life over the past sixteen years and I am so grateful that our contributors have opened their hearts and shared such wonderful life lessons. How lucky I am to have a job that provides for my family while at the same time teaching me to count my blessings, to believe that prayers are answered, to find happiness, to use my positive thinking, and to focus on gratitude. Knowing what a profound difference these stories can make has turned what started as a job into a career, and has turned a career into a privilege.

~D'ette Corona

The Power of Gratitude

Never Too Late for a Thank You

*No one who achieves success does so without acknowledging
the help of others. The wise and confident acknowledge
this help with gratitude.*
~Alfred North Whitehead

Tough Love

*Accept responsibility for your life. Know that it is you
who will get you where you want to go, no one else.*
~Les Brown

I wasn't a bad kid, but I did like to drink beer. In 1991, at the age of nineteen, it caught up with me and I was arrested for possession and consumption of alcohol by a minor. The judge threw the book at me.

I, along with three of my friends, had to perform eight days of community service, which took place on Saturday and Sunday for four weekends. The orange jumpsuits were attractive and attention grabbing as we strolled alongside the local highways. Additionally, there was a $100 fine, a $100 ten-hour school, three years of probation, and $44 in court costs.

While my pals were out drinking the very next night and telling war stories from our short time behind bars, I did not have a sip of alcohol for several months. Finally, after four months, I had a couple of drinks at a trailer park on the outskirts of town. Later in the night, a fight broke out and bad things happened. Although I was not a part of the fight, I saw the writing on the wall and knew I needed to make a change. I just wasn't sure what that change should be.

I'd been to college for one quarter but had failed miserably. I wasn't exactly the college type at that point. I was working at a drugstore running the cash register, stocking shelves, and doing whatever I was asked to do. It was neither glamorous nor rewarding. I figured that at some point I'd go to work at one of the local factories, but then a funny thing happened.

As I was driving to work the day after the party, I made an inadvertent turn into the armed services recruiting station, and the rest is history. Joining the United States Army is the best decision I ever made.

The first office I visited belonged to the Army, and it would be the last one I visited. I took a test, on which I did very well. I told the recruiter that I was walking over to talk to the Air Force guy but was told it was a waste of time because of my arrest. I believed the recruiter. I had no reason not to. Months later, I found myself working with Air Force personnel who'd been arrested for much more than underage drinking. In hindsight, I'm glad my recruiter lied to me.

Without the arrest, or more specifically the harsh penalties, the military would have been the last thing on my mind. I didn't have any close friends in the service at that time, so I joined on blind faith. Twenty-three years later, I'm still serving.

During my initial enlistment, I proudly served as an Army medic. My first assignment was in Germany at Landstuhl Regional Medical Center. The highlight of my time there was working on the Army Rangers who were injured in the Battle of Mogadishu, which was made famous by the book and subsequent movie *Blackhawk Down*. After those first four years, I decided to return home and give college another try.

I went back to my job at the drugstore, and because I was on military leave, I actually earned a raise and another week's vacation. It wasn't a bad deal. I worked full-time and went to school as often as I could. It took me five years to complete my bachelor's degree, but I did, in fact, complete it. I had no idea what to do following graduation. A month later, four U.S. airplanes were hijacked by terrorists. At that point, I knew exactly what I needed to do.

I went back to the recruiter, but this time I went to see the Air Force guy first. I had to retake my test and scored in the ninety-ninth percentile. The Air Force wanted me but said there wasn't a slot at Officer Training School at that time. I'd have to wait about a year. The Navy wanted me, too, but I'd have to first enlist and then apply for their officer program. I wasn't interested in the Marine Corps.

Ultimately, I wound up talking to the Army recruiter, who promised he'd have me back wearing the uniform in a matter of weeks. It wound up being close to fifty-two weeks, as I reported to Officer Candidate School at Fort Benning, Georgia, on September 11, 2002. I was commissioned as a Second Lieutenant the following January. It was the most exciting day of my life.

Had I not received that tough love from the judge back when I was a teenager, I never would've even considered the military as an option. The only downside was that I was told I couldn't be a good leader because of my stuttering. It's something I've dealt with my whole life.

I did three more years of active duty and deployed to Iraq along the way as the platoon leader of the third largest platoon in the Army. Afterwards, I joined the National Guard and deployed to Iraq two more times. I now hold the rank of Major in the Army Reserves. I've done quite well for someone who was told his stutter would hold him back.

When I left active duty, naturally, I transitioned into stand-up comedy. Okay, perhaps I took the road less traveled, but it was something I had to try. I talk a great deal about stuttering, working at the drugstore, and serving in the Army. Over the years, it's turned into more

> *I simply thanked him for holding me accountable.*

motivational and inspirational comedy and speaking. I've performed all over the country and have worked with some of the biggest names in comedy. I've also had multiple tours entertaining troops overseas. I've been there, so I know the importance of bringing laughter to those so far from home.

To date, the *Chicken Soup for the Soul* series has published three of my stories in five different books, and I write in several newspapers around the country.

I recently had a show in my hometown, and the judge who handed down my sentence was in the crowd. It was the first time I'd had the opportunity to address him since the fall of 1991. Some people might hold a grudge, but not me — not for someone who impacted my life in such a significant manner. In front of a couple hundred people, I simply thanked him for holding me accountable. I learned my lesson.

Too often, people are slapped on the wrist for breaking the law, and they never learn their lesson. I learned mine, made changes in my life, and am thankful for all the opportunities before me today. If not for that judge, who knows where I'd be? All of the factories that I could have worked at are now closed. I might have stayed at the drugstore. Who knows? The system worked, and I am forever grateful.

~Jody Fuller

Editor's note: To listen to Publisher Amy Newmark's Chicken Soup for the Soul Podcast interview with Jody Fuller please go to chickensoup. podbean.com/e/friend-friday-soldier-with-a-stutter-is-a-role-model/

The Hardest Kind of Saving

*Although no one can go back and make a brand new
start, anyone can start from now and make
a brand new ending.*
~Carl Bard

I stood in front of the bathroom mirror blow-drying my freshly
dyed hair and reliving the numerous painful moments that
had occurred in the last few weeks. It had all started with
Aaron. I had never had a real boyfriend before him and had
become addicted to his attention.

He was incredibly adorable but immature for his age, and like
many young teenagers, we were hormonal, overdramatic, and depressed.
I should have known how unstable that cocktail of emotions would
become, but I was in love. Desperately and insanely in love with this
sweet sandy-haired boy. I flipped my hair and continued to dry. Even
thinking about him now was giving me butterflies, but my feelings
toward him were becoming clouded with despair over everything else
that was happening.

We had been dragging each other deeper into depression though
we didn't realize it at the time. I had to admit to myself that I was out
of control. The night before, I had been getting ready to take a bath.
Knowing that I was going to be in the water and the cleanup would
be easy, I had brought one of my blades with me. I had gotten very

good at taking apart cheap disposable razors and had hidden the little blades all over my room. I had been cutting more and more often.

That night, in the bathtub, I had gone too far and the bathwater had gone red. I got out, swallowed my pride, and asked my mom for help. She was a nurse and kept gauze and thick bandages on hand. That moment was one of only a few times that I had seen her cry and it had made me hate myself more. Her eyes were clouded with worry and confusion.

She didn't understand me; no one did. Not even Aaron. He had been cutting too. When we had started dating we were both very into the "emo" lifestyle because we could identify with the pain and suffering. We were drowning ourselves in a sea of black eyeliner and dark music. We would agree to quit, but whenever one of us slipped up the other would as well and the cycle continued. I had spent many nights sitting on the floor of my closet trying to figure out how to pull myself together and the only thing that ever made sense was to cut.

> *Hope was something I had forgotten how to feel.*

This was all running through my head as I brushed my hair and surveyed my dye job. For a millisecond, I was almost pleased. Red was a good color on me.

I opened the bathroom door to find my dad leaning against the banister, waiting for me. He had tears in his eyes and immediately wrapped me in a big, safe hug. My mom had called him. Dad and I had not spoken much in the last year due to the fact that he lived six hours away and I was a moody teenager.

"Hi, Daddy." I looked into his face and tried to give him a genuine smile. I hadn't realized how much I had needed that hug.

"Let's go have a chat," he whispered in a shaky voice. I followed him down the stairs. My mom and my stepmom, Miss Kelly, were talking quietly at the table but stopped upon seeing me. I was beginning to feel cornered. I hugged Miss Kelly and sat down at the head of the table.

"Do you know why we're here, sweetie?" I could tell that Miss Kelly was trying to keep her tone light and unthreatening.

"The cutting?" I lowered my eyes to the table. I was feeling self-conscious because of the tank top I was wearing. None of the wounds on my arms were covered. I scratched nervously at the gauze wrapping my thigh under my pants.

"Yes. Your mom called us last night in tears because she thinks we're going to lose you." Mom and Dad were silent. I looked up; all three of their faces were pale and worried. Mom was scanning my face. She was trying to read my emotions, which was useless; I was pretty numb at that moment. Dad had a few tears rolling down his cheeks. His gaze was focused on a deep slice in my bicep from two or three days before.

"Honey, we need you to tell us what is going on with you. What can we do to help?" he said.

I still would not look at them, but I managed to answer. "I'm not trying to kill myself. I know that's what you think." I sighed, wishing Aaron could be there to face this with me.

"We need you to know that it doesn't have to be this way. Where did my happy little bookworm go? Your face is the same, but that light in your eyes is gone. We are here because we want you to be happy. Don't you want to be happy again?"

I could feel the tears welling up in the corners of my eyes. I could remember that girl too. The happy, little girl who was always lost in a fairytale, dreaming of the adventures she would have when she grew up. That girl seemed like a stranger now. When had things changed? When had I lost touch with myself?

"Yes." I said, but I didn't know if it was even possible to be happy again. "I don't know how."

They began to talk, each interjecting an idea, but I was only half-listening. I was thinking about Aaron again. What if I got better but he didn't? What if I didn't get better? Would I feel this way forever?

"Honey?" They were looking at me. I didn't hear whatever they had said; I was falling back into numbness. I could hardly comprehend the concept of *not* feeling like I was drowning all the time.

"Sorry. What?" I was still staring at the tabletop.

"We all think you should take a week away from everything and come back to North Dakota with us." I was completely taken aback.

Never Too Late for a Thank You | 351

Leave school? My friends? Aaron? I couldn't choke back the tears and they began collecting in a quiet little puddle on the table in front of me.

"I don't want to go."

"Honey." Mom reached over and squeezed my hand. "You may not understand now how taking some time away will help, but we all think that you need to give it a try. We are terrified that if things get worse, you will never be able to have the normal, happy life that you deserve."

"Okay, Mom," was all I could think to say.

The next hour I walked around in a daze. I packed a bag, called Aaron to tell him what was happening, and hugged my mom. We began our six-hour drive to Dad's. I buried myself in my iPod and watched the world pass by my window. It's strange that you can look into the eyes of strangers, in the next car on the road, knowing that they have no idea how much your pain is tearing you apart. You have no idea if theirs is doing the same. The trees became less and less dense. As we crossed the border into North Dakota, my heart sank a little. My memories of my father's community were not great, but I was not there to see anyone. Apparently I was supposed to take this week to rest.

"Think about what you want your life to be." That was what Mom had said when she hugged me goodbye. What did that even mean?

After three days of "rest" I was starting to get it. My numbness had subsided and I had spent an entire night crying over Aaron. I had realized how toxic we were for each other. My parents had spoken to Aaron's parents. They had all agreed that we should stay away from each other for a few weeks. I was livid, at first. They couldn't tell me who to be with! Or who to love!

Later, I realized they were right. If I had any chance of getting out of this hole, it would only happen without Aaron. That epiphany had caused such a strange mixture of anger and hope in me. Hope was something I had forgotten how to feel. The surge of emotions had exhausted me. Miss Kelly must have noticed. The next morning as I was staring at a blank page in my journal, trying to muster the brain power to write, I looked up and she was smiling down at me. She had one arm full of snacks and the other gripping a stack of DVDs.

"Come on; let's have a girl's day." I followed her to the master bedroom, where my younger sister was snuggled into the middle of the bed waiting for us. I crawled in as Miss Kelly popped in the DVD. Settling into that giant, cloud-like bed as the Disney introduction played on the TV made me feel small. I felt something take hold of me... it was the bookworm. I could feel that sweet little girl I used to be peeking out through my pain. I glanced over at my family. They were giggling, with their hands full of popcorn, and for the first time in a long time, I was happy. Genuinely happy. I could almost feel my heart glowing.

In that moment, I knew that someday I would be as happy as they were. However, it wasn't until I was an adult, with a family of my own, that I saw that entire situation for what it was. My parents had saved me from myself. The hardest kind of saving there is. They could have done what many parents do, sit back and hope it was just a phase. All three of them made the decision to actively help me through it even though they didn't understand it. They couldn't have known then how much their hard work would pay off. My heart will forever overflow with the gratitude that I wish I had shown them at the time.

~Chelsea Johnson

94

Honest Thanks

Fill your paper with the breathings of your heart.
~William Wordsworth

I sat down at my desk and started writing. I wrote an emotional letter of unadulterated gratitude. I stuffed the notecard into an envelope, sealed it, and stuck a stamp on it, but when it came to actually placing the letter into the mailbox… I froze.

I couldn't do it.

I suddenly felt this overwhelming sense of fear and insecurity. But why?

The letter was to an old high school friend with whom I kept in contact via Facebook comments and the occasional private message. For the past couple of weeks, her Facebook page had inspired me to live my life differently — for example, by volunteering more.

Her volunteer efforts weren't huge — she wasn't tending to lepers in India or building wells in Uganda, but instead she was doing small, local good deeds, such as serving as an elementary-school crossing guard. These were things that I could do, too.

She made me realize that I didn't have to go on a mission in order to make a difference in the world. I could make a difference here at home. This realization changed my outlook on the world and for some reason, deep down in my gut, I felt I should let her know how her example positively influenced my life.

I could have easily sent her an e-mail, but that seemed a bit lame for such an important thank you. That's why I ended up handwriting the letter. But now here I was, standing before the mailbox, unable to place the envelope inside — by far, the easiest step in the entire procedure. What was stopping me? Why was this so hard to do?

It suddenly dawned on me that I was afraid of being too nice.

I guess I felt weird because it wasn't like she was my best friend or a relative. I barely knew her. Maybe my message was too heartfelt and too personal. "People don't normally do this," I thought to myself.

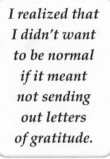

I realized that I didn't want to be normal if it meant not sending out letters of gratitude.

Mulling this over, I realized that I didn't want to be normal if it meant not sending out letters of gratitude to people who deserved them. I put the envelope in the mailbox.

A couple of weeks later I received a Facebook message from her. It turned out she was going through a tough time and my note meant the world to her. She said she had no idea she was making such a difference for others.

Not only did this letter make her happier, but her response to it increased my level of happiness as well. It literally only took me five minutes to write. I was so excited that it made such a difference to her that I decided to write a gratitude letter to someone each month.

I've been doing this for two years now and it's made a huge difference in my life. I'm more likely to seek out the goodness in others and am subsequently more thankful for this incredibly beautiful life I'm living. Cultivating gratitude is a great skill to practice. Life is too short not to do it.

~Amanda C. Yancey

95

A Hospital Visit

Forget injuries, never forget kindnesses.
~Confucius

I was born premature, under two pounds and small enough to fit in my mother's hand. I'm told that the hospital would call every day or so during the three months I was there, saying things like "come now and bring the clothes you want him to be buried in."

I grew into a small, sickly child. I had epileptic seizures, bone and joint problems, and I was bullied in school. I could have done without all that, but in reality those things made me into the man I eventually became.

Occasionally my mother and I would go to Sacred Heart Hospital in Pensacola, Florida for a test or a procedure. She would visit the neonatal intensive care unit where I spent the first three months of my life. The NICU had pictures of the babies who made it lining the walls, and mine was the first one in the line-up. I looked for it every time we were there.

I grew up and stopped visiting the NICU. In due course, I married a woman I loved and cared for very much. A week after our wedding, she had to have major surgery. That procedure dragged on, so after my prayers were completed in Sacred Heart's chapel, I decided to go look for that NICU. It had moved in the fifteen years since my last visit, so by the time I found it visiting hours were over and I couldn't go in. My mother, who was a nurse, had asked me to look up an old friend of hers who was a nurse in that unit.

I went back the next day and found an older lady with a beautiful smile sitting at the nurse's station. She looked at me and said, "You're looking for a specific person, aren't you?"

Surprised, I told her yes.

"Who are you looking for?"

I had a flash of insight, and looked at the nurse.

"Clara?" She got up and came around the counter with arms wide open for a hug.

"Yes! That's me. Your mother said that you might be coming by. Baby, you're all grown up from what you used to be. We worried and prayed over you your whole life."

> *Everyone who had taken care of me as an infant in that NICU was there.*

I hugged her, and was surprised by the tears that came to my eyes. She had another surprise for me, one that threatened to cause waterworks.

Miraculously, everyone who had taken care of me as an infant in that NICU was there. Some were to retire that week, some were working other people's shifts, and others just happened to be there. I didn't know what to say. It was an amazing coincidence.

Clara got up and called everyone together. Even my doctor was there. We took a photo that I still have. In it, you can see a curiously shining light in my eyes. I've said for years that it was the flickering fluorescent light but it really wasn't.

Those were tears in my eyes, knowing that arrayed around me were the people who helped save my life. For that I give thanks. Our paths are ordered, and not always by us. I was led full circle that day, from my birth to that moment. I will never forget that day.

~JB Steele

96

Grateful for Stew

*It's bizarre that the produce manager is more
important to my children's health than
the pediatrician.*
~Meryl Streep

When I was a young girl my mother made the same dish for supper five nights a week. She boiled potatoes, carrots, and occasionally, other vegetables, in a big, shiny pot on the kitchen stove. The vegetables were cooked fresh every day and small amounts of the roast beef that she cooked once a week were added to the bowls. She called it stew.

I would often hear the other children at school talk about the delicious meals they had for supper. Many of the children ate from fast food restaurants, which were expensive at the time. They got hamburgers, fries, and milkshakes. I wished we could eat like that once in a while, but my parents couldn't afford it. We only had take-out food once or twice a year — for special occasions.

Now I look back and I think how blessed I was. My mom took the time to cut up and prepare those vegetables and potatoes every single night. Her portions were right — focusing on the vegetables and not on the meat — and we weren't eating the grease and fat and salt we would have had in take-out food.

I'm pretty sure I had a lot fewer head colds and flus than my classmates. If I did get sick, I'd be home for a day or two, not a whole week like many of them.

When I was in my thirties I became ill and was diagnosed with hereditary high blood pressure. I have to admit I had been eating a lot of fast food, making up for not getting it as a child. But when I went back to preparing homemade meals without all the extra grease and salt I started to feel healthier.

> *My mom took the time to cut up and prepare those vegetables and potatoes every single night.*

Today I often find myself craving a bowl of my mother's stew. I realize how blessed I was to have a mother who took the time to prepare a healthy meal for her family five evenings a week. That stew was made with love and it has left me with a memory that will warm and nourish me forever.

~Shawna Troke-Leukert

97

The Gratitude Book

> *Somehow, by accident, I've realized I have lived a*
> *rich, wonderful, rewarding life. Gratitude,*
> *gratitude, gratitude for that.*
> *~Betty Sue O'Maley*

I learned the power of gratitude from my mom. When she was diagnosed with terminal cancer, she began shouting from the rooftops how thankful she was for the amazing life she'd lived. She was given a horrible prognosis—an estimated fourteen months left to live. The easy response would have been for her to choose anger. Instead, she chose gratitude.

A week after she was diagnosed with her brain tumor, my mother wrote a surprisingly upbeat analysis of her situation:

This illness gives you plenty of time to prioritize and do all the things that you might want in order to feel you have lived a complete and fulfilled life.

So far, the first and predominant feeling I've had, rather than fear or resentment, is this rush of great, overwhelming gratitude for the life I've already lived and all the people, places, and experiences in it. Everyone should be so lucky as to feel this!

I had only just begun knowing my mom as a friend, after years of rebellion in which I pretended that I didn't need her. *She* may not have been angry, but *I* was. She wouldn't get to know her grandchildren and she wouldn't be able to continue the writing career that she had just begun after raising four kids.

If there was any blessing in my mother's illness, it's that it gave her fifteen months to truly live like she was dying — and for her family, the time to tell her how much she meant to us. She was clearly flooded with gratitude, often writing about how lucky she'd been for having the life she'd lived. Another of her early musings read:

I truly am in possession, still, of a tremendous sense of gratitude for my life and the wonder of everything in it. If only the feeling could be bottled, sold, and dispensed as needed!

The more she told me how thankful she was for the life she'd been given, the more I began thinking about how very thankful I was for her. I knew it wasn't just me, though. She had a family, a large circle of friends, and a larger circle of acquaintances whose lives were better because of her.

> *She would die knowing how special her life had been to hundreds of her grateful admirers.*

My mother's influence extended far beyond the six of us in her immediate family. Everyone she met remarked on her kindness and wisdom. I had to make her understand that. I needed her to know just how incredible she was.

And that's how I got the idea for the Gratitude Book. I reached out to everyone I knew and asked them to spread the word. "If you've been touched by Betty Sue O'Maley in any way, please write a short note so she knows how she's brightened your life." It was a much larger undertaking than I'd originally thought. E-mails and letters came pouring in and I worked to put them all together as quickly as possible since there was no way of knowing when her last day might be.

I was able to put the gratitude notes together with beautiful photos of her life just in time for Christmas that year. It was the most important present I'd ever given, and the look on her face when she opened it was priceless. My mom would die five months after receiving the Gratitude

Book, but she would die knowing how special her life had been to hundreds of her grateful admirers. My hope is that everyone who wrote a piece for the book was also given a gift — the gift of slowing down and thinking about just what they have to be thankful for — particularly all the people who have made life a little better for them.

My mom was taken from this life too soon, but she still managed to appreciate all that she'd been given. I try to remember how she lived and honor her by remembering my blessings every day.

~Carrie O'Maley Voliva

A Teacher's Echo

Teachers affect eternity; no one can tell
where their influence stops.
~Henry Brooks Adams

"Can you come and read a story to my kindergarten class?" my daughter asked, preparing her lesson plans for the upcoming week.

"I'd love to," I responded, recalling the time when I was the one writing lesson plans and inviting guests to my classroom.

Entering the classroom the following morning, I was greeted by twenty lively kindergartners eager for story time. As I made my way to the story center, I passed alphabet charts in bold print, art drawn by creative five-year-old hands, and books lined up like toy soldiers on blue-painted bookshelves. Something inside me said, "I'm home."

I read the story of a little yellow duck and her puddle, witnessing the excitement and wonder in the faces of these young students. And I was convinced once again that some kind of magic happens in an environment where today's learning gives birth to tomorrow's dreams.

On my way home, I recalled how blessed I was to have so many great teachers accompany me on my own journey from kindergarten through college. My sixth grade teacher in particular was instrumental in providing me with the necessary tools I would need one day to follow my dreams. Was she still alive? Would she remember me? I set out to find her. I wanted to say "thank you."

I began my search on the Internet, looking for the order of nuns who had taught me in grade school. And I found it! I discovered that the teacher I longed to connect with after all these years was living in a monastery in Pennsylvania with her community of Sisters. She would soon be ninety years old. I could hardly wait to write to her.

I bought a large greeting card with four blank pages for writing. The cover of the card simply read: Thank You. Inside, I had all those glorious pages to fill with words of gratitude. I began… "Thank you for staying after school and helping me with my math. Thank you for showing me how to construct a sentence one word and phrase at a time. Thank you for letting me sing in the choir with the eighth graders. Thank you for…" My pen continued flowing across those blank pages, as I acknowledged the many selfless sacrifices she made for her students.

> *She said she remembered me and was thrilled to get my thank-you letter.*

On cold winter mornings, she would come to school with just a black, handmade shawl draped over her shoulders, her hands folded as if in prayer under her scapular for warmth. No matter what kind of day it was outside our classroom windows, she was always there waiting for us when the first school bell rang. I thanked her being there every morning. I told her that she was the one who first made me think about becoming a teacher.

A couple of weeks after I mailed the card, I received a letter back from her. She said she remembered me and was thrilled to get my thank-you letter. I was ecstatic. She also wrote that she had to use a large magnifying machine for reading because she was going blind from macular degeneration. But she still volunteered at their senior center doing all sorts of odd jobs. She closed her letter by saying she would pray for me and hoped I would keep her in my prayers.

We exchanged many cards and letters over the next few years, her handwriting deteriorating as her eyesight failed.

On one occasion I sent her a poem I had written celebrating the dazzling colors of spring flowers. She soon wrote back, saying, "Your description of springtime was beautiful, comparing the rainbow with your variety of flowers. I'm glad I was your teacher." She closed her letter by telling me to "Keep up the good work." I beamed. My teacher liked my poem. And for a moment I was eleven years old again, enjoying the sanctuary of sixth grade.

Sister Valeria quietly slipped away on a warm summer day in 2010. She was ninety-three years old.

I keep the cards and letters she sent me in a special place where I can visit them from time to time, recalling the memory of a special teacher who welcomed me into her sacred space and opened the world to me.

~Lola Di Giulio De Maci

Gifts

The meaning of life is to find your gift. The purpose
of life is to give it away.
~Pablo Picasso

I was in fifth grade when my father broke his hip and femur in several places. He had slipped on the morning dew while splitting wood in the back yard. The freak accident was devastating and it would take a considerable amount of time and many surgeries for my father to recover.

At the time, my father had just switched employers and our family didn't have any medical or disability benefits. So Mom became the single breadwinner supporting our family of five. She had significant health issues herself and was in and out of the hospital.

Further complicating our situation was the fact that the fixer-upper, old farmhouse we were living in was not insulated. I often found myself staring at pretty patterns of ice etched on the inside of the windows. I would use my fingernail to write my name and draw hearts in the ice. We stuffed old socks in every hole to block the cold, and we huddled in the kitchen next to the stove when Mom was cooking, as it was the only source of heat in that part of the house.

My dad stayed in a hospital bed in our living room, so we put blankets across the entranceway and heated only that room to conserve money. In the cold of an upstate New York winter of blustery winds and subzero temperatures, we could see our breaths in the other rooms of the house.

| **Never Too Late for a Thank You**

We sold everything we could to keep food on our plates, the house partly heated, and the lights on. We lived in the country and were isolated from neighbors. To my surprise, the people who did know of our difficulties didn't seem to want to get involved.

We were thankful when my mom would get the farmers' surplus food once a month from a local church — large containers of cheese, peanut butter, and powdered milk. Meat was scarce and my teenage brothers took to hunting for rabbits and deer. We couldn't afford a butcher so Mom and every one of us kids helped to butcher the deer. We were so thankful for the food and didn't let anything go to waste. My mom canned and froze whatever she could to help sustain us.

Sometimes I wondered if Dad would ever walk again. His surgery had not been successful so far, and as his pain increased, his screaming was unbearable to hear. With Mom sick too, I worried about what would become of us.

We were not being forgotten after all, and this gave us hope.

The Christmas season came along, and we knew that my parents had been whispering about how they couldn't buy us many presents. My mother had knit some items for us, and we were wise enough to know that we would be grateful for those things when we received them.

On Christmas Eve we sat in our cold dining room eating venison and peaches that Mom had canned. She had made the canned venison into a warm gravy over toast. We were enjoying our meal when we heard an unexpected knock at the door. Mom pushed her hair to the side and smoothed her shirt before taking a deep breath and answering the door.

Two men who worked with my dad walked in carrying a box wrapped in Christmas paper. They said, "Ho, Ho, Ho," with deep voices. They placed the box in front of my dad, who we had maneuvered to the table for Christmas Eve dinner. Dad looked sad and Mom had tears welling up in her eyes. Mom slowly pulled each piece of wrapping paper away. It was as if her hands were apprehensive and couldn't imagine touching something joyful

The two men said, "Open it. All the guys miss you at work. We

Never Too Late for a Thank You |

wanted to do something to let you know we care." Mom and Dad opened the box. It was stuffed with wadded up newspaper and money. Mom held her hands like she was praying. She then touched her praying hands to her heart then lips, and tears streamed down her cheeks. My father bowed his head and shielded his eyes with his hand. I saw a single tear hit the table.

They gave us $1,300. We were so thankful. That money would help us survive a few more months, until the harsh, dark winter eased into spring. The men didn't even know the true Christmas present they gave us was much bigger than money. It was the gift of feeling cared about. We were not being forgotten after all, and this gave us hope.

By the time summer arrived, each of us kids had found a job. My parents took the situation they had been handed and recreated themselves, each of them pursuing work that accommodated their medical issues. Little did our parents know that through their tragedies they blessed their children with an abundance of gifts, including resilience and compassion.

To this day, if I know of anyone struggling with medical and financial burdens I try to help them, whether it's letting them know I care or bringing them dinner. I always remember what was done for our family and how very much it meant to us.

~Kelly Hennigan

The Gratitude Party

Gratitude makes sense of our past, brings peace for
today, and creates a vision for tomorrow.
~Melody Beattie

I took a moment to step back and look around my patio. I smiled, because there, mingling in the glow of Tiki torches and citronella candles, were forty people who had earned a very special place in our hearts that year. I was struck by the perfect blend of delicious food, upbeat music and lively conversation.

I have always considered myself to be a grateful person. I was raised to thank people each time I received something as simple as a compliment and I was very conscious of this etiquette, so they knew I did not take them or their kindness for granted. In turn, I raised my children with the same values. Presents could be unwrapped but not played with until they had written a thank-you note. During dinner, we played the "Good News" game and shared the best things that happened that day. We live in a society of instant gratification and entitlement, so I wanted to slow my children down to appreciate what they had, irrespective of amount, magnitude or value.

I have been fortunate to enjoy a good life, albeit not always an easy one. I have two children who make me very happy, but each has issues that have required a good portion of my time and attention. I was divorced and living away from my family but enjoyed a network of wonderfully supportive friends. I always had a full-time job and spent countless additional hours working with my kids and volunteering.

To some, when I remarried, I lived a fairy tale. Life as we knew it changed dramatically and we happily moved near my family. It was the kind of life most only dreamt about, filled with vacations, private schools, household help, and effusive love bursting through the joints of the beautifully grand home we shared. It was perfect.

However, nothing is truly perfect, and in 2010 we were woken from our dream by a chain of events that unraveled our world in an excruciating manner with alarming speed. It began with the death of my devoted dad, whom I had been caring for over the last year. Losing the parent who was the heart of my support system and had guided me through some very difficult situations was my worst experience to date. We struggled to navigate life without his warmth, spot-on advice, and spirited wit.

> *Although the Gratitude Party is a summation of the prior year, it is the daily practice of gratitude that keeps me moving forward.*

While we mourned, we simultaneously took care of my mom, seeing her through chemotherapy as she bravely battled terminal cancer. In the midst of this, my husband abruptly left and filed for divorce. The shock of his departure and the numerous issues I now faced alone continued my slide into depression. The next few months brought the passing of my favorite aunt and then my favorite uncle. I felt lost when my kids visited their father, but in hindsight it gave me precious alone time with my mom, which was filled with long talks and laughter as our sarcastic nature deflected the pain of our circumstances.

My dream skidded into a living nightmare when shortly thereafter, my mom succumbed to her cancer and I became an overwhelmed, single, orphaned mom of two special needs kids. She was my best friend, confidante and cheerleader and her loss seemed insurmountable.

I don't remember many details from that year except that I was instantly humbled, knowing there were people smirking at my fall from grace. I have no recollection of house hunting, moving, enrolling my kids in a new school, or flying back and forth to meet with my siblings to manage the details of my parents' deaths.

I hid from the world, shopping at late hours and staying away from places frequented by people I knew. I couldn't wrap my head around all that had happened and I felt horribly alone. I had turned my kids' lives upside down, couldn't get an interview, let alone a job, and was in a house I soon wouldn't be able to afford, filled with possessions from my marriages that constantly reminded me of my failure.

I vacillated between wanting to live and hoping to die, believing my kids were better off without me. It was a daily battle with a deep depression where I struggled to get out of bed. I expressed my wish to die, be cremated and placed in the casket with my mother, where I could rest peacefully next to the one who understood and loved me unconditionally.

It was fortuitous that I had saved all of mom's voicemails from that last year and I listened to them often. At other times, I heard my mom's lilting voice in my head reminding me who I was at my core. "You were always a plugger" and "you're made of steel" she would tell me. Finally, I listened to her classic adage — "when you're done licking your wounds, you've got to pick yourself up by the bootstraps" — and I did just that. I went to a therapist, got medication, and many applications later, landed a job. Gratitude returned to my vernacular.

One day, my kids and I were discussing the positive path our lives were now on. With increasing fervor, we talked about all the people who had helped us through those dark days when nothing seemed possible. How could we ever thank them enough? Did they know just how much impact they had on our lives? Did they realize that watching the dog, meeting us for dinner, having a workout partner, hiring me for temporary work, providing oft-needed rides, a place to stay, a text to check in, a shoulder to cry on… that they had saved our lives? It was then that our annual Gratitude Party was conceived.

So, as I looked around the patio of the house I was now able to afford, during our third annual Gratitude Party, I was reminded of how far we had come. Every year we invite the people who had a positive impact on our lives in the previous year. They may have helped us in ways that seemed insignificant to them but were powerful to us. One year we read poems we had written about each person expressing why

Never Too Late for a Thank You |

we were grateful. Another year, they wore custom-made badges that contained cryptic maxims like "I give Allison a reason to get up every morning" and the other guests had to guess why.

Although the Gratitude Party is a summation of the prior year, it is the daily practice of gratitude that keeps me moving forward. I take nothing for granted and continue to encourage my kids, now with renewed purpose, to be selfless, recall the good events of every day, and pay it forward. We maintain perspective and are thankful for the little things. We know very well that the little things are sometimes all we have and are quite often worthier than the big things.

~Allison Hermann Craigie

Thanks for the Giving

Thanksgiving, after all, is a word of action.
~W.J. Cameron

My heart sank as I heard the familiar clicking sound of the electricity being shut off. It was two days before Thanksgiving. I poured a drink and sat in my room to wallow in self-pity. I had been unemployed for months, and my daughter and I were barely surviving. I grabbed my purse in a desperate attempt to fix the problem. As I did, moths flew out of it as if I were living in a cartoon. I gathered all the change that I could, but $1.75 was not going to solve our problem. How was I going to explain this situation to my daughter?

We were months behind on the rent, to the point that eviction notices were being posted on our door daily. Now we were not only going to be forced out of the only home that she had known, but we were going to make that move in the dark and cold.

I tried to be positive and look for the silver lining, but all I did was become angry as I thought through the list of all the people who had lived in my house or at least slept on my couch in the past decade — for free. I stopped counting after I hit fifty. Then I ran to the bathroom and got sick. After I washed my face, I looked in the mirror and said to myself, "You suck and Thanksgiving is ruined." I was giving up.

Just then my daughter got home from school. "Is the electricity off again?" she asked with an accusatory tone.

"Yes," was all that I could muster as I hung my head in shame.

"Mom, are we poor?"

"Only financially," I responded, choking back the tears.

At that moment, I felt a burst of energy. I had to do everything I could to make sure that Thanksgiving happened. After all, it would be our last one in our home.

During my childhood, Thanksgiving was rarely celebrated. In my family it was just another Thursday. There had been a family fight between my mom and uncle on the holiday before I was even born, so we didn't celebrate it. Instead, I usually spent the day eating frozen pizza and listening to my mother cry. When I moved out on my own, the tradition continued. It was me, alone, watching bad television, while all my friends were off with their families.

> I am living proof that the good things that you put out to the world will come back to you.

One year I decided to make my own tradition. I couldn't be the only one feeling so alone on this holiday. I started an "Orphan Thanksgiving." Those with nowhere to go were welcome. I was bound and determined to make sure no one felt alone on such a meaningful day.

As the years passed, it became my favorite time of year. I knew I would see people that I loved, if for no other reason than my grandma's famous pumpkin muffin recipe. I would cook for days to prepare for the dozens of friends and family members who would come through the front door. Now, with an eviction notice and no electricity, how would I make my fifteenth Orphan Thanksgiving a reality?

I was a woman on a mission. I had to call in favors, but slowly I was getting things done. The people living next door were generous enough to throw an extension cord over the back fence so I could charge my phone and computer. We gathered candles. I even put out an announcement that it would be the last Thanksgiving at my house. A friend who lived down the street was going out of town for the weekend, but gave me a key to use her stove and oven. All that was left was to find the money to buy food for a Thanksgiving meal.

That night, I sat in my candlelit bedroom with my daughter sleeping soundly next to me. I held my grandmother's gold locket in my hand for what felt like a lifetime. She was the woman who taught me to cook when I could barely walk. She grew up during the Depression, and she had told me many stories of hardship. I reasoned that she would have wanted me to give to those less fortunate. She would have approved. So, the next morning I sold the locket to put food on the table for one last holiday. And then I rushed to the store to buy a turkey with all the trimmings.

I spent the day traveling back and forth from the oven a block away. By the time guests started to arrive, I am sure that I looked as exhausted as I felt. But the candles were lit, the food prepared and smiles were on faces. This had become my best turnout in history. Despite the lack of heat or light, everyone was enjoying dinner and conversation. My daughter proudly announced that the thing she was thankful for was her mommy, which brought tears to my eyes. It truly was a day for which to be thankful.

As the sun came up the next morning, I had enough light to begin the cleanup of the previous night's festivities. In the darkness I had missed the suitcase sitting on my living room floor until I tripped over it. On top was a note that read simply "Thanks for the giving." Inside were cards, notes and encouragement from all of the attendees from the previous evening; plus others that I hadn't heard from in years. All with thanks for what I had done for them. More than that, inside was money. I cried, mouth agape, while counting the total. There was even information about an account that had been opened so that friends could wire money from all over the country.

To this day, I do not know who orchestrated this miracle. It was enough to get my electricity back and save me from being evicted. My daughter and I still live in the same house, with my new husband. The twentieth anniversary of "Orphan Thanksgiving" comes up this year. I am living proof that the good things that you put out to the world will come back to you, sometimes when you least expect it.

~Jodi Renee Thomas

Meet Our Contributors

Sylvia A. is a frequent contributor to the *Chicken Soup for the Soul* series. In choosing to use a pseudonym, she honors the tradition of anonymity in AA. It's just one of the valued steps and traditions of the program that has kept her sober for eighteen years and counting!

Debbie Acklin has received national attention for her frequent contributions to the *Chicken Soup for the Soul* series. She lives in Alabama with her family and two cats. Debbie loves to travel and never misses an opportunity to do so. She would love to hear from you. Contact her via Facebook at facebook.com/debbieacklinauthor.

Simone Adams holds her B.S. degree in Organizational Communication and is currently pursuing her MFA in Writing from Savannah College of Art and Design. She is a freelance writer/editor and facilitates writing courses. Simone is an avid hiker and is often joined on the trail by her teenage son or her dog.

Davina Adjani was once told to stop writing and find something she was good at — she has been writing ever since. Her Oma raised her to believe that love should always be a priority, and that, most importantly, loving yourself is essential in this crazy world. She tries to give the medicine of reality sugarcoated with a sense of humor.

Linda Allen returns to Bolivia annually to work with medical and construction teams to improve the quality of life in rural villages. She enjoys sharing her experiences, lessons learned and stories about her "second family" in Bolivia. E-mail her at lindaeallen@sbcglobal.net.

Monica A. Andermann lives and writes on Long Island where she shares a home with her husband Bill and their little tabby Samson. Her writing has been included in such publications as *Woman's World*, *Guideposts* and *Sasee* as well as many other *Chicken Soup for the Soul* books.

Elizabeth Atwater's intense love for books and storytelling as a very young child naturally developed into a love of writing. She has yet to suffer from the dreaded writer's block. Give her a little extra time and solitude, and the words will flow from her mind like a happily singing brook on a mountainside.

Katie Bangert lives in Texas with her husband, three children and many family pets. This is her fourth appearance in the *Chicken Soup for the Soul* series. In between writing and shuffling kids to activities, you will most often find her nose buried in a book with a cup of chai tea in hand. Contact her via her website at katiebangert.com.

Kathleen Basi is the quintessential jack-of-all trades writer: composer-songwriter, columnist, feature writer, essayist, novelist, and author of three short nonfiction books for families. In her "spare" time, Kate juggles disability advocacy, directing a church choir, and turning her four kids into foodies.

Thomas Behnke is a native New Yorker, writer, musician and artist. He has been published in various small press magazines, including *Talebones*. He has recently completed his first novel, *The Dark Call*, and is collaborating on a screenplay about spiritual awakening.

Susan Boltz is a retired medical lab technician and basic logic assistant. She stays young by teaching Sunday school for high school students and baking muffins. Living in Cuyahoga Falls with her husband, writing and walking keep her busy.

Jill Burns lives in the mountains of West Virginia with her wonderful family. She's a retired piano teacher and performer. She enjoys writing, music, gardening, nature, and spending time with her grandchildren.

Nancy Burrows is a freelance writer, who received her Bachelor of Arts degree, with honors, in English from the University of Pennsylvania. She lives in Maryland with her husband, seventeen-year-old daughter, and fourteen-year-old autistic son. Nancy is proud to be a co-author of *Chicken Soup for the Soul: Raising Kids on the Spectrum.*

Lorraine Cannistra received her B.S. degree in English and M.S. degree in Rehabilitation Counseling from Emporia State University. She enjoys advocating, cooking, writing, and speaking. Her passions are wheelchair dance and her service dog, Leah. Read her blog at healthonwheels. wordpress.com or learn more at lorrainecannistra.com.

Deborah Carroll is the Director of Strategic Marketing for *Grand* magazine, a former educator, and author of *Tales From The Family Crypt* and a children's book, *Real Grands: From A to Z.* She's the mother of three wonderful daughters and a grandmother who loves running and music.

Candace Carteen started writing at the age of eight. When her husband died in 2007, she became the sole support for her talented seven-year-old son. They now travel back and forth between Washington State and California for his career.

Christian Conte, Ph.D., is a renowned anger management specialist, television host, author, and professional speaker. Dr. Conte works with celebrities, college and professional athletes, and in prison systems to spread his message of compassion and conscious education.

Joy Cook is a writer, substitute teacher, and mother of four. As a girl, Joy dreamed of living in a library and becoming a children's author. She's still working on both dreams. In the meantime, you can find her wearing her favorite red shoes at school, at the library, or anywhere people are reading, learning, and creating.

D'ette Corona is the Associate Publisher for Chicken Soup for the Soul. She received her Bachelor of Science degree in business management. D'ette has been happily married for twenty-three years and has a nineteen-year-old son whom she adores.

Sasha Couch is an East Coast native living in Los Angeles since 1999. An avid writer, she is also a dialysis patient awaiting a kidney transplant who values being able to share that experience. She delights most in her volunteer endeavors, notably with the National Kidney Foundation and the literacy nonprofit, Reading Opens Minds.

Allison Hermann Craigie earned her B.S. degree in Journalism from the University of Maryland. She credits her two children, Sam and Jillian, with helping her plan these parties and most importantly as the two people for whom she will always be grateful. Allison lives in Florida and loves hockey, concerts, tennis, laughing and life.

TC Currie is a poet, writer, tech journalist, body positive activist and occasional lingerie model. Several of her tech articles made the front page of *Slashdot* and she's won a Solas Award for best travel writing. She travels, blogs, writes, and explores emerging technology. Follow her adventures at tccurrie.com.

Anita Daswani was born and raised in a small town but had big city ambitions. She aspired to one day live and work in the Big Apple while finding creative outlets to express herself through writing and performing. She and her husband are living the dream as they now reside in New York City doing what they love.

Gwen Daye is a wife, homemaker, dog rescuer, and parent of two teenagers, and is so excited to have her third piece published in the *Chicken Soup for the Soul* series!

Lola Di Giulio De Maci is grateful to the teachers who nourished her dreams of becoming a teacher and a writer. Her stories appear in the *Chicken Soup for the Soul* series, the *Los Angeles Times*, and other anthologies, newspapers, and magazines. She writes from her loft overlooking the San Bernardino Mountains.

Savannah Dee is a registered nurse in the operating room at her local hospital in central Pennsylvania. She enjoys biking, traveling and researching family ancestry. She hopes to participate in medical missions trips in the near future.

Conni Delinger spent her career in the medical profession and then returned to college, earning a bachelor's degree from Fresno State University. Now retired, she spends her time volunteering, traveling, and "paying it forward" by teaching sewing to children and adults.

Drema Drudge has an MFA in Creative Writing from Spalding University and is agented by Lisa Gallagher. Drema and her husband Barry live in Indiana, where she is working on her second novel. They are the proud parents of Mia and Zack. Contact Drema through dremadrudge. wordpress.com or on Twitter @dremadrudge.

Neither blindness at thirty-one, unthinkable tragedy nor painful injustice defeated **Janet Perez Eckles**. Rather, in spite of adversity, she has become an international keynote speaker for Spanish and English-speaking audiences. She is a #1 best-selling author, radio host, life coach, master interpreter, columnist and ministry leader.

Jenny Estes is a Christian women's retreat leader, a professional videographer, and a freelance writer. She serves alongside her husband,

Reverend Jack Estes, Rector of St. Luke's Anglican Church in Bakersfield, CA. Their daughter Zoe lives in Portland, OR.

Trisha Faye writes from North Texas when she's not rescuing kittens or antiquing. Trisha finally learned her lesson — that every day is a good day. Her favorite place is Arizona, where her grandchildren are growing too fast. You can find Trisha at trishafaye.com or on Twitter @texastrishafaye.

Carole Brody Fleet is a multi-award-winning author and media contributor. Widely recognized as an expert in life-adversity recovery and a veteran of over 1,000 radio show appearances, Ms. Fleet appears on numerous television and radio programs nationally and internationally as well as in worldwide print and web media.

Andrea Fortenberry lives near Phoenix, AZ with her husband and two children. She writes and speaks on relationships, family and faith. She was also a contributor to *Chicken Soup for the Soul: Devotional Stories for Wives*. Connect with Andrea at andreafortenberry.com.

Sharon Fuentes is an award-winning writer, author of *The Don't Freak Out Guide to Parenting Kids with Asperger's*, a special needs parenting advisor and the Founder/Editorial Director of *Zoom – autism through many lenses*, a free online magazine. Visit her website zoomautism. org to view the magazine or e-mail her at sharon@sharonfuentes. com.

Major Jody Fuller is a comedian, speaker, writer, and soldier with three tours of duty in Iraq. As a lifetime stutterer, he's an advocate for stuttering awareness. Jody has worked with some of the biggest names in comedy and has entertained troops in fourteen countries around the world. Jody lives in Alabama with his dog and cat.

Nancy F. Goodfellow is a writer and mother in Naperville, IL. As a public speaker for the National Association for Down Syndrome, she gives disability awareness presentations to children and teaches that when you understand, you accept. She writes children's books to inspire acceptance and friendship for all.

David A. Grant is a freelance writer based in New Hampshire. He is the author of *Metamorphosis, Surviving Brain Injury*. As a survivor of a cycling accident in 2010, he shares his experience and hope through advocacy work. Getting back on a bike after his accident, David can still be found cycling.

Tina Grover believes, like Socrates, that "an unexamined life is not worth living." Her life's passion is story collecting from her own life as well as the lives of her ancestors. She writes in her journal daily and just finished writing her father's biography. She is currently writing a historical novel. E-mail her at Tinadollclothes@gmail.com.

Bonnie Compton Hanson, artist and speaker, is author or co-author of over fifty books for adults and children, plus hundreds of articles, stories, and poems; including thirty-eight in the *Chicken Soup for the Soul* series. A former editor, she has also taught at several universities and writing conferences. Learn more at bonniecomptonhanson.com.

Rob Harshman has been in education for over forty years. He is married with two daughters and two grandchildren. Rob enjoys travel and photography and is planning to continue writing stories, both fiction and nonfiction.

Kelly Hennigan loves spending time with her family in upstate New York. She credits her high school English teachers Mr. Moriarty and Mr. Haynes for encouraging her writing. Kelly would like to thank Chicken Soup for the Soul for this opportunity. You can read more of her writing by following her blog at frommygut.weebly.com.

Eileen Melia Hession is a former teacher and publisher's representative whose writing has appeared in various publications. She has one daughter and enjoys running, yoga and ceramics and has not yet given up on painting. She believes there is a need for more levity in life and her writing reflects that belief.

Erika Hoffman usually writes inspirational nonfiction stories but occasionally she writes travel articles and short mysteries. She is a graduate of Duke University, a former teacher, a wife, a mother of four, and a grandma to one.

Christine A. Holliday is a licensed school librarian and Spanish teacher. She has taught students in junior high and high school for over thirty-five years, traveling with them overseas many times. She is a freelance writer for several local publications in Toledo, OH and loves traveling, photography, and anything historical.

Cindy Hval is the author of *War Bonds: Love Stories from the Greatest Generation*, which tells the stories of thirty-six couples who met/married during WWII and is available at Amazon.com. Cindy's work is featured in nine volumes of the *Chicken Soup for the Soul* series. She can be reached at CindyHval.com or dchval@juno.com.

Chelsea Johnson is a freelance writer and fitness coach. She and her family live in an RV full-time and are planning to explore the country as much as possible together!

Lynn Johnson and her husband Gerald have been married for twenty-five years and have seven children. Lynn is a Grief Recovery Specialist and Empowerment Coach, helping women heal from the devastation of loss. She is President and Founder of Gathering Friends for TLC in Brighton, MI as well as the author of *He Restores My Soul*.

April Knight is an artist and freelance writer. Her favorite pastimes are riding horses on stormy days and beachcombing when the wind is wild and the waves are crashing on the shore. She has recently written a novel titled *West of Nowhere and South of Despair*.

Kathe Kokolias is an artist, writer, and ESOL tutor who lives in St. Augustine, FL. She has published a collection of essays titled *Spandex & Black Boots: Essays from an Abundant Life*, and a travel memoir, *What Time Do the Crocodiles Come Out?* Kathe enjoys riding her bike in the sunshine and relaxing at the beach.

Mary Elizabeth Laufer has a degree in English education from SUNY Albany. As a Navy wife, she moved thirteen times in twenty years, attended six colleges, raised two children, and taught in schools across the country, from Oregon to Florida. She recently left teaching to devote more time to writing.

A criminal court reporter by day, **Jody E. Lebel** writes romantic suspense novels. Her short stories have sold to *Woman's World*, *Cosmo UK*, and dozens of others. She was raised in charming New England, was an only child who had an only child (claiming she didn't breed well in captivity) and now lives with her two cats in southern Florida.

Barbara LoMonaco has worked for Chicken Soup for the Soul as an editor since 1998. She has co-authored two *Chicken Soup for the Soul* book titles and has had stories published in numerous other titles. Barbara is a graduate of the University of Southern California and has a teaching credential.

Alice Luther is an author, a wife, mom of four, and DIY-er. She writes in an effort to capture beautiful ordinary moments of everyday life.

Michelle Mach is a freelance writer, editor, and jewelry designer. She is the author of *Unexpected Findings: 50+ Clever Jewelry Designs Featuring Everyday Components*. She sells her handmade book-inspired jewelry, key chains, and bookmarks online at michellemach.com and in selected shops and galleries.

Daniel Mangini is a resident of Philadelphia and graduate of Saint Joseph's University. He recently returned from Miami to resume working in the field that is his passion! He's a Recruiting Specialist at UPENN's HIV Prevention Research Division, where they are working to find a safe and effective vaccine against HIV.

Stephanie A. Mayberry is a freelance writer, author, and photographer who found at a young age that conventional life didn't really suit her. She and her husband are full-time RVers, enjoying the simplicity of a life unencumbered. Connect with Stephanie at facebook.com/authorstephaniemayberry.

Mary McLaurine is a writer/poet living in Maryland. She blogs at *The Heart of Sassy Lassie* trying to find humor in all of life's ups and downs. She has strong ancestral ties to Scotland and knows that although she's never been there, she has lived there all her life. She embraces all the fairy-dust moments of life.

Dean K. Miller writes poetry, creative nonfiction, and haiku coloring books. His first book of haiku, *Sometimes the Walls Cry: A Book of Haiku and Sketch*, was released in May 2016 by his own imprint MDK, Inc. Miller co-founded and volunteers for the Platte Rivers Chapter of Project Healing Waters Fly Fishing in Colorado and Wyoming.

Cathy Mogus is a freelance writer, inspirational speaker, and author of *Dare to Dance Again: Steps from the Psalms When Life Trips You Up*. She has been published in the *Chicken Soup for the Soul* series, *Guideposts*, and many other publications. She resides in Richmond, BC. E-mail her at acmogus@shaw.ca.

Ann Morrow is a writer, speaker and former corporate employee. She and her husband live in western South Dakota where they run their own business. Ann's stories have appeared in numerous books in the *Chicken Soup for the Soul* series and she is currently at work on her first novel.

Andrea Mullenmeister writes about her family's story of love, hope, and survival at AnEarlyStartBlog.com. Her essays about motherhood, prematurity, and parenting a child with extra needs have been featured nationally. She loves to grow good food, play in the woods, and laugh with her family.

Annie Nason is so grateful to be published for a second time! She also had a story in *Chicken Soup for the Soul: Think Possible*. She is passionate about sharing her story with others affected by cerebral palsy. Annie loves spending time at the beach and sipping on iced coffees. Her motto is "Go confidently in the direction of your dreams...."

Linda Newton is a counselor and the author of *12 Ways to Turn Your Pain Into Praise*. She speaks all over the country at women's, couples', and pastors' retreats. Visit her at LindaNewtonSpeaks.com, and check her out on Facebook at facebook.com/answersfrommomanddad.

Ronda Nuñez, a former teacher with several awards to her credit, recently resigned as administrator of the preschool she founded to write full-time. Her book, *In Awe and Wonder* and the first children's book of *Ms. Ronda's Alphabet Teaching Series* are available on Amazon. Learn more at TrueIssuesoftheHeart.com.

Katie O'Connell is a writer, teacher, blogger, mother of two, and lover of all things creative. Her greatest joy comes when stories written from her heart help others on their journey. Her work has appeared in *Sasee* magazine, *Chicken Soup for the Soul: It's Christmas!,* and Patheos. Follow her work at heartwiredwriting.com.

Judy O'Kelley's work appears in magazines, newspapers, greeting cards and musicals from the Midwest to Beijing. A passionate tutor, Judy finds inspiration in her insightful students and enjoys sunrises, storm chasing, midnight board games, and every moment with her adult kids. E-mail her at judyokelleycards@gmail.com.

Mary C. M. Phillips is a caffeinated wife, mom, and writer. Her stories have appeared in numerous anthologies including *Chicken Soup for the Soul*, *Cup of Comfort*, and *Bad Austen: The Worst Stories Jane Never Wrote*. She blogs at CaffeineEpiphanies.com. Follow her on Twitter @ MaryCMPhil.

Connie Pombo is a freelance writer and author of three books. She is a regular contributor to the *Chicken Soup for the Soul* series and *Coping with Cancer* magazine. As a professional speaker, she loves to encourage cancer survivors, their families, and healthcare professionals. Learn more at conniepombo.com.

A Texas attorney working in Houston, wine, beer and spirits aficionado **Amy Corron Power** writes for the internationally acclaimed *Another Wine Blog* and is a contributing writer at Snooth.com. She and husband Joe live in the Clear Lake area, where she enjoys gardening, nature walks, live music, entertaining and home brewing.

Jennifer Reed received her MFA in Writing from Vermont College of Fine Arts in 2013. She has published over thirty books for children, with a focus on educational nonfiction books. Jennifer enjoys traveling, gardening and paper quilling. She lives in Maryland with her husband and two dogs.

Cara Rifkin received her Bachelor of Science degree from DePaul University in Chicago. She spends much of her time working with philanthropic organizations and volunteering for nonprofits focused on humanitarian causes and social justice. Her writing is inspired by personal experiences and day-to-day encounters.

Alicia Rosen's stories have appeared in journals, magazines and anthologies throughout America. She lives in a tiny apartment in Brooklyn with her pup and more than 1,000 books.

Carolyn Roy-Bornstein is a doctor and writer. Her memoir *Crash: A Mother, a Son, and the Journey from Grief to Gratitude* was published by Globe Pequot Press in 2012. She is at work on her second memoir titled *Last Stop on the Struggle Bus* about taking in two of her patients as foster daughters.

Larry Schardt, Ph.D., is an author, speaker, and the creator of The Success That Rocks series. Larry encourages people to live with passion, lead with excellence, and explore the world with a sense of wonder. He is a professor at Penn State. He loves socializing, walking, reading, music, and the outdoors. Learn more at LarrySchardt.com.

Lindy Schneider inspires people to express their gratitude with her Amazon best-selling watercolor thank you cards. Her artwork has won national awards and is featured in the children's book *Starfish on the Beach*, also a bestseller. You can see her work at peakspublishing.com or by searching her name on Amazon.com.

Thom Schwarz, RN, CHPN, has been a registered nurse for forty years, working in hospice and palliative care for the past nine. E-mail him at Thomapl@Yahoo.com.

Joyce Newman Scott worked as a flight attendant while pursuing an acting career. She started college in her mid-fifties and studied screenwriting at the University of Miami and creative writing at Florida International University. She has short stories in the *Chicken Soup for the Soul* and *Not Your Mother's Book...* series.

Jay Seate writes everything from humor to the macabre, and is especially keen on transcending genre pigeonholing. He lives in Golden, CO with the dream of enjoying the rest of his life traveling and writing.

Mickey Sherman is a criminal defense lawyer in Greenwich, CT. He has been a legal commentator on most every TV network except The Food Channel. His first book, *How Can You Defend Those People?*, has been universally praised by the legal and literary community. Learn more at mickeysherman.com or e-mail him at ms23@aol.com.

Haylie Smart holds a Bachelor of Arts in Liberal Arts and has worked in community journalism as a reporter since June 2013. She plans to teach English and creative writing. She enjoys cooking, reading for knowledge, serving in church and loving her nine nieces and nephews. E-mail her at haylie.smart@yahoo.com.

Jessica Snell is a writer who lives in sunny Southern California. She's the editor of *Let Us Keep the Feast: Living the Church Year at Home* and *Not Alone: A Literary & Spiritual Companion for Those Confronted with Infertility & Miscarriage*. She blogs about faith, fiction, and family at jessicasnell.com.

Laura Snell, her husband Dave and their dog Gus Gusterson live in Wasaga Beach, ON where they operate their business GeorgianBaySelect at GBSelect.com. Her son Ryan lives in Melbourne, Australia. This is her fifth contribution to the *Chicken Soup for the Soul* series. E-mail her at laura@gbselect.com.

Diane Stark is an award-winning writer, a wife, and mother of five. She is a frequent contributor to the *Chicken Soup for the Soul* series. She loves to write about the important things in life: her family and her faith. E-mail her at Dianestark19@yahoo.com.

JB Steele was born and raised in Florida, where mosquitoes can carry a person away and it gets really humid. He swears it's literally possible to fry an egg on the sidewalk, but doesn't recommend eating it after that. He writes science fiction and fantasy, with side trips into other genres for something different.

Annmarie B. Tait resides in Conshohocken, PA with her husband Joe Beck. Annmarie is published in several *Chicken Soup for the Soul* books, *Reminisce* magazine, *Patchwork Path*, and many other anthologies. She also enjoys cooking, crocheting, and singing and recording Irish and American folk songs. E-mail her at irishbloom@aol.com.

Johnny Tan is a talk show host, professional keynote speaker, consultant, author and founder of *From My Mama's Kitchen*. His Internet FMMK Talk Radio show has amassed over one million listeners. Johnny's bestselling and award-winning book, *From My Mama's Kitchen*, honors his nine moms. Connect with him at JohnnyTan.com.

Jodi Renee Thomas has published stories on many subjects, from relationships to women's rights. She is a featured speaker for the women's movement and award-winning author of *aMused*. She lives happily in Florida with her teenage daughter, husband and three dogs that like to bother her while she types.

Charlotte Triplett graduated from school with a Culinary Arts degree, but currently works in the modeling industry as a clothing model. Her hobbies are swimming, reading, writing, cooking and drawing. She has nine pets and a husband who inspires her every day.

Shawna Troke-Leukert is a published writer and an Infinite Possibilities trainer. She grew up in Sydney, Nova Scotia and today lives in beautiful Codroy Valley, Newfoundland with her husband Eric and two dogs. She enjoys gardening, working on writing projects, and visiting her mother Viola every summer in Nova Scotia.

Kathy Shiels Tully is a regular contributor to *The Boston Globe*. Her stories have been published in *FamilyFun*, *The Christian Science Monitor*, *The Writer*, and *Chicken Soup for the Soul: Celebrating Brothers & Sisters*. Kathy lives north of Boston with her husband and two daughters. Learn more at kathyshielstully.com.

Carrie O'Maley Voliva is a public librarian, writer, and mother in Indianapolis, IN. She received her B.A. degree in Journalism from Butler University and her MLS degree from Indiana University. Carrie misses her mother every day, but feels grateful for the time they shared and all the lessons her mother passed on.

Pat Wahler is a retired grant writer and proud contributor to twelve *Chicken Soup for the Soul* books. Pat resides in Missouri and draws writing inspiration from family, friends, and the critters who tirelessly supervise each minute she spends at the keyboard. Connect with her at critteralley.blogspot.com.

Dorann Weber is a freelance photographer for a South New Jersey newspaper and a contributor to Getty Images. She has a newfound love for writing short stories and greeting cards. Dorann lives in the Pine Barrens with her family, which also includes three dogs, two cats, and a flock of chickens. E-mail her at dorann_weber@yahoo.com.

Richard Weinman is an Emeritus Professor at Oregon State University. Following a disabling motor vehicle accident in 2005, he has become an advocate for elders living in long-term care facilities. His work includes a video documentary, available on YouTube, and bi-monthly blogs for AARP.org.

Johnny Wessler has spent his career in the hospitality industry, which is perfect for him because he loves traveling, good food, entertainment and good company. He is the proud father of two grown children and has three grandchildren.

Helen Wilder, a former kindergarten/first grade teacher in southeastern Kentucky, is married with one daughter, a son-in-law, and a grandpuppy, Paco. She is passionate about teaching young children, storytelling, journaling, reading, scrapbooking, and writing.

Amanda Yancey lives off of adventures, thought-provoking books and films, and has a weakness for tacos. She is a storyteller of sorts. She has written several stories for the *Chicken Soup for the Soul* series and has written a memoir about all her summer camp experiences she hopes to publish soon.

Luanne Tovey Zuccari lives in Niagara Falls, NY. She is the grandmother of eight and retired from a long career as a newspaper reporter and public relations coordinator for public schools. She is a freelance copywriter who serves her community as a DWI Victim Impact speaker and organ donation advocate.

Meet Amy Newmark

Amy Newmark is the bestselling author, editor-in-chief, and publisher of the *Chicken Soup for the Soul* book series. Since 2008, she has published 125 new books, most of them national bestsellers in the U.S. and Canada, more than doubling the number of *Chicken Soup for the Soul* titles in print today.

Amy is credited with revitalizing the Chicken Soup for the Soul brand, which has been a publishing industry phenomenon since the first book came out in 1993. By compiling inspirational and aspirational true stories curated from ordinary people who have had extraordinary experiences, Amy has kept the twenty-three-year-old Chicken Soup for the Soul brand fresh and relevant.

Amy graduated *magna cum laude* from Harvard University where she majored in Portuguese and minored in French. She then embarked on a three-decade career as a Wall Street analyst, a hedge fund manager, and a corporate executive in the technology field. Her return to literary pursuits was inevitable, as her honors thesis in college involved traveling throughout Brazil's impoverished northeast region, collecting stories from regular people. She is delighted to have come full circle in her writing career—from collecting stories "from the people" in Brazil as a twenty-year-old to, three decades later, collecting stories "from the people" for Chicken Soup for the Soul.

When Amy and her husband Bill, the CEO of Chicken Soup for the Soul, are not working, they are visiting their four grown children. Follow her on Twitter @amynewmark and @chickensoupsoul. Listen to her free daily podcast, The Chicken Soup for the Soul Podcast, at www.chickensoup.podbean.com, or find it on iTunes, the Podcasts app on iPhone, or on your favorite podcast app on other devices.

Meet Deborah Norville

Bestselling author Deborah Norville credits many of the successes in her life to a positive mental attitude. She is the anchor of *Inside Edition*, the nation's top-rated syndicated news magazine, a two-time Emmy winner, and serves on the Board of Directors for the Viacom Corporation, the global provider of entertainment content.

Deborah is also the author of a half-dozen books including the New York Times bestseller, *Thank You Power: Making the Science of Gratitude Work for You. Thank You Power* brought together for the first time the growing body of academic research proving the benefits of gratitude. Similarly, *The Power of Respect* presented research detailing the benefits of respectful behavior with real-life stories. She also coauthored *Chicken Soup for the Soul: Think Possible* and wrote the forewords for *Chicken Soup for the Soul: Think Positive* and *Chicken Soup for the Soul: Find Your Happiness.*

Deborah is also a growing force in the craft industry. A lifelong seamstress and crafter, her Deborah Norville Collection of fine hand yarns and finely crafted hooks and needles for knitting and crochet is available online and in craft stores nationwide. She is also the host of

Knit and Crochet Now, broadcast on public television stations.

Deborah Norville is a *summa cum laude* (4.0) graduate of the University of Georgia. She is married and the mother of three.

Deborah can be reached via her website www.DeborahNorville.com.

Thank You

We are grateful to all our story contributors and fans, who shared thousands of stories about how they use the power of gratitude to improve their lives. We loved reading all the submissions and choosing the 101 that would appear in the book.

We owe special thanks to D'ette Corona, Barbara LoMonaco, Ronelle Frankel, and Susan Heim, the team of editors who read all the submissions. They narrowed down the list of finalists for Amy and Deborah to make some difficult decisions. As always, we had way more great stories than would fit in this volume, and many of them will end up appearing in future *Chicken Soup for the Soul* titles.

Associate Publisher D'ette Corona continued to be Amy's right-hand woman in creating the final manuscript and working with all our wonderful writers. Barbara LoMonaco and Kristiana Pastir, along with outside proofreader Elaine Kimbler, jumped in at the end to proof, proof, proof. And yes, there will always be typos anyway, so feel free to let us know about them at webmaster@chickensoupforthesoul.com.

The whole publishing team deserves a hand, including Executive Assistant and sometime editor Mary Fisher, Senior Director of Production Victor Cataldo, and graphic designer Daniel Zaccari, who turned our manuscript into this beautiful book.

Sharing Happiness, Inspiration, and Wellness

Real people sharing real stories, every day, all over the world. In 2007, *USA Today* named *Chicken Soup for the Soul* one of the five most memorable books in the last quarter-century. With over 100 million books sold to date in the U.S. and Canada alone, more than 200 titles in print, and translations into more than forty languages, "chicken soup for the soul" is one of the world's best-known phrases.

Today, twenty-three years after we first began sharing happiness, inspiration and wellness through our books, we continue to delight our readers with new titles, but have also evolved beyond the bookstore, with super premium pet food, a line of high quality soups, and a variety of licensed products and digital offerings, all inspired by stories. Chicken Soup for the Soul has recently expanded into visual storytelling through movies and television. Chicken Soup for the Soul is "changing the world one story at a time®." Thanks for reading!

Chicken Soup for the Soul

Share with Us

We all have had Chicken Soup for the Soul moments in our lives. If you would like to share your story or poem with millions of people around the world, go to chickensoup.com and click on "Submit Your Story." You may be able to help another reader and become a published author at the same time. Some of our past contributors have launched writing and speaking careers from the publication of their stories in our books!

We only accept story submissions via our website. They are no longer accepted via mail or fax.

To contact us regarding other matters, please send us an e-mail through webmaster@chickensoupforthesoul.com, or fax or write us at:

Chicken Soup for the Soul
P.O. Box 700
Cos Cob, CT 06807-0700
Fax: 203-861-7194

One more note from your friends at Chicken Soup for the Soul: Occasionally, we receive an unsolicited book manuscript from one of our readers, and we would like to respectfully inform you that we do not accept unsolicited manuscripts and we must discard the ones that appear.

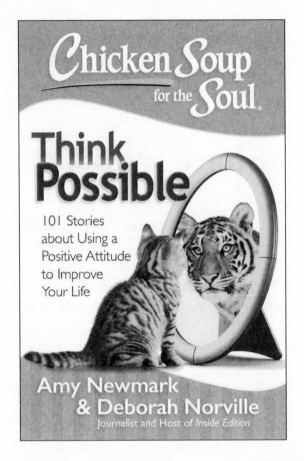

It's always better to look on the bright side. The true stories in *Chicken Soup for the Soul: Think Possible* will encourage and inspire readers to follow their hearts and dreams with these 101 stories of optimism, faith, and strength. In bad times and good, readers will find encouragement to keep a positive attitude, reach higher and accomplish more than they ever thought possible.

978-1-61159-952-7

More classic inspiration

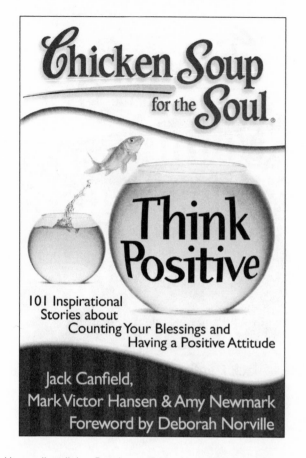

Every cloud has a silver lining. Readers will be inspired by these 101 real-life stories
from people just like them, taking a positive attitude to the ups and downs of life,
and remembering to be grateful and count their blessings. This book continues
Chicken Soup for the Soul's focus on inspiration and hope, and its stories of
optimism and faith will encourage readers to stay positive during challenging times
and in their everyday lives.

978-1-935096-56-6

to improve your life

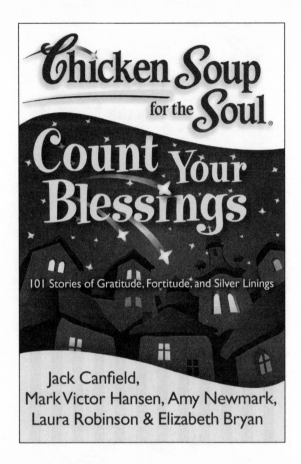

Chicken Soup for the Soul
Count Your Blessings
101 Stories of Gratitude, Fortitude, and Silver Linings

Jack Canfield,
Mark Victor Hansen, Amy Newmark,
Laura Robinson & Elizabeth Bryan

This uplifting book reminds readers of the blessings in their lives, despite financial stress, natural disasters, health scares and illnesses, housing challenges and family worries. This feel-good book is a great gift for New Year's or Easter, for someone going through a difficult time, or for Christmas. These stories of optimism, faith, and strength remind us of the simple pleasures of family, home, health, and inexpensive good times.

978-1-935096-42-9

Great tips and advice

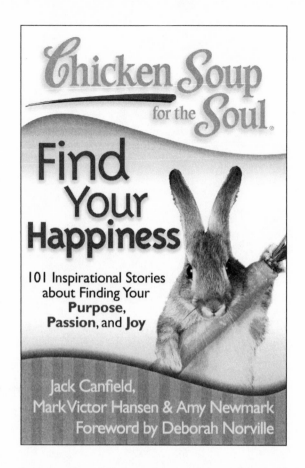

Chicken Soup for the Soul
Find Your Happiness

101 Inspirational Stories
about Finding Your
**Purpose,
Passion,** and **Joy**

Jack Canfield,
Mark Victor Hansen & Amy Newmark
Foreword by Deborah Norville

Others share how they found their passion, purpose, and joy in life in these 101 personal and exciting stories that are sure to encourage readers to find their own happiness. Stories in this collection will inspire readers to pursue their dreams, find their passion and seek joy in their life. This book continues Chicken Soup for the Soul's focus on inspiration and hope, reminding readers that they can find their own happiness.

978-1-935096-77-1

that you can use every day

Chicken Soup for the Soul

Changing your life one story at a time®
www.chickensoup.com